Aromatherapy and Chakras
balancing your body's energy centres
for optimal health and wellbeing

Salvatore Battaglia

Aromatherapy and Chakras
balancing your body's energy centres for optimal health and wellbeing

Salvatore Battaglia

Black Pepper Creative

First published in 2020 by
Black Pepper Creative
7 Guardhouse Road
Banyo QLD 4014
www.salvatorebattaglia.com.au

ISBN 978-0-6482606-4-6

All rights reserved.

No part of this publication may be reproduced, stored in a retrieval system or transmitted, in any form or by any means, electronic, mechanical, photocopying, recording or otherwise, without the prior permission of the publisher.

Note to the reader

The therapeutic benefits of the essential oils outlined in this book are based on traditional knowledge and many years of experience. The concepts outlined herein are not intended as a substitute for medical advice. Any application of the ideas and information contained in the book is at the reader's sole discretion.

To the fullest extent of the law, neither the author nor the publisher, contributor or editor assumes any liability for any injury and/or damage to people or property as a matter of product liability, negligence or otherwise, or from any use or operation of any methods, products, instructions or ideas contained in this book.

Copyright © 2020 Salvatore Battaglia

 A catalogue record for this book is available from the National Library of Australia

Cover artwork by Paola Milani
Edited by Kyoko Mizoguchi
Proofread by Gail Cartwright
Text design by Bill Adrisurya
Typeset in EB Garamond 11pt by Watson Ferguson and Company, Brisbane
Printed in China by Everbest Printing Investment Limited

by the same author
The Complete Guide to Aromatherapy, Volume I — Foundations and Materia Medica.
The Complete Guide to Aromatherapy, Volume II — Science and Therapeutics.
The Complete Guide to Aromatherapy, Volume III — Psyche and Subtle.
Aromatree — a holistic guide to understanding and using aromatherapy.

Tantrika painting. CC by Wellcome Collection.

Small is the number of them that see with their own eyes
and feel with their own hearts.

Albert Einstein

Contents

Acknowledgements — ix
Foreword by Jennifer Jefferies — xi
Introduction — xii
    Why are chakras so popular? — xii
    About this book — xiii
    Are we losing our humanity? — xv
    My personal journey — xviii
    The need for new sciences — xx

Part 1: Energy, Subtle Bodies and Subtle Therapies — 1
    1. Defining Energy Medicine — 2
    2. Defining Energy — 7
    3. Energy Systems of the Human Body — 10
    4. The Future of Medicine is Energy — 20
    5. Subtle Therapies — 22

Part 2: A Brief Overview of Chakras — 45
    6. The 'True' History of Chakras — 46
    7. Eastern Chakra System — 55
    8. Western Chakra System — 70
    9. The Relationship between Chakras and Physical Anatomy — 78
    10. Chakras and Consciousness — 86
    11. Chakras and Lifespan Development — 95
    12. Chakras, Yoga and Meditation — 98
    13. Chakras and the Human Biofield — 101

Part 3: The Chakras — 109
    14. Base Chakra — 110
    15. Sacral Chakra — 122
    16. Solar Plexus Chakra — 135
    17. Heart Chakra — 149

18. Throat Chakra	162
19. Third Eye Chakra	175
20. Crown Chakra	187

Part 4: Chakra Healing 203
    21. Chakra Imbalances 204
    22. How to Balance your Chakras 208
    23. How to Use essential oils to Balance the Chakras 214
    24. Afterword 221

Part 5: Resources 223
    Glossary 224
    Potions to keep your chakras balanced 228
    Books by Sal 231
    Stay inspired 233

References 235
Statement to readers 241
Image credits 243
Inspiration behind the chakra collage 245
About the poems 246
Index 247

Acknowledgements

I would like to extend my sincere gratitude to everyone who has attended my aromatherapy and chakra workshops. It is an honour to share with you my passion for aromatherapy and chakras.

In preparing this book, I have drawn upon the teachings and information from so many educators, scholars and therapists involved with chakras. I am ever so grateful to everyone who has contributed to helping us understand chakras and how chakras can be used to transform our lives.

I would like to thank all the yoga teachers who have incorporated aromatherapy into their yoga practice and classes.

I am ever so grateful to be surrounded by incredibly creative individuals. I would like to thank Paola Milani for creating the beautiful art for the cover that I have also used throughout the book. My sincere thanks to Jill Psenitza for allowing me to use her beautiful chakra collage and sharing with us the inspiration behind the art. There is always something magical about poetry. I would like to thank Marzena Skowronska for writing the poems at the beginning of each chakra. Her poems beautifully reflect the essence of each chakra.

I often receive comments about the graphic design of my books. For this I am sincerely indebted to another talented individual, Bill Adrisurya who has beautifully designed this book. Special thanks to Kyoko Mizoguchi for editing the book and Gail Cartwright for the proofing.

I am grateful for the amazing team at Perfect Potion who embrace our purpose to support the individual, community and environment to flourish by listening, guiding and reconnecting body, mind and spirit.

I would like to thank all my friends and family who have been encouraging and last but not least my wife Carolyn, for her constant support and encouragement.

Foreword

My introduction to energetics and chakras came when I first read *Wheels of Light* in about 1989. Immediately, I was excited to learn of chakras and what I felt could extensively influence the health of the body depending on their state of balance. The chakra system simply made sense to me. We are energetic beings, and chakras and energy work became a solid foundation to my work with essential oils and the body. I am a visual person — and in this book, Sal paints the pictures in my mind of how chakras and energetics work. He truly is a wonderful storyteller.

Sal was the first one to ignite my interest in the subtle uses of aromatherapy and the energetics of oils. He was my teacher in aromatherapy decades ago. He has such vast experience not only in aromatherapy but also in Eastern philosophies and therapies. His clinical experience is not limited to that of aromatherapy. Sal's studies in TCM and acupuncture bring an even more holistic approach to aromatherapy. I remember in lectures he would bring the subtleties of oils into our learning. To this day Sal continues to inspire my career in aromatherapy as I spread my work around the world, especially with the *Aromatherapy Insight Cards*.

Sal has applied the knowledge to the practical application with his students around the world, and his teaching and writing style makes people lean in hungry for more. His passion for the subject of this book and aromatherapy oozes through his writing.

Sal has mined through his library of life experiences and used his talent for research to bring us a comprehensive book written from the heart. The world is evolving. We are energetic beings and we are waking up. This book is perfectly timed for the practitioner wanting to further their knowledge and also for the layperson to further their knowledge and passion, opening up and aligning their chakras as they dive in.

Jennifer Jefferies ND
Author — *The Aromatherapy Insight Cards*

Introduction

Why are chakras so popular?

The aromatherapy and chakras workshop that I have been teaching for over 20 years has always been one of the most popular workshops. It is an excellent way to incorporate my passion for essential oils within a holistic framework that promotes personal and spiritual growth.

However, I have often found the history and origin of chakras a little perplexing. Chakras are based on the teaching of Indian Tantra. Why is this rarely discussed in many of the contemporary books written on chakras? My first encounter with chakras was after coming across a book published by the Theosophical Society. Why is this rarely acknowledged in many of the New Age books on chakras? Why are there so many inconsistencies in the assignment of colours or the endocrine glands with the chakra centres?

A little while ago I discovered a book, *Rainbow Body — A History of the Western Chakra System from Blavatsky to Brennan* by Kurt Leland. This was my 'ah ha' moment. All of a sudden, everything that I had known about chakras made sense. Leland does not attempt to justify the existence of chakras, what they are or how they interact at a physical, emotional, spiritual or subtle level. However, what he does effectively do is present us with a detailed history of chakras, or more accurately the Western Chakra System.

I did note a hint of cynicism when Leland described his experience browsing through the local food co-op and discovering a brochure promoting a range of chakra balancing aromatherapy blends. He states:

> *Several half-amused questions came to mind: could a scent really "open the floodgates of compassion and understanding" associated*

with the heart chakra. Why was the "empowering" third chakra associated with "delicate citrus blend"? How would a fully enlightened being smell when wearing all seven scents at once?[1]

I could be cynical and suggest that Leland may not understand how essential oils work at a subtle level. However, he does have a point. How did something that has its origins in ancient Indian spiritualism and Tantric practice come to this? He explains that when you look into the traditional teachings involving chakras in India, scent was not involved or the idea of chakra balancing was never mentioned. This, claims Leland, was the catalyst to write a book for people who want to know the real history of the Western chakras.

This made me question what I have been doing all these years. Had I fallen under the spell of the New Age movement and perpetuated many of the Western constructs associated with chakras?

But then I said to myself: *Hold on, I have seen, time and time again, how so many people's lives have been profoundly changed when they use essential oils and how essential oils have empowered them, acted as a catalyst to improve their health or simply provided clarity and direction in their life.*

While Leland has written a book that traces the true history of chakras, I felt it was important to write a book to help us to understand a holistic approach to using essential oils within the framework of the Western concept of chakras as psycho-energetic centres and energy medicine.

About this book

In Part 1, I explain how I became involved in Traditional Chinese medicine (TCM), aromatherapy and natural therapies and my fascination with energy medicine. I introduce you to the concept of energy medicine, we examine the origins of energy medicine and some of the traditional and contemporary practices using energy medicine such as TCM, homoeopathy, flower essences, crystals and of course aromatherapy. We also examine the science supporting the evidence for energy medicine and chakras.

In Part 2, I provide you with a brief overview of the origins of chakras and how we have come to understand and use them. In order to do this, we examine the traditional Indian origins of chakras, and I introduce you to key Sanskrit terms such as *tantra*, *kundalini*, *chakras* and *nadi* and the role of yoga. I introduce you to a Sanskrit scholar who suggests that almost everything Westerners know about chakras is gobbledygook and that if we really want to know about chakras we must learn about Tantra.

We examine how the West came to discover chakras and the important role that the Theosophical Society played in introducing chakras to the West. We explore how the contemporary understanding of chakras emerged based on the work of individuals such as Caroline Myss, Barbara Brennan and Anodea Judith.

Leland defines two systems of chakras. The Eastern Chakra System, whose origins lay in the teachings of the traditional Tantric texts, and the Western Chakra System that has appropriated much of the traditional knowledge of the Eastern Chakra System and developed a more contemporary interpretation of the meaning of the chakras. Sanskrit scholar Christopher Wallis, I believe, is not so upset with the fact that this has happened, but is more concerned that many yoga practitioners and those who use chakras in their practice believe what they know about chakras to be the ultimate truth.

Contemporary historians who specialise in traditional subtle body practices of the East are sometimes critical of Western New Age appropriation of these teachings.[2]

However, I like Leland's explanation that describes the fusion of philosophies that has led to the development of the Western Chakra System:

> ... the embodiment of a deeply meaningful archetype of enlightenment, common to East and West — that of the spiritually perfected being, graphically represented by the image seen so often on covers of books on chakras: a resplendent, meditating human form, shining with the rainbow-colored light of having fully realized our spiritual potential, each chakra representing an evolutionary stage on this sacred developmental journey.[1]

In Part 2, we will also examine the relationship between chakras and our physical anatomy. We search for scientific evidence of the existence of chakras. Be prepared to be surprised and excited when we examine the result of a Gas Discharge Visualisation (GDV) test and learn about the latest research into biophotons or ultraweak photon emissions. I get excited when we discuss the role of the pineal gland and its association with the third eye, and its role in secreting compounds that may lead to mystical and spiritual experiences. We examine research that has found that meditative practices may play a role in the pineal gland being activated to produce neurotransmitters that lead to altered states of consciousness.

We examine how Western psychology and transpersonal psychologists are using traditional Vedic concepts of consciousness to explain how chakras can provide us with a more holistic framework for understanding human consciousness.

In Part 3, we examine each of the chakras in detail, examining the origins and meaning of their Sanskrit name, their purpose, the psychospiritual associations, and the various concordances such as colour location and element association. We explore the meaning of the traditional symbology associated with each chakra and the influence that the chakra can have on our psyche and level of consciousness and what to expect if the chakra is not balanced. We examine how aromatherapy can help to balance the chakras, and discuss a range of activities that we should consider to balance the chakra.

In Part 4, we conclude with some practical advice on how to use essential oils to balance our chakras.

Are we losing our humanity?

It is so exciting to see aromatherapy make a positive contribution within the medical health care framework. Around the world, doctors and nurses are embracing and introducing aromatherapy into many areas of their practices. However, it is frustrating that while aromatherapy has become an intrinsic element in many sectors of integrative health care practices, it is only accepted if it complies with the conventional medical framework — that is, the pharmacological model.

I have spoken at many international aromatherapy conferences about the need for a more integrative approach to the practice of aromatherapy. At these conferences, I have met so many amazing speakers. Their research is fascinating; however, it is mostly based on the pharmacological model. This means understanding essential oils at a physiological level.

At one conference, I challenged the current medical paradigm by suggesting that when it comes to the current health care model 'we are losing our humanity'.

What did I mean by this?

A comment by Schnaubelt back in 1999 clearly explains what I meant when I said 'we are losing our humanity':

> *Through the disintegration of family, private life is coming less of a place to turn for quietude and regeneration. Quiet, connection to nature, holistic health and happiness, and many other contributing factors to well-being are in short supply. Alternative methods such as aromatherapy offer great potential where physical healing and psychological regeneration intersect, because they provide integrated solutions. So far, this potential has been suffocated by restrictive legislation.*[3]

He continues:

> *Industrialization created an enormous abundance of goods, but it also created most of the psychological and physical health problems discussed in this book. With material goods readily available and the information technology unable to fill the void of content, the desire for physical and psychological health will be the biggest demand in the future. Only alternative, holistic modalities lead to an improved command of the phenomena of the soul, which is necessary to satisfy these needs.*[3]

Like Schnaubelt, I believe that aromatherapy can be a powerful catalyst to help us reconnect with our humanity. To reconnect with our humanity, we must integrate our emotional, spiritual and physical wellbeing. The Western chakra model provides us with the ideal framework to achieve this.

Technology and greater advancements made in medicine have not led to better health outcomes. The costs of conventional health care in most Western countries continue to spiral out of control and are on the rise. What is more disturbing is that the incidence of chronic diseases such as diabetes, heart disease, chronic fatigue, irritable bowel syndrome and chronic pain syndromes also continues to escalate.

Ted Kaptchuk, author of *The Web That Has No Weaver*, an excellent book introducing us to the philosophies and principles underpinning TCM, is also critical of the current biomedical system:

> *The current turning away from biomedicine, however, cannot be explained solely on the basis of unrealistic expectations. It is more likely that many people have begun to see that too often biomedicine is simply not concerned with general wellbeing because it can only assess very small, discrete bits of information. Also it is rooted in a society whose routine processes not only provoke stress but contaminate the environment to such an extent that every new comfort may conceal a new threat to life. Our medicine parallels our society. New cures often produce side effects of unexpected virulence.*
>
> *Moreover, our central medical institution, the hospital, is structured like nothing so much as a health factory — a contradiction in terms. And probably most important, people feel that there is no place for their feelings, intentions, beliefs, and values in the biomedical perspective. Biomedicine often leaves the 'person' in the waiting room.*[4]

This statement highlights the weaknesses and challenges of the Western medicine model of healing. In regards to TCM, Kaptchuk asks: Can a system of knowledge rooted in 'metaphysics' have anything to communicate to Western medicine? He explains that Western medicine has been very slow and very reluctant to embrace any 'metaphysical' aspect of TCM.[4]

Unfortunately, this does not only apply to TCM; it applies to all holistic therapies that attempt to integrate the physical, emotional and spiritual aspects of health into the health care model. I agree with Kaptchuk, who states that when there is no room for feelings, intentions, beliefs and values, there can be no true healing.

It is not surprising that many individuals are beginning to demand more focus on the health and healing of the whole person. Many people are drawn to complementary approaches that are more aligned with their own values, beliefs and philosophical orientations towards health and life.

A holistic practitioner of any particular therapy must have a deep respect for the individual's inherent capacity for self-healing. This, claims

Hoffmann, facilities a relationship of active partnership in the healing process, as opposed to an unequal dynamic between expert healer and passive healer.[5]

Hoffmann states that the mere use of herbal medicines does not make a treatment holistic. In fact, using a herbal remedy as a natural alternative to a prescription medication relegates the herb to the status of an organic drug delivery system. What makes herbs part of a holistic treatment is the context within which the herbs are prescribed and used.[5] I agree with Hoffmann and suggest that the same principles apply to the use of essential oils.

A holistic treatment aims at treating the whole person. A holistic approach may include identification and treatment of the disease, but it does not focus exclusively on symptoms. It should focus on the development of wellbeing and enjoyment of life in a system of self-responsibility.

This is where I get really excited, as an understanding of chakras can help us understand and use essential oils at a physiological, psychotherapeutic and metaphysical level to promote the self-healing process.

My personal chakra journey

My journey into natural therapies began with an interest in TCM and acupuncture. In my past life, that is, my life before I discovered natural therapies, I studied electrical engineering. Therefore, the concept of energy or *Qi* was not foreign to me. As an engineer, the idea of using crystals to amplify energy was not some New Age concept; it was based on sound scientific principles. The idea of energy flowing through meridians made so much sense. I came to learn of the incredible work that Russian scientists were doing in the field of Kirlian photography. How amazing is it that we could actually photograph this subtle energy? I felt it was my destiny as an engineer to develop devices that could measure the subtle energy channels of our body. While studying anatomy and physiology, I naively was frustrated that there was not a chapter on *Qi* and the meridians in my anatomy and physiology textbook.

In 1984 while fossicking around in my favourite secondhand bookstore in Hobart, looking for some guidance and direction in life, I found a very interesting book by Arthur E Powell called *The Etheric Double*. This book immediately caught my attention. Written in 1925 and published by the Theosophical Society, it was my first encounter with chakras.

At that time, there was very little information available on chakras; however, I soon discovered the local chapter of the Theosophical Society and attended some of their classes to expand my understanding of the subtle body.

The catalyst for change in my life was a small little blue book, *Heal Thyself — An Explanation of the Real Cause and Cure of Disease*, by Dr Edward Bach, creator of the Bach flower remedies. While part of me was excited to use my electrical engineering skills to build Kirlian photography equipment and electronic devices to measure or stimulate *Qi* along the meridians, I knew I had found my calling. I wanted to dedicate my life to healing and helping others. Bach's words resonated with me with such clarity:

> *Disease is in essence the result of conflict between soul and mind ... that so long as our souls and personalities are in harmony all is joy and peace, happiness and health. It is when our personalities are led astray from the path laid down by the soul, either by our worldly desires or by the persuasion of others, that conflict arises. This conflict is the root cause of disease and unhappiness.*[6]

Over the years I expanded my repertoire of skills: I studied herbal medicine with Kerry Bone, who provided me with a sound foundation in chemistry and pharmacognosy of herbs, and Simon Mills, who taught me how to integrate my two loves — herbal medicine and TCM. Then I discovered aromatherapy. It was like falling in love. Suzanne Fischer-Rizzi best describes my feeling towards aromatherapy:

> *Getting to know these heavenly scents is something like falling in love. They will touch your heart, make you keenly aware of the beauty surrounding you, and open the door to your soul. Suddenly, every facet of your life will be touched by magic.*[7]

Starting in the late 1980s, books such as *Hands of Light* by Barbara Brennan, *Vibrational Medicine* by Richard Gerber in 1988, and *Anatomy of the Spirit* written in 1996 by Caroline Myss became available.

During these years, I maintained my interest in chakras, always looking for ways of integrating my love of aromatherapy with chakras. I came to understand the incredible properties of essential oils such as their effective pharmacological properties, and the effect that they have on our psyche and emotional wellbeing, and our spiritual wellbeing and subtle energy. Each essential oil has its own unique energetic fingerprint that has the ability to balance our body's subtle energy.

I am disappointed that many of the books written on chakras nowadays do not acknowledge the early history of chakras. In 2016, I was delighted to discover Kurt Leland's book, *Rainbow Body*. This book helped me fit all the pieces of the chakra puzzle together. Leland, in a true investigative journalism style, traces the history of the Western Chakra System from its original roots in Indian Tantra, through to the early pioneers of the Theosophical Society such as Blavatsky and Leadbeater, through to Jung, the Esalen Institute and contemporary writers such as Brennan and Judith.

The origins of chakras lay in ancient traditional esoteric and Tantric practices of India. However, most of what we know of chakras today is a Western construct. Whatever the origins of chakras, they are a very effective tool to help us understand the relationship between our subtle energetic body, our emotions, our physical wellbeing and our spiritual wellbeing. It is not surprising that they are often referred to as the seven centres of consciousness.

The need for new sciences

Science has helped us to make some remarkable discoveries. Science is important for the advancement of humankind; however, a purely scientific approach to health care is an extremely alienating paradigm. Within an aromatherapy context, science has helped us to understand the chemical nature of the essential oils and how the essential oils work at a pharmacological level. However, you might be surprised to know that we still do not fully understand the mechanisms of olfaction or the intricate relationship between smell, the limbic brain and our emotions.

Schnaubelt states that the current scientific method is unable to make meaningful statements regarding the role of scent and emotions. He suggests the need for new sciences that would allow us to understand the existence of psychosomatic networks.[3]

For example, the currently accepted model of olfaction is based on shape theory — that scent is recognised by the molecular shape of the aroma molecules. However, in 1996 a biophysicist and chemist Luca Turin challenged this olfactory theory. Turin suggests that olfactory villa detect smell by molecular vibration rather than molecular shape.[8]

How interesting!

Yes, you heard right — vibrations. Vibrations, which are frequencies, are the basis of subtle energy medicine and energy healing. Perhaps one day in the near future, energy medicine will become part of mainstream medicine.

Smith explains how all energy medicines such as homoeopathy, acupuncture and healing are all linked through the commonality of frequencies. He provides us with a sound scientific framework for understanding how frequencies affect our health and wellbeing.[9]

There are people doing some excellent scientific research into vibrational and energy medicine. Dr Konstantin Korotkov, professor of physics at St Petersburg State Technical University in Russia, has developed the Gas Discharge Visualisation (GDV) technique to study the human energy field. He has also conducted studies examining the subtle energetic influences of essential oils on our subtle body.[10] Wisneski and Anderson provide us with a detailed scientific investigation of subtle energy therapies in their book *The Scientific Basis of Integrative Medicine*.[11]

Oschman, author of *Energy Medicine*, and Gerber, author of *Vibrational Medicine*, are pioneers in establishing a scientific basis for understanding subtle therapies. They both provide us with a comprehensive framework for understanding and integrating bioenergetic principles within mainstream medicine.

It is not surprising that Bone and Mills state the need for new physiology to study the complex dynamic living organism.[12] I suggest that any new physiology considers the principles of the subtle body that we are about to read about.

Part [1]
Energy, Subtle Bodies and Subtle Therapies

1. Defining Energy Medicine
2. Defining Energy
3. Energy Systems of the Human Body
4. The Future of Medicine is Energy
5. Subtle Therapies

1. Defining Energy Medicine

Gerber is adamant that energy therapies will ultimately be proven to be effective because they positively influence the human body's subtle energetic pathways. These pathways include the acupuncture meridian system, the chakras and the etheric body. He states that these energetic systems contribute to the final expression of the human form in both health and disease. Only when we are able to understand the role that these systems play in maintaining physiological balance will we realise the true relationship between 'wholeness' and 'disease'.[1]

I believe that the National Center for Complementary and Alternative Medicine has perfectly described the categories of natural, complementary and alternative medicines.[2] I am excited that they have acknowledged energy therapies.

Alternative medical systems: refer to complete systems of theory and practice such as homoeopathic and naturopathic medicine, traditional Chinese medicine and Ayurveda.

Mind–body interventions: include patient support groups, meditation and mindfulness, prayer, spiritual healing and therapies that use creative outlets such as art, music or dance.

Biological-based therapies: include herbs, food and nutritional supplements.

Manipulative and body-based therapies: include chiropractic, osteopathy and massage therapy.

Energy therapies: involve the use of energy fields such as qi gong, chakras, therapeutic touch and the use of electromagnetic fields.

Chaoul states that subtle therapy concepts remain problematic for biomedical science, and that mainstream Western medicine supposes a far more ironclad division between illness and energetic or mental obstacles. Thus, it becomes difficult for most Western doctors to accept the connection that Eastern traditional healing practices see between the health and meditative benefits, including those of Yogic practices and integration of the subtle or energetic body, mind and spirit.[3]

Silvia Binder explains that energy medicine involves energy of particular frequencies, intensities and wave shapes that stimulate the repair of one or more tissues. She lists examples of energy such as heat, light, sound, gravity, pressure, vibration, electricity, magnetism, chemical energy and electromagnetism.[4]

Binder explains that many traditional systems such as TCM and Ayurveda incorporate concepts of energy medicine. For example, Ayurvedic understanding of physiology differs from modern Western thought.[4]

> *Human beings are spiritual beings living in the temple of physical body prompting the care of health to focus on spiritual healing to affect the physical body. Another idea unique to the Eastern philosophy and yogic doctrine is the ideas of chakras.*[4]

She claims that the chakras are functional rather than structural, and states that numerous researchers have recorded and identified these locations, particularly in people in a higher state of consciousness or with extrasensory abilities.[4]

Oschman provides us with a detailed definition of energy medicine:

> *Energy medicine is defined as the diagnostic and therapeutic use of energy, whether detected by or produced by a medical device or by the human body. Energy medicine recognizes that the human body utilizes various forms of energy for the internal communications that maintains and organize vital living systems and for powering processes such as sensation, digestion, circulation and movement. Energy medicine involves the use of energies of particular intensities and frequencies and other characteristics that stimulate the repair of one or more tissues, or that enable built-in healing mechanisms to operate more effectively. Such energies can come from the environment, from another human being or from a medical device.*[5]

Rubik et al. suggest that the term biofield may be more appropriate than energy medicine. They state that biofield science is an emerging field of study that aims to provide a scientific foundation for understanding the complex homodynamic regulation of living systems. They state that many complementary and alternative therapies utilise 'laying-on-of-hands' and other minimally invasive procedures to improve endogenous energy flows. Many practitioners use terms from non-Western models to evoke a vital force or vital energy. Terms such as *Qi* and *prana* are descriptions of life energy that originate from metaphysical considerations of the nature of consciousness and its interaction with mental, emotional and physical systems.[6]

Most energy healers report utilising energy awareness not only to sense imbalances in patients' energy fields but to regulate energy flow and release energy blockages perceived to be impeding the healing process. Most traditional healing practices maintain that disease starts with an energetic imbalance such as a blockage or other irregularity in the energy flow of the body.[6]

Kafatos et al. hope that integrative biophysics and associated field processes, including electromagnetic fields (EMFs), biophotons and possible quantum interactions, will soon be seen as necessary, fundamental and complementary aspects of molecular biology and biochemistry.[7]

Jain et al. state that such a network may be found in what is currently being referred to as the biofield, a field of energy that reflects and guides the homeodynamic regulation of a living system, and as such influences and is influenced by consciousness. Biofield concepts are deeply rooted in many traditional and indigenous healing systems. It is not surprising that biofield science is highly controversial, not yet well understood and often academically contentious.[8]

Binder reminds us that mainstream medicine is already using energy medicine:

> Looking at today's diagnostic approaches, one couldn't imagine a hospital without ultrasound, X-Ray, and MRI capabilities, or even a private practice without an EKG, EEG, or ultrasound devices. All these devices measure the energy of the body in different ways and from different perspectives for diagnostic purposes.[4]

However, Binder expresses her disappointment that medical schools do not teach their students about the energetic body or energy therapies. She is adamant that if doctors understood this, then more doctors would confidently embrace energy medicine.[4]

Srinivasan states that it may not be possible to measure subtle energy as it is not of a physical nature:

Here the energies activating a person are subtle or of very low intensity. Such low levels may not be measurable at this time ... There is yet another notion of subtle energy; that is, the energy may not be a physical one.[9]

For example, Srinivasan explains that the effects of prayer and therapeutic touch are well documented and reported; however, the energy can only be surmised. The energy of the *Qi* or *prana* is not measurable; however, the interaction of the *Qi* or *prana* with the biological system may be deduced. Srinivasan explains that indirect measurement of the subtle energy of the body is possible with highly specialised equipment; however, the instruments must undergo many trials and clinical evaluation so that one day their use maybe acceptable in medical diagnostics and therapy.[9]

Warber et al. state that healing research and biofield science has contributed to advances in understanding energy healing practices. While they acknowledge that energy healing practices are very diverse, there are some common assumptions:[10]

- the existence of a universal lifeforce or vital energy flowing through and available to all beings
- the existence of a subtle energy system or biofield that interpenetrates the physical anatomy of the human body and extends outward beyond it
- the idea that in ill health, the human energetic field is out of balance or congested, free flow is blocked, which diminishes the normal self-healing capacity
- the belief that the practitioner can detect abnormalities in the energy system, sometimes before physical manifestations, and can restore the capacity of self-healing
- the contention that the practitioner's conscious healing intent and compassion are essential to the effectiveness of therapy
- the assertion that the healing outcome is not dependent on the client's belief.

Hover-Kramer and Halo Shames, authors of *Energetic Approaches to Emotional Healing*, state that while the human energy field is subtle, it can be measured by developing technologies. They cite the research of nurses who used Therapeutic Touch to examine the human energy field:[11]

> *While the healthy human energy field is full, vibrant, symmetrical, and smooth to the hands of the person who does an energetic assessment, the ill person's field may be bumpy, rough, diminished, asymmetrical, or irregular in shape.*

Binder explains that in the peer-reviewed literature, we can find evidence that certain electromagnetic fields have an impact on the physiological process including melatonin secretion, nerve regeneration, cell growth, collagen production, DNA synthesis, cartilage and ligament growth, lymphocyte activation and more.[4]

According to Binder, Wilhelm Reich noted that memory of traumatic episodes is stored in body cells. She explains that physical therapists have discovered that deep joint and skeletal massage releases memories of traumatic emotional episodes.[4]

Candice Pert, author of the *Molecules of Emotions*, is a pioneer in the field of mind–body medicine. Pert received her doctorate in pharmacology from John Hopkins University and later worked as a neuroscientist and was involved in the discovery of the opioid receptor. Pert came to the conclusion that virtually all illness has a psychosomatic component. Pert explains that the 'molecules of emotion' run every system in our body, creating a 'bodymind' intelligence.[4]

Binder also refers to the work of Valerie Hunt who is internationally recognised for her pioneering research of human energy fields. As professor at UCLA, California, she was one of the first researchers to measure the vibrational patterns of the bioenergetic field surrounding the human body.[4]

2. Defining Energy

Vibrations underlie every aspect of nature. The vibrations of atoms create sound and heat. Light is another form of vibrating energy. These are examples of the different types of energy that make up the electromagnetic spectrum, which also includes radio waves, television signals, X rays, ultraviolet radiation, ultrasonic waves and microwaves. The only difference between all these forms of energy is their frequency or rate of vibration.[12]

It was Albert Einstein who created the famous equation $E=mc^2$ that describes how energy and matter are interrelated. In fact, energy and matter are two different forms of the same thing. It is from here that we can begin to conceptualise that human beings are multidimensional energy systems.

The concept of 'energy' or 'subtle energy' that has been used in alternative and complementary therapies is one that has come under a great deal of criticism.

The concept of energy is used in many cultures, and these terms are often used interchangeably in a mix-and-match way in much of New Age

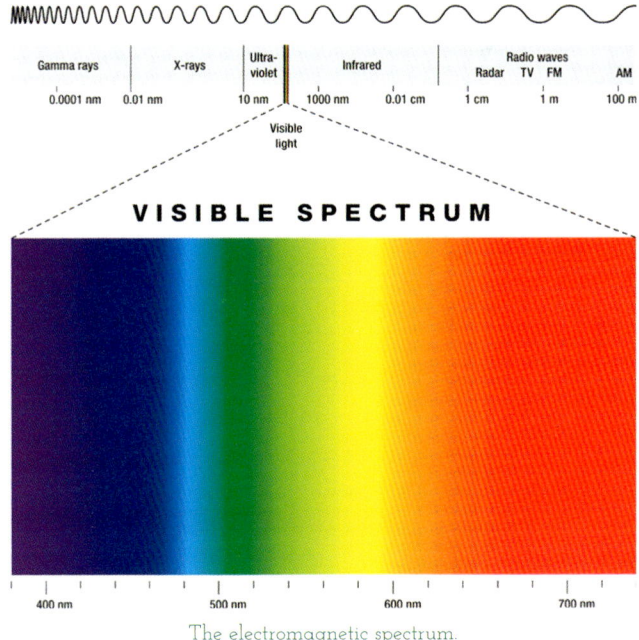

The electromagnetic spectrum.

thinking. The Chinese use the term *Qi* while in India the term *prana* is used. These are all labels for the energy that many complementary and alternative therapy practitioners say they work with to precipitate healing.

However, modern science only recognises four forms of energy: gravity, strong and weak nuclear forces, and electromagnetic force. Wright & Sayre-Adams claim that much of the energy that has been spoken about in the field of complementary therapies is not clearly definable or measurable.[13]

Oschman documents an extensive range of scientific studies that have been able to quantify the subtle energy of the body. He explains that all life depends upon molecules interacting through vibrating or oscillating energy fields.[5] This is supported by Gerber, who states:

> *In the living body, each electron, atom, chemical bond, molecule, cell, tissue, organ (and the body as a whole) has its own vibratory character. Since living structure and function are orderly, biological oscillations are organized in meaningful ways, and they contribute information to a dynamic vibratory network that extends throughout the body and into the space around it. Energy medicines and vibrational medicines seek to understand this continuous energetic matrix, and to interact with it to facilitate healing.*[12]

In search of scientific evidence for the existence of the energy field around living beings, Gerber discusses the work of neuroanatomist Harold S Burr:

> *Burr was studying the shape of energy fields around living plants and animals. Some of Burr's work involved the shape of electrical fields surrounding salamanders. He found that salamanders possessed an energy field roughly shaped like an adult animal. He also discovered that this field contained an electrical axis which was aligned with the brain and spinal cord.*
>
> *Burr wanted to find precisely when this electrical axis first originated in the animal's development. He began mapping the fields in progressively earlier stages of salamander embryogenesis. Burr discovered that the electrical axis originated in the unfertilised egg. This discovery contradicted the conventional biological and genetic theory of his day.*[12]

Research has lent further credibility to Burr's theories of bioenergetic fields from experimental work in the areas of electrographic photography, otherwise known as Kirlian photography. This is a technique whereby living objects are photographed in the presence of a high frequency, high voltage and low amp electrical field. This technique was pioneered by the Russian researcher Semyon Kirlian.[1]

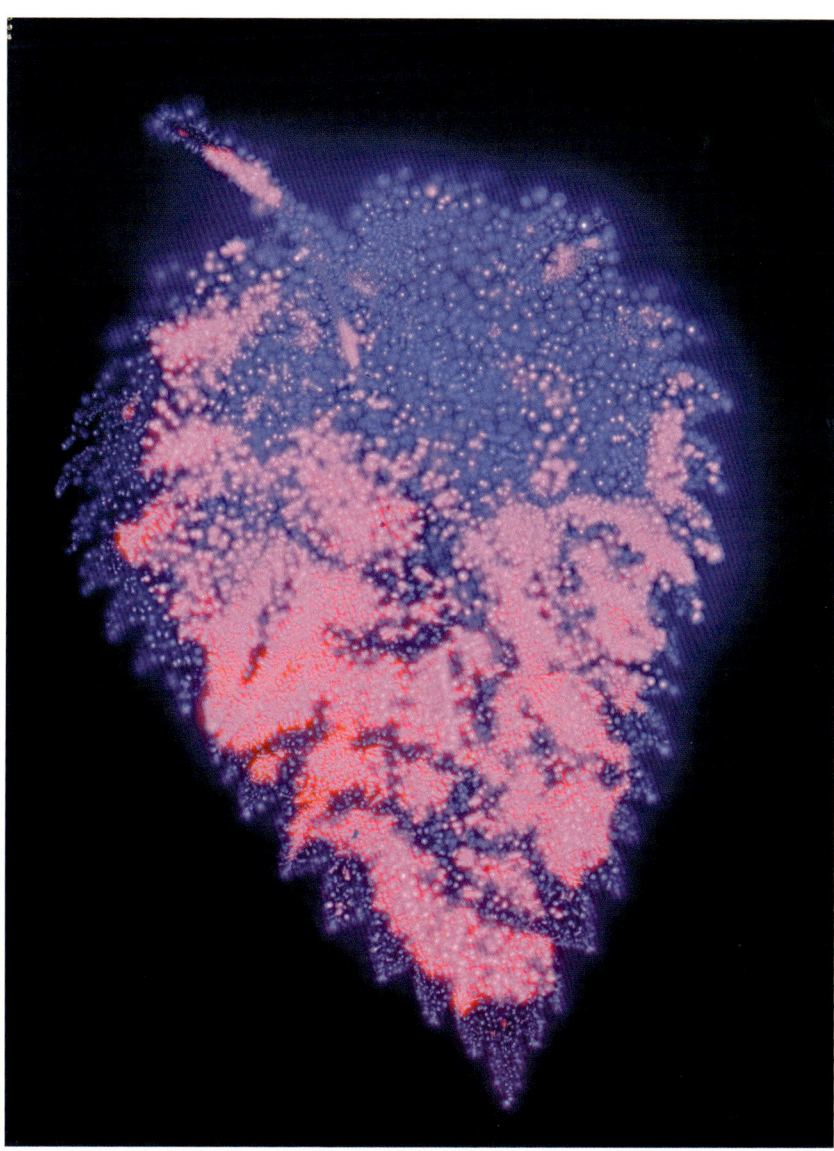

Kirlian photograph of a leaf.

3. Energy Systems of the Human Body

Throughout history, humanity has found different ways of exploring, describing and working with this subtle anatomy. Much of our knowledge of energy systems, sometimes referred to as 'subtle energy' systems, comes from sacred and spiritual knowledge of Asia.

The most common systems or models used in vibrational healing today are the meridian system of Traditional Chinese medicine (TCM), and the subtle body as defined in Indian and Tibetan Tantric traditions.

Gerber states that Western science has long ignored descriptions of subtle anatomy and physiology because their existence cannot be documented within the current medical framework. He explains that only recently has Western technology evolved to the point where we are beginning to understand that the subtle energy systems do exist and that they influence the physiological behaviour of cellular systems.[1]

Chaoul states that the globalisation of the twentieth century has not only allowed many Asian mind–body practices to take root in the West, but some practitioners have also adopted what anthropologist Joseph Alter called the 'medicalisation' of mind–body practices such as meditation and yoga, sometimes more than the original texts would.[3]

Mind–body practices such as meditation and yoga have become very popular in the West in the last decade as a way of reducing stress and enhancing spiritual growth. Chaoul states that many people with cancer believe that stress plays a role in the aetiology and progression of their disease.[3]

Chaoul cites Tenzin Wangyal Rinpoche's description of how one can connect the subtle body by focusing on meditation and breath:

> *We can sense prana directly at the grosser levels in the air we breathe. We can also sense its flow in our bodies. It is at this level, in which prana can be felt both in its movement and in its effects, that we work on Tantra. We become sensitive to and develop the flow of prana using mind, breathing, posture, and movement. By guiding*

the grosser manifestations of prana, we can affect the subtle levels. As our sensitivity increases, we can directly experience prana in subtler dimensions.[3]

Chaoul states that while all traditions do not necessarily agree on all the details of the subtle dimensions, all agree that they are composed of subtle channels through which subtle energy travels.[3]

Samuel and Johnston state that the concept of the subtle bodies used within New Age and alternative medical circles is often based on the interpretation of the subtle body of theosophists, who developed their own concepts based on psychic and clairvoyant insights, and their own interpretation of Sanskrit terminology. They state that neither theosophy nor anthroposophy were part of the scientific mainstream of Western thought, although they had many influential followers and significant scholars. This, they claim, makes the scholarly study questionable and even unworthy of serious consideration.[14]

Traditional Chinese medicine

The principles of TCM are extremely interwoven and complex. It embraces the ideas of *Qi* — the life force or subtle energy that permeates the universe and sustains all living things. It embraces the ideas of the Five Elements, of *Yin* and *Yang* and the meridians that are the channels through which *Qi* flows. All of these factors are delicately interrelated.

The philosophy underpinning TCM includes:

- The human body is a miniature version of the larger, surrounding universe.
- Harmony between two opposing yet complementary forces, called *Yin* and *Yang*, support health, and disease results from an imbalance between these forces.
- Five Elements — Fire, Earth, Wood, Metal and Water — symbolically represent all phenomena, including the stages of human life, and explain the functioning of the body and how it changes during disease.
- *Qi*, a vital energy that flows through the body, performs multiple functions in maintaining health.

12 Aromatherapy and Chakras

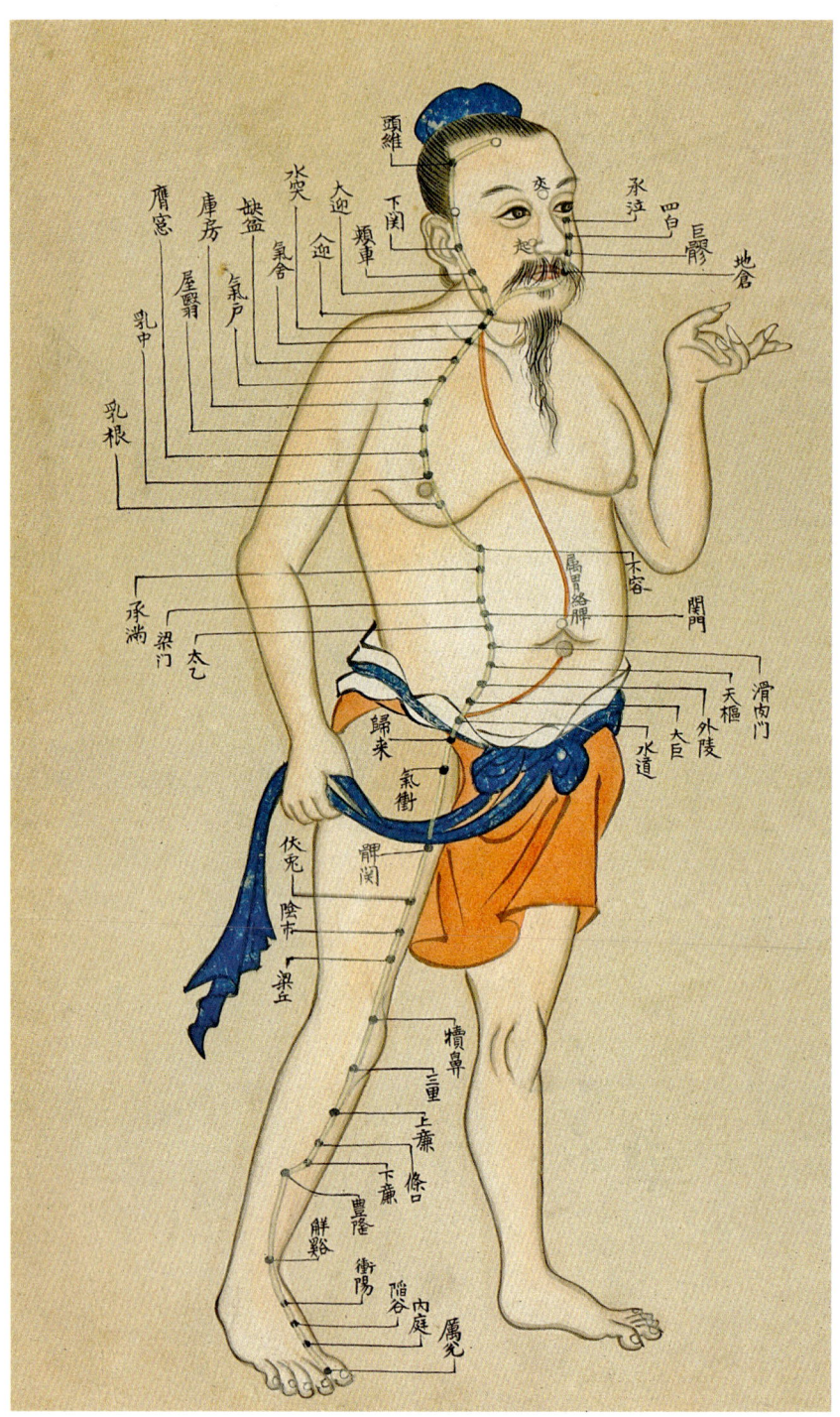

Acupuncture chart.

The greatest difficulty for the Western student of TCM lies in the tremendous difference between Western and Chinese patterns of thought. In the West, the word 'body' indicates the physical aspect: 'the body' as distinct from 'the mind' or 'the spirit'.

In TCM, the word 'body' implies not only the complex of physical, emotional, mental and spiritual aspects, but also the ongoing interaction between this complex and the external environment.

TCM recognises the acupuncture meridian system consisting of a series of channels, known as meridians, which acupuncturists are able to manipulate by inserting fine needles into special points along the meridians. The meridians carry the life force or energy, known as *Qi*, and according to TCM, illness can result from an imbalance of *Qi* energy to the organs and body. Therefore, the goal of acupuncture is to rebalance the flow of *Qi* throughout the body.

The subtle body in India – chakras and nadis

Samuel and Johnston state that the subtle body practices, found in Indian and Tibetan Tantric traditions, are similar to those of Chinese practices, involving the idea of an internal subtle physiology of the body made up of channels through which substances of some kind flow, and points of intersection at which these channels come together. The substance that flows through the channels or *nadis* is referred to as *prana*. The term *prana* is commonly understood as breath or respiration; however, it is also associated with the mind and with the emotions. It is considered a form of subtle energy.[14]

In Buddhist Tantric practices, the circulation of *prana* through the *nadi* and the chakras of the subtle body are associated with a series of meditative practices. It is understood in Tantric practices that there is a connection between *prana* and physical, mental and emotional correlates.[14]

The word *chakra*, traditionally spelt *cakra*, comes from Sanskrit and means circle. Chakras are described as wheels of forces arranged vertically on the trunk and head; they are transfer points for our thoughts and feelings and the physical functioning of specific endocrine glands. Chakras appear to be involved in the flow of higher energies via specific subtle energetic channels to the cellular structure of the physical body.[12]

XXIII

The astral body as revealed by higher clairvoyance, from the 1920 edition of Charles Leadbeater's *Man Visible and Invisible*.

Samuel states that the main chakras within the body are points of focus in Tantric internal practice. The chakras are often depicted as lotus-like, with multiple petals from which the *nadi* emerge. These petals are also the seats for a circle of deities associated with that particular chakra.[15]

The number of chakra and *nadi* varies between different Tantric traditions. The set of six or seven main chakras familiar in modern Yogic and New Age practices has gradually become the norm within Hindu practice.[15]

Saiva	Buddhist	Position in the body
Sahasrara	Mahasukha	crown of the head
Ajna	-	eyebrows
Vishuddha	Sambhoga	throat
Anahata	Dharma	heart
Manipura	-	navel
Svadhisthana	Nirmana	genitals
Muladhara	-	anus

Typical Saiva and Buddhist chakra systems.[15]

Samuel states that the question of how far these chakras are seen as physically existing at specific points within the body is difficult to answer. He states that Tantric practitioners do not consider the material existence of chakra as central to their practice. The central issue for Tantric practitioners is how one uses a particular system as a meditative device for personal transformation or other rituals.[15]

Samuel states that both Buddhist and Saiva traditions had developed a set of physical yoga exercises to prepare the mind–body for sexual practices. The Saiva versions of these exercises were the origins of the hatha yoga and similar traditions that gave rise to modern postural yoga. However, he states that modern hatha yoga practices have generally been divested of their Tantric and sexual associations, although they are still present in various Indian ascetic traditions.[15]

British High Court Judge Sir John Woodroffe, under the name 'Arthur Avalon', provided the West with the first accurate translation of Tantra and the role of the chakras.[16]

Originally published in 1919, *The Serpent Power* was the first English translation of Tantric practices and chakras. It is easy to see how this original text provided the foundations of our contemporary understanding of chakras. For example, in describing chakras Woodroffe states:

> *Each of these "astral" centres has certain functions: at the navel, a simple power of feeling; at the spleen, "conscious travel" in the astral body; at the heart, "a power to comprehend and sympathise with the vibrations of the other astral entities"; at the throat, power of hearing on the astral plane; between the eyebrows, "astral sight"; at the "top of the head", perfection of all faculties of the astral life.*[16]

Gerber claims that the flow of *prana* through our chakra system is influenced by our personality and our emotions, as well as our state of spiritual development. Anatomically each chakra is associated with a major nerve plexus and a minor endocrine gland. The seven major chakras are located in a vertical line ascending from the base of the spine to the head.[12]

The human subtle bodies – the auras

In addition to the life energy and the spiritual energies from the acupuncture meridians and the chakras, other energy systems also influence our health and wellbeing.

Marques, author of *The Human Aura* published in 1896, explains:

> *Theosophy claims that we are, all of us, as well as all things animate and inanimate, enveloped, surrounded, by a very complex, yet subtle, emanation, which (to the clairvoyant eye) is not only luminous, but tinted with the most variegated colors, these colors indicating our constitution, our passions, our ideas.*[17]

He claims that materialistic tendencies tend to destroy the psychic faculties. He also quotes Helena Petrovna Blavatsky's definition of aura:

> *A subtle, invisible essence or fluid that emanates from human and animal bodies and even things; it is a psychic effluvium, partaking of both the mind and the body, as it is the electro-vital and at the same time an electro-mental aura, called in Theosophy the akasic or magnetic.*[17]

Gerber suggests that our soul or our 'true self' expresses itself through a physical body that is influenced by higher spiritual bodies. The first of these higher spiritual bodies or auras is known as the etheric body. The etheric body is described as a kind of duplicate of the physical body that actually occupies the same space as the physical body, but at a higher vibratory rate or frequency.[12]

The etheric body is invisible to the naked eye, but can easily be seen by some psychically gifted people who are able to see auras. Most people working in subtle healing can sense the aura in non-visual ways. It is not difficult to feel with your hands the energy emanations, especially the etheric and astral bodies.[9] Kirlian photography is a technique that can be used to take an image of the etheric body.[12]

Besides the etheric body, there is the astral body, which participates in how we feel and how we express ourselves, and how we are influenced by our emotions. Some clairvoyants refer to the astral body as the emotional body.[12]

While the etheric body is strongly attached to the physical body, the astral body appears to be more mobile and can move about independent from the physical body.[12]

Beyond the etheric and astral bodies resides another spiritual body known as the mental body. The mental body is composed of subtle magnetic energy that vibrates faster than astral energy. The mental body is involved in the energy of thought, creation, invention and inspiration.[12]

Finally, the human energy field extends to an even higher spiritual plane known as the causal body. Gerber explains that the causal body might be considered the closest thing to the soul. The record of all that a soul has experienced on the physical earth plane, in its current life as well as past lives, is said to be contained in the causal body.[12]

Gerber cites a number of spiritual philosophies that suggest the soul lives different lives through a variety of different physical bodies over the course of the earth's history. He states that to truly understand the causal body, one must believe that the human soul is immortal and that it progressively becomes more spiritually enlightened by returning to earth numerous times in different physical bodies. This is the cornerstone of reincarnation, a belief system shared by millions of people throughout many different cultures of the world.[12]

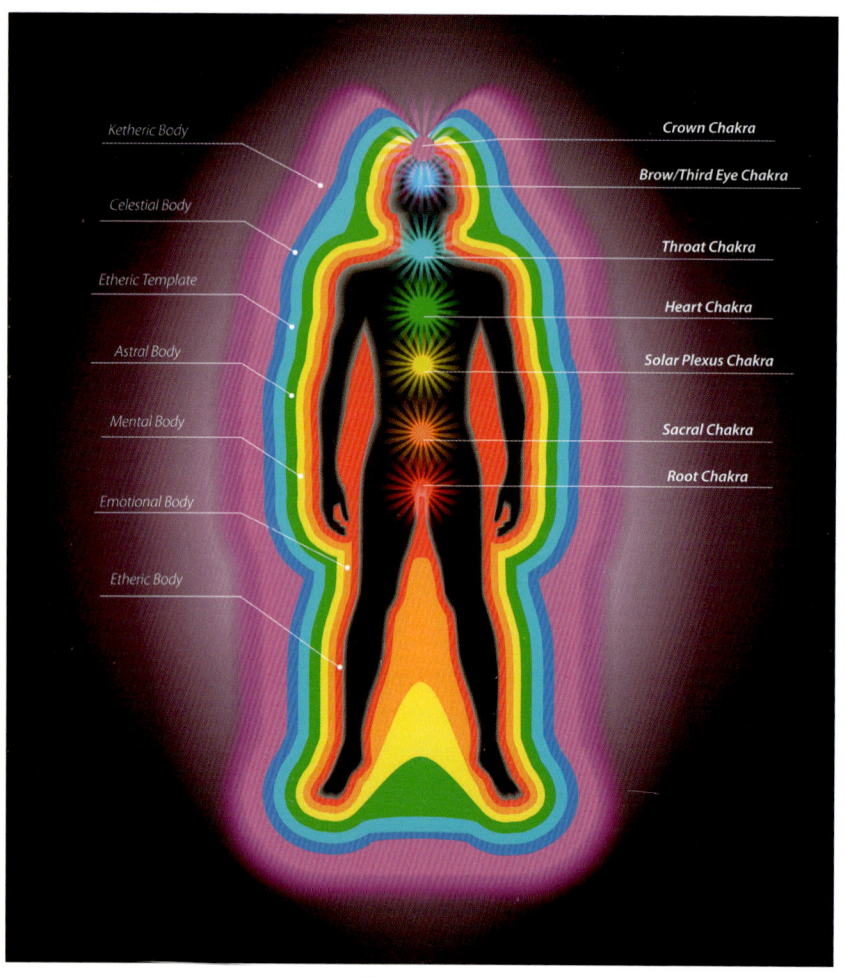

Human aura.

Gerber states that the causal body retains a memory of our past lives, and unresolved traumas and conflicts may be carried over from one lifetime to affect the body and life patterns of another lifetime. The unique types of health problems, related directly to the causal body, are known as 'karmic illnesses'.[12]

Leland states that according to theosophical teachings, the seven planes of existence are arranged in hierarchy from lower (more physical, dense and earth-oriented) to higher (more subtle-oriented). He explains that each of these planes may be accessed by a vehicle of consciousness or energy body.[18]

The list of bodies and planes is as follows:[18]
- the physical body and the etheric body (etheric double), on the physical plane
- the astral body, on the astral plane
- the mental and causal bodies, on the mental plane
- the buddhic (intuitional) body, on the buddhic (intuitional or unity) plane. Leland explains that buddhic does not refer to the Buddha or Buddhism, but to the Sanskrit word *buddhi*, which means higher mind or faculty of wisdom
- the nirvanic (*atmic* or spiritual) body, on the nirvanic (*atmic* or spiritual) plane. Leland explains that *atmic* is a theosophical term, based on the Sanskrit word *atman*, which refers to our whole self, or soul
- the monadic body, on the monadic (*anupadaka* or paranirvanic) plane
- the divine (or logoic) body, on the divine (*adi*, logoic or mahaparanirvanic) plane.

Leland explains that theosophy has gone through a number of stages in which the names of the energy bodies have changed from long Sanskrit terms to simplified English terms.[18]

Sturgess offers us a more traditional interpretation of the subtle bodies. He explains that the individual soul-consciousness expresses itself through five sheaths (*koshas*), which are divided between the three bodies — the physical, astral and causal body.[19]

Sturgess states that the chakras are situated within the astral body — the subtle body that mirrors the physical body. The chakras energetically connect the five sheaths (*koshas*) that embody the soul to the function of the physical body, primarily through the endocrine glands and the nerve plexuses of the spine.[19]

An understanding and appreciation of the higher spiritual bodies — our etheric, astral, mental and causal bodies — as well as the chakras and the meridians give us a holistic way of looking at concepts of health and wellness from a multidimensional perspective.

4. The Future of Medicine is Energy

I am drawn to Gerber's explanation of the subtle energy systems. He describes the relationship between our subtle energy system and our body as follows:

> *The brain, albeit a complex biocomputer, still needs a programmer to instruct the nervous system how to perform and what acts to accomplish. That conscious entity which uses this biomechanism of the brain and body in the human spirit or soul. That which we refer to as the spiritual domain is part of a series of higher dimensional energy systems which feed directly into the computer hardware we call the brain and body. It is these higher dimensional systems, our so-called subtle energetic anatomy, that science has yet to recognize. Alternative systems of healing are often effective because they can correct abnormal patterns of function in the higher dimensional systems which control cellular physiology and behavioral patterns of expression.*[12]

Gerber claims that Western science has long ignored descriptions of ethereal components of physiology because their existence could never be documented by anatomical dissection. However, acupuncture meridians, chakras and *nadis*, the etheric body and other systems of the human multidimensional anatomy have long been described in traditional healing systems.[12]

I agree with Gerber who claims that, as our understanding of our multidimensional nature develops, the application of subtle energetic therapies will become mainstream, lessening our need for drugs and surgery. He states:

> *In addition, the recognition of our relationship to these higher frequency energy systems will ultimately lead to a fusion of religion and science as scientists begin to recognize the spiritual dimension of human beings and the laws of expression of the life-force. The trend of 'holism' in medicine will ultimately move physicians toward the*

> *recognition that, for human beings to experience health, they must enjoy an integrated relationship between body, mind, and spirit.*[12]

I have no doubt that the future of medicine will one day be energy-based.

We now know that all cells, plant matter and living organisms emit biophotons, known as ultraweak photon emissions (UPEs). Researchers have been examining the relationship between biophotons and their connection to disease and wellbeing. Scientists state that measuring the UPE levels has the potential to be a powerful non-invasive diagnostic tool.[20]

It appears that UPEs are a natural bioproduct of oxidative reactions that release free radicals. Biophoton emissions are therefore considered normal as the body is constantly undergoing oxidative reactions. However, there will be some disease states in which oxidative stress is higher, meaning that there would be higher levels of UPEs.[20]

More exciting is the fact that biophotons could be used as a target of treatment for a disease. For example, studies involving the adaptogen *Rhodiola rosea* found that it is associated with reduction of oxidative stress inflammation and depression, and enhancement of cognitive performance. Researchers also found that it significantly decreased biophoton emissions.[20]

In one study using GDV, I was able to see how just inhaling essential oils was enough to influence the biophoton emissions. I look forward to sharing the full details of this study later in the book.

Researchers have also found that biophoton emissions from the body decrease after meditation, which indicates that meditation leads to reduced oxidative stress and production of free radicals. It is known that oxidative stress is the indication of many metabolic syndrome disorders and that biophoton measurements could be an easy and non-invasive method of measuring oxidative process in the body.[21,22]

5. Subtle Therapies

Subtle therapies are often referred to as vibrational or energy medicine. There are many subtle, vibrational or energy therapies and many theories explaining subtle energy. Much of our knowledge of subtle therapies comes from the Eastern traditional healing arts such as Ayurveda and TCM.

Some of the therapies commonly used nowadays incorporating the use of subtle energy include flower remedies, gem elixirs, homoeopathy, acupuncture, crystal healing, colour therapy, therapeutic touch, spiritual healing and, of course, subtle aromatherapy.

A brief history of subtle therapies

Various forms of healing are described in the Bible and other spiritual texts from the world. The 'laying on of hands' practised by Jesus continues today in some churches. Modern versions of this technique include therapeutic touch, healing touch, reiki and polarity therapy, to name just a few.

In 1773, Franz Anton Mesmer began using magnets for healing. Mesmer's patients frequently noticed 'unusual currents' flowing through their bodies prior to the onset of a 'healing crisis' that led to a cure. Oschman states that Mesmer discovered that he could produce the same phenomena without the magnets, simply by passing his hands over the patient's body.[5]

In 1873, Edwin D Babbitt, a minister in East Orange, New Jersey, published his classic treatise *The Principles of Light and Colour*. He had secluded himself in a darkened room for several weeks, and when he emerged, he discovered he had acquired a greatly heightened visual sensitivity and could see energy fields around human bodies.[5]

By the turn of the twentieth century, a wide range of electrical and magnetic healing devices were on the market, providing therapies for every disease imaginable. Unfortunately, there was no system in place to verify the efficacy of any of these devices. In 1906, the FDA considered electrotherapy scientifically unsupportable and they were legally excluded from clinical practice.[5]

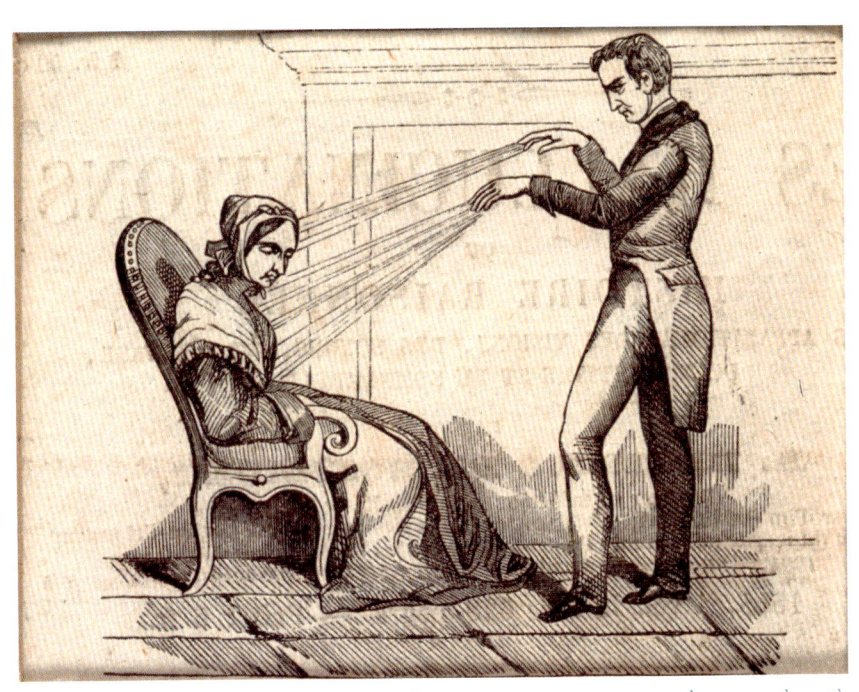

A practitioner of mesmerism using animal magnetism on a woman who responds with convulsions.

One cannot discuss subtle energy therapies without reference to Blavatsky (1831–1891), the founder of the Theosophical Society. Theosophists believe in the presence of life and consciousness in all matter, the ability of thought to affect the reality we live in, and a concern for the welfare of others.[5]

Blavatsky encouraged the study of Western mystical traditions such as Gnosticism, the Kabbalah, Freemasonry and Rosicrucians, as well as Buddhism and other Eastern philosophies. It was one of the theosophists, Charles Leadbeater, who in the 1920s published one of the first books on the chakras. It was the theosophists who introduced the concept of the chakras as energy vortexes that have an independent objective existence associated with particular endocrine glands and nerve plexuses.[5]

I am fascinated with the work of Harold Saxton Burr. He obtained his PhD at Yale in 1915 and became a Professor of Anatomy in 1933 and remained in the post for 40 years. According to Oschman, Burr began a series of important and controversial studies of the role of electricity in development and disease. Burr was a pioneer in linking biology and physics, and his research laid the groundwork for the development of the magnetic resonance imaging (MRI).[5]

Candice Pert and Valerie Hunt were both extraordinary individuals who passionately researched the field of energy medicine within the framework of rigorous adherence to the highest scientific standards. As a professor at UCLA, Hunt ran the first laboratory studies measuring and recording the energy of vibrational patterns of the bioenergetic field surrounding the human body.[4]

Homoeopathy

The discovery and development of homeopathic medicine is credited to Samuel Hahnemann (1755–1843), a brilliant German physician. Gerber explains how Hahnemann came up with the principle of 'like cures like', which is the very foundation for homoeopathy:

> *According to this new principle of "like cures like", cinchona was ideal for treating malaria because it reproduced malaria's symptoms in someone healthy. A homeopathic remedy was chosen to treat an illness based upon its ability to reproduce the patient's "total symptom complex" in an otherwise healthy person.*[1]

Gerber states that in homoeopathy the mental and emotional symptoms were given equal or greater weight than the physical symptoms. He explains that from this perspective, homoeopathy was one of the first holistic disciplines that gave attention to alterations of both mind and body in search for a cure.[1]

Hahnemann treated many diseases with great therapeutic success utilising the principle of 'like cures like'. He also experimented with diluting the remedies that he gave his patients and he was surprised to find that the greater the dilution, the more effective the remedy. The remedies were so diluted that in many of the remedies, not a single molecule of the original herb is present.[1]

> *Homeopaths believe that microdoses interact with the human subtle energies system which is integrally related to the physical cellular structure.*[1]

Gerber explains:

> *Homeopathy aims to match the correct single remedy with the totality of the patient. This includes not only physical, but emotional and mental symptoms as well. This allows for the closest "vibrational match" between illness and cure.*[1]

Gerber suggests that homoeopathy can be best summarised as representing an alternative evolutionary pathway in the application of medicinal plant therapies. Where pharmacologists chose to isolate single, active molecular agents from herbs, homoeopaths work with the vibrational essences of the whole plant.[1]

Flower remedies

Dr Bach is credited with the discovery of the now-famous Bach flower remedies. These flower essences are used to treat a variety of emotional disorders and temperaments. Like homoeopathic medicines, flower essences contain very little of the physical substance.

Before becoming a homoeopathic practitioner, Bach was an orthodox physician specialising in bacteriology at a major hospital in London. In his work, he found that patients carrying different intestinal bacterial pathogens displayed particular personality types or temperaments. Based on this insight, he began to treat his patients with nosodes. He assigned the nosodes strictly on the basis of the patients' emotional temperaments. He ignored the physical aspect of their disease and dealt with their mental/emotional symptoms.[1]

He was able to conclude that individuals of the same personality type would not necessarily come down with the same disease. Rather, patients in the same personality group would react to their illness in a similar fashion with the same behaviours, moods and states of mind, regardless of the disease. He suggested that different emotional and personality factors contribute towards a general predisposition to illness. He found that the most significant of these factors were emotional tendencies such as fear and negative attitudes.[1]

He did not like prescribing nosodes (prepared from disease-producing agents), so he began searching for more natural plant-derived remedies. Bach identified 38 essences in all. The 38th essence was a combination remedy known as Rescue Remedy. He perceived that the illness-personality link was an outgrowth of dysfunctional energetic patterns within the subtle bodies:

> *He felt that illness was a reflection of disharmony between the physical personality and the higher self or soul. Reflections of this inner disharmony could be found within particular types of mental traits and attitudes which the individual displayed. This mental and energetic disharmony between the physical personality and the higher self was seen as outweighing the particular disease process.*
>
> *Bach felt that the subtle vibrational energies of the flower essences could assist in realigning the emotional patterns of dysfunction. By increasing the alignment of the physical personality with the energies of the higher self, greater harmony can occur within the individual as reflected by greater peace of mind and the expression of joy. By correcting these emotional factors, patients would be assisted in increasing their physical and mental vitality and thus be aided in resolving any physical disease.*[1]

Gerber explains that qualities of the mind and emotion that are expressed through the brain and physical nervous system are a product of energetic input from the etheric, astral and mental bodies. He suggests that flower essences are able to have an energetic impact upon these higher bodies; their effects are ultimately able to filter down to the physical body.[1]

Gerber describes Bach's process of making the flower remedies:

> *He collected the morning dew from flowers that were in sunlight, and the dewdrops from flowers that were still in the shade. He examined them for differences in their ability to affect his subtle energy bodies. By comparing the two solutions, he found that the water from the flowers exposed to sunlight had the most marked effect. To his delight, he found that he could place the flowers of a particular species upon the surface of a bowl of spring water for several hours in sunlight and obtain powerful vibrational tinctures. The subtle effects of sunlight were critical in charging the water with an energetic imprint of the flower's vibrational signature. This may relate to the subtle energetic qualities in sunlight which the Hindus have referred to as "prana".*[1]

Gerber describes how flower essences work:

> *Utilizing the Bach flower remedies, many practitioners have achieved clinical success in relieving long-standing patterns of emotional distress and personality dysfunction. Unlike conventional drug therapies which impact solely at the level of physical cellular pathology, the energetic patterns contained within the flower essence work at the level of the emotional, mental and spiritual vehicles. The subtle bodies influence the physical body by altering its susceptibility to illness from any external or internal noxious agent. What Bach was doing with his vibrational essences was working to increase the host resistance of his patients by creating internal harmony and an amplification of the higher energetic systems that connect beings to their higher selves. Bach's flower remedies had little direct effect upon cellular systems of the physical body.*[1]

The 38 Bach flower remedies can address one of seven psychological causes of illness: fear, uncertainty, insufficient interest in present circumstances, loneliness, oversensitivity to influences and ideas, despondency or despair, and overcare for the welfare of others.[23]

Colour therapy

Colour therapy is not new to vibrational healing. Colour therapy has been used in the healing temples in Egypt, Greece, China and India.

Colour therapy utilises the vibrational frequency of the colours of the spectrum to correct the imbalances or disharmony in the body. Colour has a powerful effect on our emotions. Colours activate the chakra system. Each chakra resonates in harmony with one of the spectrum colours. The chakras can be stimulated and energised with their particular colour vibration to restore balance and harmony.

Colour therapy and aromatherapy work together in synergy. Essential oils and colour can recharge the aura and cleanse negative vibrations from the subtle bodies. Each essential oil has its own colour vibration or signature, so you can blend a harmonious mix of essential oils that resonate at the same frequency as the colours you wish to use. You can complement the treatment with the use of a colour lamp, coloured towels and the colour of the room.

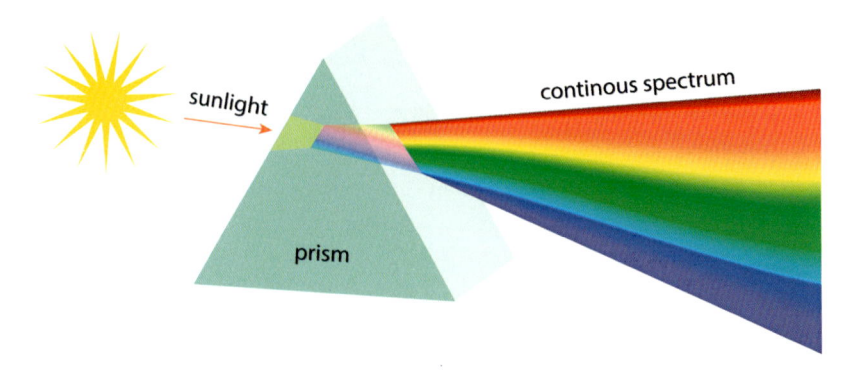

Light split by a prism.

Keim Loughran and Bull state that colours have a unique, vibrational and energetic signature that produces a specific effect in subtle energy therapy. There are seven colours in the visible light spectrum: red, orange, yellow, green, blue, indigo and violet. These correlate to the seven primary energy centres.[24]

Visualising and sending the appropriate colour combined with subtle energy techniques can be helpful in bringing balance and harmony. Generally, the cooler colours of blue, indigo and violet relax us while the warmer colours of red, orange and yellow energise us. They state that colours can be visualised on parts of the body to achieve a particular result. The soothing, vibrational qualities of blue can calm an inflamed condition, such as a sprained ankle. Red energises and can help an area that has poor circulation, such as cold feet, while orange can bring joy to the heart and relieve emotional depression.

Red

Red is the colour associated with the element of fire. It is the colour of the base chakra. Red governs the genitals and reproductive organs, blood and circulation. It is drive and willpower.

Cooper states that the colour red is associated with energy, procreation, zest for life, dangers, construction and destruction, being alive and sexuality. It produces restlessness, anger, might and aggression and the will to win, sometimes at all costs.[25]

Newton states that red rays produce heat that is vitalising and energising, excellent for contracted muscles. Red activates blood circulation, raises the pulse and heartbeat. It tends to motivation, stimulation and power. Red light can be used when one is feeling tired and rundown. It rids the body of toxins and any psyche negativity.[26]

Newton states that essential oils that reflect the red ray are benzoin, black pepper, cedarwood, jasmine, myrrh, rose, sage and thyme.[26]

Orange

Orange is a combination of red and yellow rays, and its healing power is greater than the two individual rays. Orange is the colour of the sacral chakra. Orange governs the area of the lower back and lower intestines, the abdomen and kidneys. It has an antispasmodic effect and it stimulates the pulse rate without affecting the blood pressure.

Cooper states that the colour orange is about feeling and sensations, good-natured and flamboyant, giving one back their self-esteem, worth and importance, emotional force, and pleasurable experiences. It is related to being sociable, ambitious and enthusiastic and leads to a concern for others. It helps in cases of identity crisis by promoting self-assurance. Orange is the colour for dealing with grief, bereavement and loss.[25]

Newton states that essential oils that reflect the orange ray are aniseed, benzoin, bergamot, caraway, cardamom, carrot seed, cedarwood, cypress, ginger, mandarin, marjoram, neroli, nutmeg, orange, patchouli, pine and sandalwood.[26]

Yellow

Yellow is the colour of the solar plexus chakra. The solar plexus is the part of us that absorbs emotions. Yellow governs the pancreas, spleen, middle stomach, liver, gall bladder, digestive system and the nervous system.

Gerber states that yellow is associated with the colour of intellect and the use of the mind in concrete, scholarly ways. Because many individuals with stress-related disorders, such as ulcers, tend to be mentally focused and sometimes emotionally repressed, the yellow ray can be helpful in treating various types of stomach problem and indigestion.[12]

Cooper states that the colour yellow is associated with the search for self-knowledge. It is the re-energiser of the mind, promoter of mental activity, ingestion and assimilation, study and thought. Yellow is associated with those who can be stubborn and opinionated, have a good business head and are the protectors of innate wisdom. It relates to higher emotions like joy and happiness, emotional sensitivity, reactivity and reaction.[25]

Yellow is the colour of the mind and the ego. It is an excellent colour for the nerves and brain. It is a good eliminator, ridding the body of toxins. It can help to relieve constipation. Psychologically, yellow is uplifting, bringing hope and light, giving a feeling that everything will be alright.

Newton states that essential oils that reflect the yellow ray are aniseed, basil, bergamot, cajeput, cardamom, carrot seed, citronella, dill, fennel, ginger, grapefruit, lemon, lemongrass, petitgrain, sandalwood, tea tree and vetiver.[26]

Green

Green is the colour of peace and healing and the colour of the heart chakra. Green governs the thymus gland, heart, shoulders, chest and lower lungs. Green is made up of yellow and blue. Gerber states that green exercises some control over the distribution of blood supply through its effects are on the heart.[1]

Cooper states that green helps prevent stagnation and represents a new place and pace, affections of the heart, freedom, adaptability and harmony, and brings good judgements, balance and understanding, maturity and self-control, love for humanity, generosity, nature, regeneration, karma or opportunities for new beginnings, breathing space, compassion, cooperation, understanding, caring, stability, giving, growth, willingness and a positive expression of the inner self.[25]

Green is cooling, soothing and calming on all levels. It is emotionally stabilising and balancing and is also regulating on the metabolism. It is a muscle builder and tissue builder. It helps to dispel negativity. It soothes headaches.

Newton states that essential oils that reflect the colour green are aniseed, bergamot, eucalyptus, geranium, lemon, melissa, palmarosa, peppermint and petitgrain.[26]

Blue

Blue is the colour of the throat chakra; it rules the throat area and is linked to upper lungs and arms, the base of the skull and weight. Blue is peaceful and cool.

Cooper states that the colour blue is associated with nurturing, communicating, peace, faith, idealism, sincerity, expression of thoughts, languages and images, the mother, cool and calm, a natural antiseptic, stability, gentleness and meditation.[25]

The blue vibration is very helpful for throat problems, helping to dispel the fear of 'speaking out' or 'speaking the truth'. Blue increases vitality, the coolness of blue makes it an excellent colour for treating inflammatory diseases. Blue can reduce stress and anxiety and can help to reduce blood pressure.

Newton states that essential oils that reflect the blue ray are German chamomile, Roman chamomile, cypress, eucalyptus, hyssop, mandarin, sweet marjoram, myrtle, pine and rosemary.[26]

Indigo

Indigo is made up of dark blue and dark violet; it is the colour of the third eye chakra. Indigo rules the endocrine system, the spine, lower brain, eyes and sinuses.

Cooper states that the colour indigo is about pacifying and calming, pure spiritual thoughts, devotion to an ideal, psychic matters, the eye of the soul and contact with the higher self, spiritual communications, a higher level of intellect, insight, imagination and self-realisation.[25]

Indigo provides the greatest analgesic benefits in the spectrum. It is useful for treating sciatica, migraine, bruising and inflammations. It promotes skin repair. It is a balancer for high blood pressure and is said to be great for insomnia. Newton states that essential oils that reflect the indigo ray include bay laurel, cinnamon, clove, myrtle, tea tree and yarrow.[26]

Violet

Violet is a light shade of purple. Violet is the colour of the crown chakra. It governs the pineal gland. Violet is considered a very spiritual colour and has a spiritual dedication. Violet is intuition. It calms emotional upsets. It aids psychic ability and is a great colour for meditation.

Cooper states that the colour violet is associated with creativity, inspiration, mental strength, inspired leadership, evolution of the soul, religion, spirituality, the gateway to attainment, aspiration, humanitarianism and devotion.[25]

Violet is good for bone growth. It is a blood purifier and helps to build up white blood cells. It is used as a treatment for varicose veins, inflammation and pain. Because violet vibrates at such a high frequency, it has the ability to break down fears associated with the mind. Newton states that it is a cleanser of impure thoughts and emotions in the mind as well as the room. Essential oils that reflect the violet ray include basil, frankincense, grapefruit, hyssop, juniper, lavender, patchouli, sage and sandalwood.[26]

Utilising colour therapy in healing

There are intricate systems and approaches to colour healing that are utilised by various practitioners. Colours may be applied alone or in special therapeutic combinations that tend to enhance the potential of colour therapy through synergistic effects. The methods by which the frequencies of colour may be transmitted to patients are numerous. According to Gerber, the methods include:[12]

- direct light from electric lamps (or natural sunlight) that has passed through various colour screens and filters
- coloured tinctures or flower essences
- colour breathing.

Gerber outlines a procedure for colour breathing and the benefits of visualisation and affirmations. This could be utilised with the appropriate essential oils that reflect the colour you are visualising:

> *Color breathing involves visualising oneself breathing in a particular color during the inspiratory phase of respiration. Following inspiration, the visualised color is mentally directed to areas of illness, blockage and dysfunction, or those bodily systems which are in need of visualisation. There are many variations on this particular technique of colour breathing which allow visualised color to be used for altering the level of one's consciousness and for cleansing the*

chakras, as well as achieving particular types of healing. Color breathing at the mental level involves directing energies that work with the mental and astral bodies and chakras.

In general, visualisation of the color, gem, or flower being vibrationally applied can powerfully augment the effectiveness of the treatment. Mental affirmations — inwardly spoken statements that reaffirm the desired physical or emotional change — can also be helpful in amplifying the efficacy of the various vibrational therapies ... The more the individual becomes actively involved with the therapy, as in the use of visualisation and affirmations, the greater the chances are for a successful healing outcome to occur.[12]

Colour and the human aura

Leadbeater, author of *Man, Visible and Invisible* written in 1902, examines the subtle bodies of humans, identifying how the colours of the aura change with different emotions. He explains that the appearance of the etheric body or 'healthy aura' is symptomatic of the general state of a person's health, as the vital energy of *prana* or *Qi* is seen flowing through it.[27]

I find the qualities that he assigns to the different colours in the subtle body fascinating. They most definitely relate with the contemporary associations often given to colours of the aura.

Leadbeater, for example, states that red signifies anger, while crimson is the manifestation of love. Orange is always associated with pride and ambition. Yellow implies intellect, while green indicates a kind of adaptability. A dark clear blue usually is associated with religious feelings, while a light blue indicates devotion to a noble spiritual ideal.[27]

Klotsche, author of *Color Medicine: The Secrets of Color/Vibrational Healing,* explains that our personality and state of health are reflected in our aura:

As the patterns of our personalities change, we monitor the progress in life, our frustrations and, for our purposes, our state of health. As the patterns of our personalities changes, we can monitor the progress or lack thereof, determine if we have missed or used opportunities. Although the long-term vibration of personality is in the aura, our current state of being is readily visible as well.[28]

He suggests that the mind and our emotions are likely to be the governing factors that determine the colour of the aura; however, the environment can also play a part. He states that the colours in the aura are constantly changing and are a blend representing temporary or permanent imbalance.[28]

Klotsche assigns the following meanings to the various colours expressed in our aura:[28]

- Red in the aura indicates a physical and more materialistic orientation, with a strong concern for physical life. It often shows a vigorous, active, forceful person, often with a warm and affectionate nature, yet impulsive and passionate; may be domineering or angry. Red in the aura may indicate low energy level and problems with the nervous system.
- Orange in the aura indicates thoughtfulness and consideration, vitality and health.
- Yellow indicates a healthy person who takes care of themselves and is happy and unworried. It shows mental force and concentration.
- Green is the colour of vegetation and tolerance. It is the colour of independence, peace and regeneration.
- Blue is a positive colour of inspiration in the aura. Darker shades represent more depth and dedication, while lighter shades denote a struggle towards maturity.
- Indigo represents intuition, integrity, devotion, sincerity, spirituality and often an urge to help others on a deeper level of being.
- Violet is seldom seen in the aura, for it belongs to highly developed souls with open crown chakras. Violet combines the blue of religious search and devotion with the vitality of red. It is also the colour of greatness, transcendence, spiritual power and authority.
- White is considered the colour of perfection or integration. All the healing colours blend in perfect harmony to create white.

Klotsche correlates the colours with the seven major chakras:[28]

- red — base chakra
- orange — sacral chakra
- yellow — solar plexus chakra
- green — heart chakra

- blue — throat chakra
- indigo — brow chakra
- violet — crown chakra
- white — perfect colour blend.

Crystals

Kristine Carlos, author of a very insightful research thesis examining crystal healing practices in the Western world, explains that there are three overwhelmingly important cultures that have contributed to the New Age practices involving crystals. The three cultures are Indian, British and Native American. She suggests that many of the New Age practices have borrowed rituals involving crystals from these traditions.[29]

It is interesting that many books on crystals do not make any attempt to examine the origins of knowledge regarding their healing qualities. On the other hand, Gerber, in *Vibrational Medicine,* provides us with a scientific basis for the healing properties of crystals. He points out that technology has embraced the unique electrical qualities of crystals and explains about the important role of crystal technologies in the development of electronic systems.[1]

> *From utilizing crystals for communication, information storage, solar power, and laser applications in industry and medicine, we are slowly discovering that the gems and minerals of the Earth hold undreamt-of potentials for serving humankind.*[1]

According to Gerber, the reason that quartz crystals are so good at keeping the time is that when they are stimulated with electricity (a form of energy), their oscillations are so regular and precise that they form a handy reference by which bits of time may be measured and displayed. This property of quartz crystals is a reflection of what is known as the 'piezoelectric effect'. When quartz crystals are subjected to mechanical pressure, they produce a measurable electric voltage.[1]

Conversely, when an electric current is applied to a crystal, it will induce mechanical movement. Most electronic devices utilise a slice or plate of quartz. Each plate of quartz has a particular natural resonant frequency that is dependent upon its thickness and size. This is the basis for crystal oscillator components used in many electronic systems to generate and maintain very precise energy frequencies. Of particular interest is the way in which crystals affect the subtle energetics of the body.[1]

Gerber quotes crystal researcher Marcel Vogel, a senior scientist with IBM for 27 years:

> *The crystal is a neutral object whose inner structure exhibits a state of perfection and balance. When it is cut to proper form and when the human mind enters into relationship with its structural perfection, the crystal emits a vibration which extends and amplifies the powers of the user's mind. Like a laser, it radiates energy in a coherent, highly concentrated form, and this energy may be transmitted into objects or people at will.*
>
> *Although the crystal may be used for 'mind to mind' communication, its higher purpose ... is in the service of humanity for the removal of pain and suffering. With proper training, a healer can release negative thought forms which have taken shape as disease patterns in a patient's physical body.*

Quartz crystals.

As psychics have often pointed out, when a person becomes emotionally distressed, a weakness forms in his subtle energy body and disease may soon follow. With a properly cut crystal, however, a healer can, like a surgeon cutting away a tumor, release negative patterns in the energy body, allowing the physical body to return to a state of wholeness.[1]

Dr Vogel suggests that the quartz crystal is capable of amplifying and directing the natural energies of the healer.[1]

Gerber explains that the healing energies transmitted by crystals work at the subtle level of our subtle energetic bodies. When healing energy is focused through the quartz crystal, it is sent into the body of the patient and distributed to the area most in need of an energy balancing.[1]

The quartz crystal may be held in the hand while touching the patient, and the healing energies sent through the palm chakra. As the energies pass through the crystal, they are both amplified and directed to those parts of the subtle anatomy that require energetic healing.[1]

Quartz crystals may also be used for rebalancing and cleansing abnormally functioning or 'blocked' chakras. When cleansing a chakra, the crystal is placed over the particular chakra region and energy is sent through the crystal. The cleansing action may be induced by the energy of the therapist or the individual in need of chakra balancing.[1]

If the therapist is the active energy source, subtle energy is transmitted from the therapist's palm chakra, through the crystal, and into the individual's unbalanced chakra, while the therapist focuses his/her mind on the task at hand. Conversely, an individual can use the crystal to cleanse his/her own chakras by placing a single terminated crystal over the chakra with the point facing away from the body. In this technique, the individual directs energy from inside the body out through the chakra and the overlying crystal.[1]

Another method of utilising the energies of crystals is through the application of gem elixirs (similar to flower essences but made by using crystals). The energy imprint of the crystal is transferred to the water.[1]

In the realm of personal healing, the quartz crystal is an excellent tool to assist in meditation. Gerber states that in meditation, the crystal should be held in the left hand. He states that the reason for this practice is that

Amethyst crystals.

the left hand is neurologically connected to the right cerebral hemisphere, which is attuned to the higher dimensional fields of consciousness of the higher self because the right brain has unique crystalline connections to the pineal gland.[1]

Crystals and chakras

Gerber explains that crystals, gems and stones are classified according to their unique molecular arrangement or crystalline lattice structures. There are seven categories — the triclinic, monoclinic, orthorhombic, tetragonal, hexagonal, cubic and trigonal systems of crystalline structures. He claims that each crystalline category has an affinity with subtle energy resonances.[1]

While many relate the colour of the stone or the crystal to the colour typically assigned to the chakra, Gerber states the different crystals belonging to the same crystalline classification scheme correspond to the energies of the seven chakras.[1]

For example, crystals of the cubic system such as diamonds, garnets and fluorites possess qualities of a very fundamental or basic nature. These crystals are often used for meditation or other states of consciousness to deal with issues of an earth-plane nature. He explains that these crystals possess a quality that radiates a basic building block type of energy. On the other hand, crystals of the hexagonal classification such as emeralds and aquamarines are more complex in nature than those with cubic lattice arrangements. They tend to give off energies, and encourage processes of growth and vitality. Gerber suggests that crystals of the hexagonal classification can be used for healing, energy balancing and communicating.[1]

Stones such as zircon, wulfenite and chalcopyrite belong to the tetragonal system. Gerber states that these crystals are of a balancing nature. They can absorb many negative energies of the earth, yet they are also able to give forth positive vibrations. These crystals correspond to the heart chakra.[1]

Stones belonging to the orthorhombic system such as topaz and alexandrite have a unique aspect of encircling and encompassing energy patterns, problems and thought forms. Gerber states that they can bring far things closer, or project near things further away. This means that they can bring greater perspective on issues that may be out of focus. Gerber suggests that they help to magnify and clear away that which is not relevant.[1]

Crystal system	Colour	Energetic nature	Chakra
Triclinic	Yellow	Completion	Crown
Monoclinic	Blue violet	Pulsation movement	Third eye
Orthorhombic	Orange	Protecting, encompassing	Throat
Tetragonal	Pink	Balancing	Heart
Hexagonal	Green	Growth & vitality	Solar plexus
Cubic	Cobalt blue	Fundamental earth nature	Sacral
Trigonal	Red	Energising	Base

The subtle energies of crystals and chakra correspondences.[1]

On the other hand, azurite, jade, malachite and moonstone are crystals of the monoclinic system and have a unique constant pulsating action. Gerber suggests that these stones correspond to the third eye chakra.[1]

Crystals of the triclinic system, such as turquoise and rhodonite, possess aspects of completion within their makeup. Gerber claims they can be used to balance the *Yin* and *Yang* energy within an individual. These stones can allow individuals to attune to a higher spiritual dimension.[1]

Crystals of the trigonal system, such as bloodstones, carnelians, agates and amethysts, continually give off energy. Gerber claims they are useful in balancing subtle energies of the human body.[1]

Gerber reminds us that each crystal is unique:

> *Each class of crystal structure assists in transforming the energies of human consciousness in very special and unique ways. More important than the class, however, is the particular crystal or stone itself. Each gemstone possesses unique spiritual, energetic, and healing properties which may assist us in our search for balance and wholeness.*[1]

Crystals and aromatherapy

According to Davis, crystals will enhance the action of the essential oils that you are using. She explains that the quartz crystal is but one of many stones and gems that can be used for the purpose of healing, energising and gaining access to higher dimensions of consciousness. The quartz crystal that we have been discussing up to now is the rock crystal of the quartz family. All crystals in the quartz family are composed of silicon dioxide.[30]

There are many different colours and variations of quartz, because within the mixture of silicon dioxide there are also traces of other elements. For instance, amethyst is a violet type of quartz; there is also a smoky quartz, rose quartz, green quartz, blue quartz etc. Each variety of quartz has its own special subtle energy and healing properties.[30]

Many of the coloured crystals correspond to various essential oils. For example, Davis states that rose quartz harmonises exquisitely with rose absolute and both relate to the heart chakra. German chamomile has a strong affinity with blue stones such as lapis lazuli and blue agate, which share the ability to calm and soothe. Davis explains that the clear quartz crystal can be used with any essential oil.[30]

Therapists use crystals in many different ways. One of the simplest ways of using crystals with aromatherapy is to place a small crystal in the bowl of massage oil to potentiate it. Davis suggests that you should only use 1% or less dilution when using crystals in this way.[30]

Another way of using crystals is to place a crystal at each corner of the massage table while you are massaging the client. Davis states that it is important to use evenly matched crystals for this purpose.[30]

Keim Loughran & Bull state that crystals should be cleared and then programmed before use. They recommend swabbing the crystal with cedarwood oil, then putting it in a bowl of salt water, preferably in the sun, for a few hours to clear it. The crystal can then be programmed by the use of affirmation and anointing with a drop of essential oil.[31]

Subtle aromatherapy

It is interesting to look back at some of the rather esoteric definitions of essential oils. For example, Robert Tisserand described essential oils as:

> ... like the blood of a person ... the essence is the most ethereal and subtle part of the plant ...[32]

Shirley Price described essential oils as the:

> ... life force of the plant which we introduce into the body by aromatherapy ... It has been said that essential oils are actually the hormones of the plants.[33]

However, by the 1990s, aromatherapy was rapidly becoming popular, and there was a need to validate it in order to keep legislators satisfied. We began to focus on the science, chemistry and pharmacology to understand how the essential oils worked. Science could even explain how essential oils make a person feel good emotionally through its work in the area of olfaction and brain chemistry.

By 1995, Price provides us with a more scientific definition of essential oils:

> ... of these secondary metabolites the essential oils have the greatest commercial significance ... whatever else they may do, they give the plant its aroma and flavour and often have a significant physiological effect on people.[34]

Jean Rose provides us with a very functional yet esoteric definition:

> ... but what is this elusive essence of plant material called essential oil? It is the heart and soul of the plant. It is the essence that deters

> *bugs from eating the plant. It is the fragrant aromatic heart of the plant that attracts bees and pollinating insects. It is the chemical component contained in the tiny plant cells that are liberated during the extraction process.*[35]

In each of these definitions, the authors are attempting to encompass some of the subtle aspects of essential oils.

Holmes states that whether we are trying to describe how an essential oil works on the body or soul, or whether we are trying to explain why a particular blend has such a miraculous effect on a certain client, we are usually attempting to validate aromatherapy in terms of chemistry or pharmacology, yet aromatherapy is essentially an energy medicine.[36]

The chemistry of the essential oils can help us understand the pharmacology of essential oils, olfaction can help us understand the psychological benefits of essential oils, and an understanding of the concepts of vibrational medicine can help us understand how essential oils work at a subtle level.

Worwood explains that the notion of subtle aromatherapy promoted nowadays implies the use of aromatherapy to purely influence the subtle body, the psyche and the soul. However, it must be emphasised that you cannot practise 'subtle aromatherapy' on its own because holistic aromatherapy includes 'physical aromatherapy', 'emotional aromatherapy' and 'subtle aromatherapy'.[37]

> *... there are those who will set up practice as "energetic" or "vibrational" aromatherapists on the basis of the idea that "all illness starts in the etheric". It does not matter where the illness starts, the point is that it is there — manifesting in the physical, mental, emotional and spiritual, or all four.*
>
> *To treat a person energetically, all aspects of the person must be understood. Energetic therapies cannot make shortcuts bypassing the physical, because vibration is part of essential oils and the physical body. You cannot ignore it. The subtle and physical bodies of a person work together like a color printer's primary colours — one does not make sense without the other, and you need all the colours, or "bodies" to see the whole. Vibrational or subtle aromatherapy is aromatherapy.*[37]

Worwood believes that essential oils are 'thoroughfares for transactions': They have their own vibrations, which connect with the frequencies in the human energy field, causing effects in the physical, emotional and spiritual body.[37]

Worwood describes that when the energy field from the essential oil and the person are connected, there is an expansion of the human aura. It is not surprising that scent has been used since time immemorial to connect people with the divine, lifting us to finer, higher vibrations, in touch with wider consciousness.[37]

In selecting essential oils for use in subtle therapies and chakra healing, I am drawn to the advice of Davis, who states that no two experts will ever completely agree on the choice of essential oils to influence the chakras.[30]

Davis suggests this is because we are dealing with ever-changing energies and because those authors who have complied lists or charts matching essential oils to chakras may not have the same purpose or end result in mind. She explains that it really depends on how you intend to use essential oils to influence the chakras. For example, is it necessary to energise, calm or balance a chakra?[30]

There are many ways we can arrive at the relationship between essential oils and chakras. Davis explains:

> *Sometimes colour is the link, and this may be the colour of the actual oil, the colour of the flower it came from or the "colour" of the aroma (as in "a green smell" or "a dark brown smell"). Sometimes the part of the plant from which the oil is derived, or even the type of plant, its shape, size, etc. may lead you to make a connection with a particular chakra ... You might perceive a connection by applying what you know about the oil's subtle properties, you could dowse, you might wish to meditate on each chakra in turn or you may simply feel intuitively that an oil is right. All of these paths are valid, and most therapists will use several of them.*[30]

L'HOMME TERRESTRE NATUREL TENEBREUX.

SELON LES ET LES
ETOILES ELEMENTS

L'ELEMENT... Reside dans...

... du Feu △ ... le Coeur
__ de l'Eau ▽ ___ le Foie
__ de la Terre ▽ ___ les Poumons
__ de l'Air △ ___ la Vessie

Part [2]
A Brief Overview of Chakras

6. The 'True' History of Chakras

7. Eastern Chakra System

8. Western Chakra System

9. The Relationship between Chakras and Physical Anatomy

10. Chakras and Consciousness

11. Chakras and Lifespan Development

12. Chakras, Yoga and Meditation

13. Chakras and the Human Biofield

6. The 'True' History of Chakras

Chakras are based on the ancient teachings of Indian Tantra; however, Leland suggests that everything that we know about chakras in the West only came together as recently as 1977. Leland in *Rainbow Body* provides us with the most comprehensive history of the Western Chakra System, from its roots in Indian Tantra, through Blavatsky, Leadbeater, Woodroffe, Steiner, Alice Bailey, Carl Jung, Joseph Campbell, Ramakrishna to Aurobinda, and the influence of the Esalen Institute, Shirley MacLaine and Barbara Brennan.[1]

Christopher Wallis, a Sanskrit scholar who has written an excellent blog, *The Real Story on the Chakras*, states that the West has almost totally failed to come to grips with what the chakra-concept meant in its original context and how one was supposed to practise with them.[2]

Wallis defines chakras (*cakras*) in Tantrik tradition, from which the concept of chakras derives, as focal points for meditation within the human body, visualised as structures of energy resembling discs or flowers at those points where *nadis* converge. He reminds us that they are conceptual structures yet phenomenologically based, since they tend to be located where humans experience emotional and/or spiritual energy.[2]

Wallis claims that most of what we know about chakras originates from Western yoga and Western occultism. He claims that 'Western yoga understands almost nothing about the original concepts of the chakras'.

Wallis states that if you have read books on chakras such as the very popular *Wheels of Life* by Anodea Judith, it is important to realise that you are not reading a work of yoga philosophy but of Western occultism, based on three main sources:[2]

1. earlier works of Western occultism that have borrowed Sanskrit terms without really understanding them (like theosophist CW Leadbeater's *The Chakras*, 1927)
2. John Woodroffe's flawed 1919 translation of a text on chakras that was originally written in Sanskrit in 1577

3   20th century books by Indian yoga gurus, which themselves are based on sources 1 and 2.

Wallis claims that books on chakras based on sound comprehension of the original Sanskrit sources exist only in the scholarly world. He does not imply that there is no spiritual value to Western occultism or the westernisation of the chakra system; however, he states that it is helpful to have a better appreciation of chakras if we know their true history.[2]

Leland uses the term 'source amnesia', which means that one intentionally or unintentionally neglects to refer to the source of their information.[1]

Wallis provides us with six fundamental facts about the chakras that we need to know:

1. *There's not just one chakra system in the original tradition, there are many.*

Wallis points out that there is not one chakra system in the original tradition, there are many. The theory of the subtle body and its energy centres called chakras comes from the tradition of Tantric yoga, which flourished from 600–1300 CE and is still alive today.[2]

All of the many branches of Tantrik yoga articulated a different chakra system, and some branches articulated more than one. Five chakra system, six chakra system, seven, nine, 10, 15, 21, 28 and more are taught, depending on what text you are looking at. The seven-chakra system that Western yogis know about is just one of many and it became dominant around the sixteenth century.[2]

Wallis states that it is tempting to think — so how many chakras are there really?

He explains that chakras are not like organs in the physical body. The subtle body is an extraordinary fluid reality and can have any number of energy centres, depending on the person and the yoga practice they are performing. Wallis states that there are a few centres that are found in all the chakra systems — the solar plexus, the heart and the crown of the head. He suggests that this is because these are three places in the body where humans all over the world experience both emotional and spiritual sensations. He also explains that one is not more correct than another — basically it is specific to the practice.[2]

2. *The chakra systems are prescriptive, not descriptive.*

English sources tend to represent the chakras as existential fact using descriptive language in terms of the location, endocrine gland, relationship with organs, and so on. However, Wallis states that most original Sanskrit sources did not provide lessons on the individual chakras. You were given a specific yoga practice and told to visualise a subtle object made of coloured light, shaped like a lotus or a spinning wheel at a specific point in the body, and then activate mantric syllables in it, for a specific purpose.[2]

3. *The psychological states associated with the chakras are completely modern and Western.*

We also see countless books associate psychological states with each of the chakras. Wallis suggests that this is a modern and Western construct, most likely associated with Carl Jung.[2]

4. *The seven-chakra system popular today derives not from an ancient scripture, but from a treatise written in 1577.*

According to Wallis, the chakra system that Western yogis follow is found in a Sanskrit text written by Purnananda Yati in 1577.[2]

5. *The main purpose of a chakra system is to function as a template for nyasa — installation of mantras and deities.*

Wallis states that the main purpose of any chakra system was originally to function as a template for *nyasa*, which means the installation of mantras and deity-energies at specific points of the subtle body.[2]

6. *The seed mantras that you think go with the chakras actually go with the elements that happen to be installed in those chakras.*

Wallis states that we may have been told that the seed mantra of *Muladhara* chakra is LAM; however, it is not.[2]

> Not in any Sanskrit source, not even in Purnananda's somewhat garbled syncretic account. And the mantra of Svadhisthana chakra is not VAM.[2]

He explains that the fundamental mantras associated with the first five chakras do not belong to those chakras per se; they belong to the five elements installed in them. Furthermore, he states that the geometric figures associated with the chakras today belong to the elements. Earth element is traditionally represented by a square, Water by a crescent

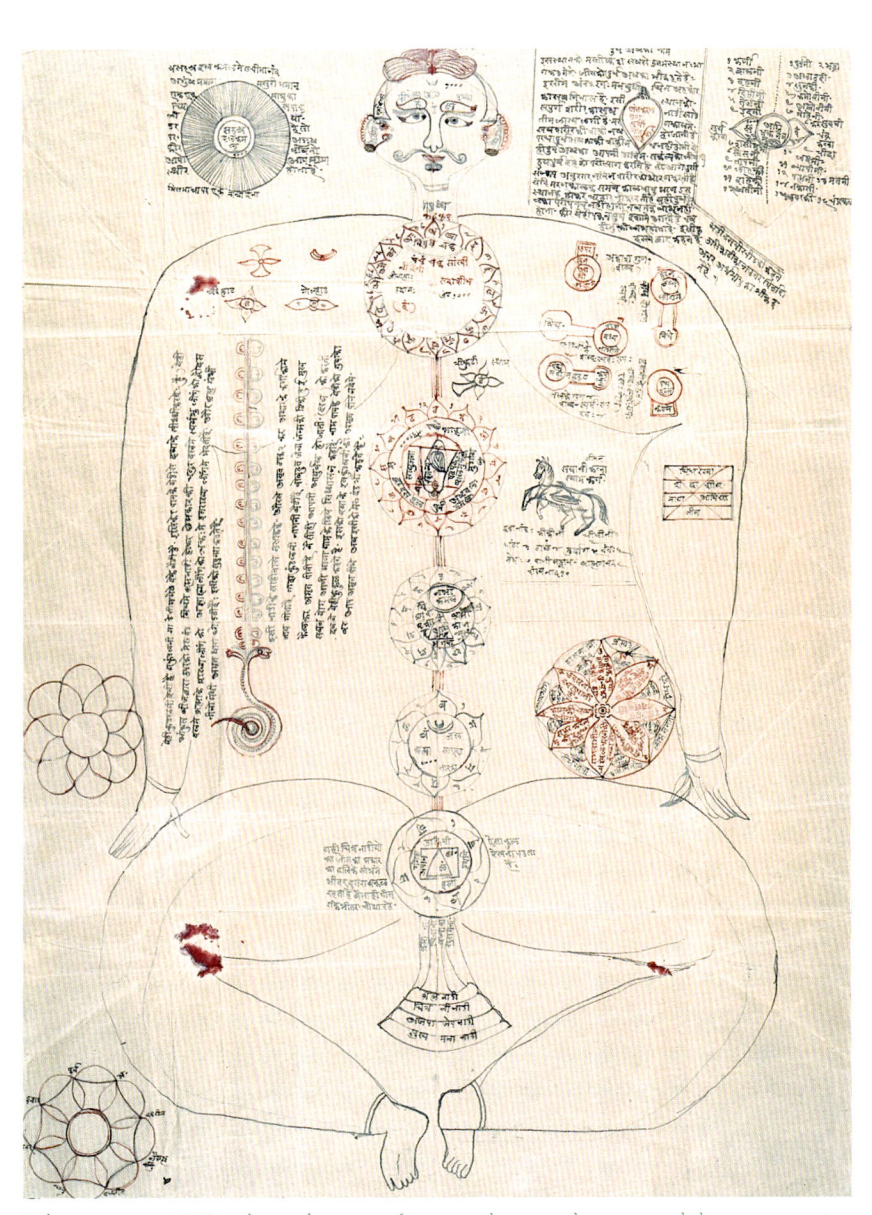

Indic manuscript 347, a large drawing of a man showing the seven subtle energy centres (cakras) within the body, the main subtle veins (nadis), and the coiled serpent energy at the base of the spine.

moon, Fire by a downward-pointing triangle, Wind by a hexagram or six-pointed star and Space by a circle. Wallis states that when you see these figures inscribed in illustrations of the chakras, you now know that they are actually representations of the respective elements, not of a geometry inherent in the chakra itself.[2]

Perhaps his best advice to yoga teachers is:

> *So, when it comes to chakras, don't claim you know it. Tell your yoga students that every book on the chakras presents only one possible model. Virtually nothing written in English is really authoritative for practitioners of yoga. So why not hold more gently the beliefs you've acquired about yoga, even while you keep learning? Let's admit we really don't understand these ancient yoga practices yet; and instead of seeking to be an authority on some oversimplified version of them, you can invite yourself and your students to look more clearly, more honestly, more carefully, and more non-judgementally at their own inner experience.*[2]

Leland also states that what we know of the Western Chakra System began in the 1880s in the writings of Madame Blavatsky, founder of the Theosophical Society, and was more or less complete by 1990, when actress Shirley MacLaine appeared on the *Tonight Show* and amused a national TV audience by affixing coloured circles representing the chakra system onto Johnny Carson's clothing and head.[1]

Leland explains that the chakra system we are most familiar with in the West first appeared in *The Serpent Power*, a book originally published in 1919 by Sir John Woodroffe, a British judge on the high court of Calcutta who was also a student of Tantra. Woodroffe wrote under the name Arthur Avalon. According to Leland, this was to protect himself and his Indian co-authors and co-translators from exposure during a period when Tantra was vilified by Indians and Europeans alike.[1]

He explains that *The Serpent Power* presented to us the Eastern Chakra System. This book was an exposition of Tantra as it related to chakras, including an annotated translation of *Sat-Cakra-Nirupana* (description of the six centres), a famous Bengali treatise in Sanskrit from 1577.[1]

The 'True' History of Chakras 51

Leland concludes that the Western Chakra System was an unintentional collaboration between the following:[1]

- esotericists and clairvoyants (many linked to the Theosophical Society)
- scholars of Indology (the study of Indian culture, including religious beliefs)
- mythologist Joseph Campbell
- psychologists (Carl Jung and the originators of the human potential movement at the Esalen Institute in Big Sur, California)
- Indian yogis (some of whose 'ancient' teachings made use of Leadbeater's work)
- energy healers (Barbara Brennan and others).

Leland provides us with a chronological development of the Western Chakra System:[1]

- a seven-chakra system (1880s)
- association of each chakra with a nerve plexus (1880s)
- a list of vernacular (non-Sanskrit) names (1920s)
- association of each chakra with a gland of the endocrine system, with minor variations from system to system, especially with regards to the pituitary and pineal glands (1920s)
- single colours attributed to each chakra in order of the colour spectrum — either seven colours, including indigo, or six colours plus white (1930s)
- an evolutionary scale of psychological and spiritual attributes, functions or qualities assigned to each chakra, eventually becoming the familiar single-word list often seen nowadays (1970s).

Leland claims that the following are more recent attributes to the chakra system:[1]

- associations with layers of the aura, subtle bodies and planes
- development stages in the evolution of humanity
- development stages in the evolution of the individual
- diseases of the mind or body associated with each chakra
- elements, in the form of westernised interpretations of the *tattvas*
- positive and negative emotions for each chakra
- states of consciousness and psychic powers.

Leland states that the list of correspondences tends to develop along the lines of the writer's interest and their motivation for the use of the chakra system. He notes the following approaches:[1]

- acquisition of psychic or spiritual powers, such as seeing auras or experiencing astral projection
- application to postural yoga practice, in which the chakras are used to enhance the effects of the postures or postures are used to activate the chakras
- esoteric theorising, such as absorbing the chakras into existing Western esoteric systems such as astrology, Kabbalah, magic or tarot, as did Myss, in her book, *Anatomy of the Spirit: The Seven Stages of Power*, which absorbed Kabbalistic teachings into the chakra system
- healing of physical, emotional or psychological disease through alternative modalities associated with the chakras
- intuitive diagnosis of physical, emotional, psychological or spiritual problems in self or others
- scientific validation of the existence of chakras and use in therapeutic settings
- self-help in achieving balanced personal development and greater satisfaction and happiness
- self-realisation through tapping unrecognised or underdeveloped human potential
- self-transcendence through achieving spiritual liberation.

Leland gives us an insight into the complex web of the development of chakras, which infuses what he refers to as the Eastern Chakra System with the Western Chakra System:

> *Thus, a Western scholar of comparative religion, such as Mircea Eliade (Yoga: Immortality and Freedom, 1958), may write legitimately about the Eastern chakra system. An Indian writer, such as Harish Johari (Chakras: Energy Centers of Transformation, 1987), may develop a new set of painted images based on imagery from Sat-Cakra-Nirupana and write a book on the chakras that appeals to Western audiences yet remains firmly rooted in the Eastern tantric tradition. A Western student of an Indian spiritual master, such as Sivananda Radha (Kundalini Yoga for the West,*

1978), may seek to explain Eastern teachings for Western minds and yet remain in the Eastern tantric tradition. Furthermore, an Indian spiritual master, such as Satyananda Saraswati (Kundalini Tantra, 1984), may absorb theosophical teachings into an explanation of the chakras yet still present an Eastern system.[1]

Frawley is critical of the New Age appropriation of chakras. He explains that there is a big gap between the way chakras are viewed today and how they are regarded in traditional Yogic literature. He states nowadays the chakras are often used for physical healing, whereas within traditional yoga practices, the opening of chakras requires a radical change in consciousness and only occurs after many years of meditation. It's not a simple matter of emotional or physical cleansing.[3]

He is critical of the New Age concept that considers imbalanced or blocked chakras as the root cause of disease, and that it can then be treated by rebalancing the associated chakra. This misconception, he claims, has spawned a whole group of practitioners who claim to heal our chakras for us. He states that the Yogic approach of opening chakras is not for healing

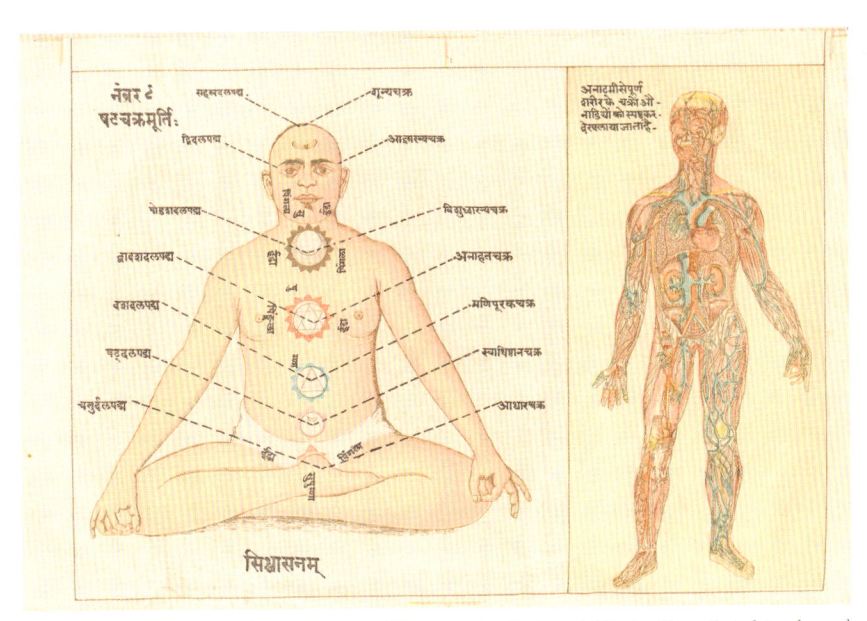

Illustration of the six chakras of Tantric Yoga in Sanskrit and Hindi. One of eight coloured plates, drawing explicit parallels between the Yogic view of chakras and the medical/anatomical view of the body. Drawings by Shri Swami Hansa Swaroop. Author: Svami Hamsasvarupa. Sanskrit MS 391.

purposes or gaining occult knowledge, but as a part of the process of self-knowledge.[3]

He claims that according to yoga practice:

> ... in the ordinary human state, which is rarely transcended except by sustained spiritual practice, the chakras are closed; that is, they do not truly function. The result of this is not disease, but ignorance. This ignorance consists of regarding the external world as the true reality and living without awareness of one's true Self which is neither body nor mind but thought-free awareness. One's chakras can be closed and yet one can be healthy, emotionally balanced, mentally creative, and successful in many areas of life. The purpose of opening the chakras is not to improve one's capacity in the ordinary domains of human life but to go beyond our mortal and transient seeking to the immortal essence.[3]

Furthermore, Frawley states the current tendency to confuse the chakras with corresponding functions in the physical body is based on a lack of understanding of the subtle body. He describes the subtle body:

> It belongs to another plane of existence, which we normally access only in dream states or after death. The subtle body allows the life force to enter into the physical body; without it the body could not even move. The subtle body is always active within the physical body, as the source of its vitality, though its activity is obscured by the veil of physical conditions.[3]

He claims that the chakras are not part of the ordinary functioning of the subtle body and that they only take on a significant role in states of heightened awareness or spiritual awakening.[3]

7. Eastern Chakra System

Tantra

Any discussion of the Eastern Chakra System must examine Tantra. In his book, *Tantra Illuminated: The Philosophy, History, and Practice of a Timeless Tradition*, Wallis explains the significance of Tantra and the basic spiritual and philosophical ideas that underpin it.[4]

Wallis states that Tantra has become a buzzword in the modern Western world. He states:

> *Though almost everyone has heard this word, almost no one — including many people claiming to teach something called Tantra — know anything about the historical development of the Indian spiritual tradition that scholars refer to as Tantra. What these academics study as Tantra bears little resemblance to what is taught under the same name on the workshop circuit of American alternative spirituality.*[4]

Wallis explains that there is a lot of misunderstanding in the yoga world today about the historical facts of the development of the Yogic and Tantric traditions. The word *tantra* is a Sanskrit word with various meanings such as 'theory', 'doctrine' or simply 'book'. Generally, this refers to scriptural texts that are purported to have been divinely revealed by gods or goddesses. He states that 'tantra' simply refers to a system of spiritual practice articulated within a specific sacred text. These sacred texts began to appear in India around the sixth century of the Common Era and continued to be composed in large numbers for the next thousand years.[4]

Wallis states that when we break down the word into the verbal roots *tan* and *tra*, the former means 'propagate, elaborate on or expand on' and the latter means 'save, protect'.[4]

He states that the second verbal root has a double meaning:

> *For it alludes to the fact that Tantrik practices give us a means of strengthening and protecting ourselves from worldly harm, as well as bestowing the ultimate spiritual liberation.*[4]

He goes on to explain that a *tantra* is a device *(tra)* for expanding *(tan)*, as a *mantra* is a device for working with the mind *(man)*, and a *yantra* is a device for controlling *(yan)*.[4]

Wallis shares how Rama Kantha, Tantrik scholar and guru who lived around a thousand years ago, defines tantra:

> *A tantra is a divinely revealed body of teachings, explaining what is necessary and what is a hindrance in the practice of the worship of god; and also describing the specialised initiation and purification ceremonies that are necessary prerequisites of Tantrik practice. These teachings are given to those qualified to pursue both the higher and lower aims of human existence.*[4]

Wallis summarises some of the features that characterise Tantra as a spiritual movement:[4]

- alternative path/new revelation
- evocation and worship of deities
- visualisation and self-identification with the deity
- centrality of mantras
- installation of mantras on specific points of the body
- ontological identity of mantras and deities
- necessity of initiation and importance of esotericism
- yoga — referring to meditation and visualisation practices
- ritual use of mandalas and yantra, especially in initiation
- spiritual physiology — subtle body, chakras and *kundalini*
- mapping deities and pilgrimage sites onto the practitioner's body
- linguistic mysticism
- importance of the teacher (guru)
- bipolar symbology of god/goddess
- revaluation of the body
- revaluation of 'negative' mental states
- revaluation of the status and role of women
- utilisation of 'sexual yogas'
- nondualism

- importance of Shakti (power, energy, goddess)
- cultivation of bliss
- special types of meditation that aim to transform the individual into an embodiment of the divine after a short span of time.

Leland states that Tantra is difficult to define. He cites Anagarika Govinda, a twentieth century German scholar and practitioner of Tantric Buddhism:

> *The word 'tantra' is related to the concept of weaving and its derivatives (thread, web, fabric, etc.) hinting at the interwovenness of things and actions, the interdependence of all that exists, the continuity in the interaction of causes and effects, as well as in spiritual and traditional development, which like a thread weaves its way through the fabric of history and of individual lives.*[1]

He also quotes David Gordon White's definition of Tantra:

> *Tantra is that Asian body of beliefs and practices which, working from the principles that the universe we experience is nothing other than the concert manifestation of the divine energy of the godhead that creates and maintains the universe, seeks to ritually appropriate and channel that energy, within the human microcosm, in creative and emancipatory ways.*[1]

Woodroffe explains that the basis of Tantra yoga is highly metaphysical and of scientific character. He explains that, for its understanding, we need to be fully acquainted with Indian philosophy, religious doctrine and ritual in general.[5]

Perhaps it would pay to heed the advice of Satyananda:

> *The attributes that we have assigned to each chakra are very, very rough. Do not take them too seriously, otherwise you may build up too many preconceptions without personal experience of the actual chakras. Remember also that the actual individual expression at a particular level will depend on personal dharma.*[6]

Chakras, yoga, kundalini and nadi

VanSteenhuyse's paper, *Understanding the Subtle Body: Examining How Chakras Are Most Generally Understood, Through the Lens of Tantric/Hatha/Kundalini Yoga, in the Modern West*, examines how chakras have been interpreted in the Western world within the framework of Tantric, Hatha and Kundalini yoga. She explains that chakras are intimately connected to our subtle bodies as swirling vortices of concentrated metaphysical energy at various points along our spinal column alignment, called *sushumna nadi*. Each chakra is connected to various bodily, mental, emotional and spiritual functions.[7]

Chakras are mentioned in many ancient Hindu texts such as the *Hatha Yoga Pradipika, Siva Samhita, Gheranda Samhita* and the *Yoga Sutras of Patanjali*, leaving much room for vast interpretation and experimentation. However, the Western interpretation of the seven-chakra system is based on Woodroffe's translation of the *Satcakranirupana*.[7]

VanSteenhuyse states that the meaning and purpose behind understanding our chakras is primarily to understand our individual, as well as a universal call to action. The call to action is described in the *Yoga Sutras of Patanjali*.[7]

The first chapter begins by stating that the purpose of the practice of yoga is to resist fluctuations of the mind (v.1.2), and the only way we can achieve this necessary resistance of fluctuations is to practise and release desire (v.1.12). Repeating this practice will result in a self-understanding and subjective, defined purpose in the form of inner consciousness attainment (v.1.28–29). Because this attainment has been successfully achieved, obstacles and distractions of the mind such as sickness, dullness, doubt, carelessness, laziness, sense addiction, false view and instability do not arise (v.1.29–30). However, if one has not achieved attainment, they may suffer some, or all, of these ailments. The only way to counteract these symptoms, and the obstacles of the mind, is through repetitive, fruitful, and intentional practice (v.1.32–13). The understanding obtained from this practice will finally be strong enough to grow long-lasting roots after a long, uninterrupted period of practice (v.1.14). These roots will release you from your desires, resulting in the desired internal peace and harmony and a mastery over thirsts (v1.15).[7]

Satyananda explains that there are many practices belonging to Tantra, but Kriya yoga is considered to be the most powerful and suitable for awakening the *kundalini*. He claims that the knowledge of this system of yoga has been revealed to very few. He explains that the main purpose of Kriya yoga is to create awakening of the chakras, to purify the *nadis* and awaken the *kundalini*. The *kriyas* are intended to subtly awaken the *kundalini* in stages. When the *kundalini* is abruptly awakened, the experiences you have may be too difficult to handle. Satyananda explains that the practice is based on Hatha yoga, which aims at controlling *prana*.[8]

He explains that Kriya yoga offers a unique approach:

> *Kriya yoga means "the yoga of practice, movement of action". Unlike the various religious, mystical or yogic practices which demand mental control, the special instruction in the system of kriya yoga is "Do not worry about the mind". If your mind is dissipating or if there are distractions in your mind and you are not able to concentrate even for one second, it does not matter. You only have to continue with your practices, for even without confronting, controlling or trying to balance the mind, you can still evolve.*[8]

He states that Kriya yoga emphasises that you do not need to try anything with the mind.

> *If your body protests about maintaining a fixed posture, change it. If your mind objects about closing the eyes, keep them open. However, you must continue with the kriya yoga practices because they have a direct effect on deeper processes of the body which are responsible for the state of your mind.*[8]

Kundalini

Woodroffe provides us with the first English translation of *Paduka-Panchaka*, a form of Tantric yoga, which he called Kundalini yoga. Woodroffe refers to chakras as lotuses that are centres of universal consciousness and describes *kundalini* as the static form of creative energy, which is the source of all energies, including *prana*. However, he goes on to explain that *kundalini* is a force distinct from *prana*.[5]

Woodroffe describes the activation of the *kundalini*:

> *When vivified by the "Serpent Fire" they become gates of connection between the physical and "astral" bodies.*[5]

Woodroffe goes into much detail in describing the various *tattvas*. He explains that the chief centres of consciousness are to be found in the chakras of the cerebrospinal system and in *Sahasrara*.[5]

VanSteenhuyse states that the *Yoga Upanishads* describe *kundalini* as a lying coiled serpent in our *Muladhara* chakra, awaiting its awakening. The *kundalini* is understood to be a dormant potential force and is one of the four components of the subtle body (*nadis*, *chakras*, *prana* and *bindu*).[7]

According to VanSteenhuyse, the *kundalini* can be awakened in one of two ways:[7]

- *shaktipat* — the spiritual transmission by a guru
- spiritual practices, such as yoga and meditation.

Once awakened, the *kundalini* is understood to rise up from its starting point within the *Muladhara* chakra, and travel up through the central *sushumna nadi*. As it reaches each chakra, it, in turn, releases different mystical experiences and awakening, until the *kundalini* reaches the *Sahasrara* chakra at the crown of the head. When the *kundalini* reaches the *Sahasrara*, a profound mystical experience occurs, unlike anything the person has been able to experience previously.[7]

Satyananda states that everyone should know something about *kundalini* as it represents the coming consciousness of humankind. He states that to awaken *kundalini* you must prepare yourself through yoga — by practising the *asanas*, *pranayama*, Kriya yoga and meditation.[8]

He describes the awakening of the *kundalini*:

> *With the awakening of kundalini there is an explosion in the brain as the dormant or sleeping areas start to blossom like flowers.*[8]

He goes on to state that whatever happens in our spiritual life is related to the awakening of *kundalini*. Satyananda states that in Tantric texts, *kundalini* is considered as the primal power or energy and in terms of modern psychology, it is called the unconscious in man. In Hindu mythology, *kundalini* corresponds to the concept of Kali. In the philosophy of Shaivism, the concept of *kundalini* is represented by the *shivalingam*, the oval-shaped stone or pillar with a snake coiled around it.[8]

Satyananda explains that the serpent has always been a symbol for efficient consciousness. He explains the meaning of the three coils of the serpent:

> *The three coils represent the three mantras of Om, which relate to the past, present and future; to the three gunas — tamas, raja and sattva; to the three states of consciousness — waking, sleeping and dreaming; and to the three types of experience — subjective experiences, sensual experience and absence of experience. The half coil represents the state of transcendence, where there is neither waking, sleeping nor dreaming. So, the three and a half coils signify the total experience of the universe and the experience of transcendence.*[8]

Most classical descriptions suggest that the awakening of *kundalini* begins in *Muladhara* chakra and that the *kundalini* must be awakened and made to travel through and awaken all the chakras in turn. However, Satyananda states that the seat of *kundalini* is actually *Sahasrara* and that *Muladhara* is only a manipulating centre, or like a switch. According to Satyananda, each of the chakras is independent — they are not connected with each other. *Kundalini* can be awakened in an individual chakra or it can be awakened through all the chakras collectively. He explains that if *kundalini* awakens in an individual chakra, the experiences which are characteristic of that chakra will be brought to consciousness. This may also occur when one does practices for one individual chakra.[6] He explains:

> *For example, svadhisthana practices will raise joy; manipura practices will increase self-assertion; Anahata stimulation will expand love; vishuddha practices will awaken discrimination and wisdom, and ajna practices will increase the flow of intuition, knowledge and perhaps extrasensory abilities and so on.*[8]

According to Satyananda, some yogis say that *kundalini* is the flow of *prana* along the *sushumna nadi* associated with the spinal axis. He explains that there is a flow of *prana* within the meshwork of the pranic body and that there is no anatomical counterpart. Other yogis relate their perception of *kundalini* to the flow of messages along the nerve fibres and that these arise in the networks of the autonomic plexuses and ascend along tracts in the spinal cord to the brain.[8]

Satyananda states that one thing is certain about *kundalini*:

> Kundalini has the ability to activate the human consciousness in such a way that a person can develop his or her most beneficial qualities, can enter a much more intimate relationship with nature and can become aware of oneness with the whole cosmos.[8]

The awakening of Kali

Satyananda states when the *kundalini* has just awakened and you are not able to handle it, it is called Kali. Kali is depicted as a female deity, naked, black or smoky in colour, wearing a mala of 108 human skulls, representing the memories of different births. The sacrificial sword and the severed head held in her left hand are the symbols of dissolution.[8]

In Hindu mythology, the awakening of Kali has been described in great detail. When Kali rises in anger, all the gods and demons are stunned and everyone keeps quiet. They do not know what she is going to do. They ask Lord Shiva to pacify her, but Kali roars furiously, throwing him down and standing on his chest with her mouth wide open, thirsty for flesh and blood. When the *devas* hold prayers to pacify Kali, she becomes calm and quiet.[8]

The skulls around her neck are not dead victims, but the letters of the Sanskrit alphabet, through which she manifests both liberating mantras and deluding ideas. The hands on her apron represent the karmic tendencies she removes from her devotees. The head that she holds, which she has just lopped off, is the ego that separates us from her. Her nakedness shows that she has cast away illusion; even her colour is esoteric. The dark colour stands for the ultimate void state, where all differences dissolve into the absolute beyond all form. Her sword is the force that slices through delusion, ignorance, false hope and lies. Her position on top of Shiva implies that she is the dynamic force in the universe.[9]

According to Sally Kempton, author of *Awakening to Kali — The Goddess of Radical Transformation*, Kali first appears as a frenzied, battle-maddened demon-slayer, who comes into the world at moments when dark forces — demons — threaten civilisation and especially the feminine.[9]

Kali brandishes a sword and a severed head in two of her four arms as she tramples her consort Shiva underfoot in a display of her dominance.

Kempton describes the myth of Kali's emergence:

> ... *she appears out of Durga's third eye at one of the key moments in the Devi Mahatmya, when the Devi is threatened by two demons called Chanda and Munda. Durga's face darkens, and Kali*

> *emerges with a roar, her sword swinging, cutting down the demons and crunching them in her teeth. At last, she slashes off the heads of Chanda and Munda, and presents them to Durga. Later in battle, Kali confronts the demon chief Raktabija. Raktabija has magical powers: when drops of his blood spill, they turn into warriors. Kali, with her long tongue, licks up his blood before it can touch the ground.*[9]

Kempton states that Raktabija's blood is a symbol of our uncontrollable desires that agitate our minds, and Kali's tongue eats up desires and thoughts so that luminosity of our essential awareness can reveal itself. According to Kempton, Kali appears differently depending on the level of consciousness with which you approach her.[9]

The nadis

The etheric body channels of *prana* run through a network of fine subtle channels called *nadis*. Satyananda explains that according to Tantra there are more than 72,000 *nadis* covering the whole body, and through them the rhythms of activity of all the organs of the body are maintained. Within this network of *nadis*, there are three important *nadis* that control the flow of *prana* and consciousness within all the other *nadis* and the body. These *nadis* are *ida*, *pingala* and *sushumna*. *Ida nadi* controls all the mental processes, while *pingala nadi* controls all the vital processes. The third *nadi*, *sushumna*, is for awakening spiritual consciousness. Satyananda asks us to think of these three *nadis* as pranic force, mental force and spiritual force.[8]

Ida, *pingala* and *sushumna nadis* begin at *Muladhara*. From here, *sushumna nadi* flows directly upwards within the central canal, while *ida* passes to the left and *pingala* to the right, at *Svadhisthana* chakra the three *nadis* once again come together and the *ida* and *pingala* cross over one another. The three *nadis* come together again at *Manipura* chakra, and once again *ida* and *pingala* cross. This occurs again and again until the three *nadis* meet at the *Ajna* chakra.[8]

Satyananda states that when *kundalini shakti* awakens it passes through the *sushumna nadi*. The moment it is awakened, the energy makes its way through *sushumna* up to the *Ajna* chakra.[8]

Eastern Chakra System 65

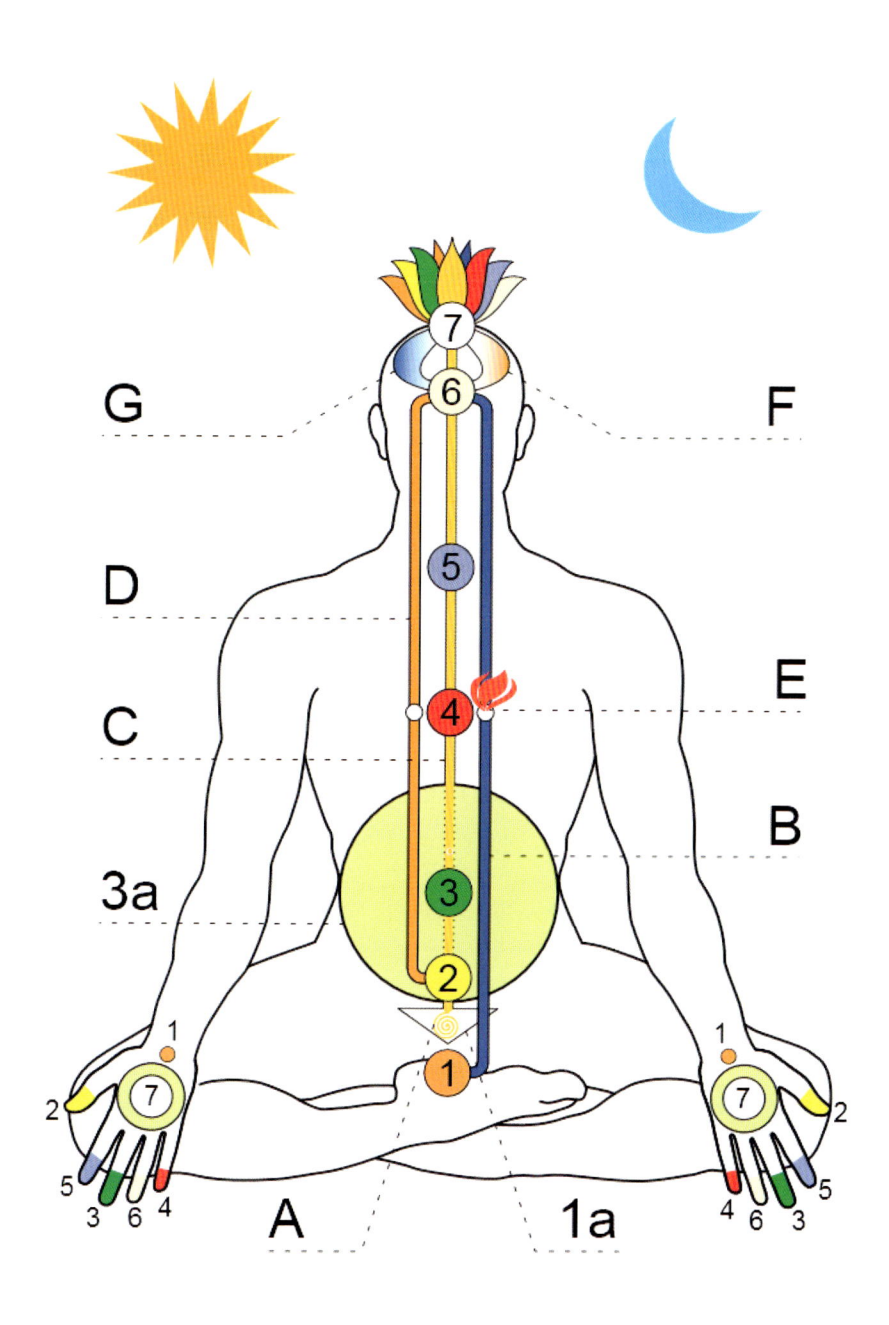

A simplified view showing the three major nadis, the ida, sushumna and pingala which run vertically in the body. 1. Muladhara chakra. 2. Svadisthana chakra. 3. Manipura chakra. 4. Anahata chakra. 5. Vishuddha chakra. 6. Ajna chakra. 7. Sahasrara chakra. A. Kundalini. B. Left channel (Ida nadi). C. Central channel (Sushumna nadi). D. Right channel (pingala nadi). E. Spirit. F. Ego. G. Superego.

Kundalini yoga is concerned with the awakening of *sushumna*, because once it is activated, it is a means of communicating the higher and lower dimensions of consciousness. *Shakti* then travels up the *sushumna nadi* to become one with Shiva in *Sahasrara*.[8]

Satyananda states that the three nadis roughly translate as mind, body and spirit. He suggests that the recent explosion in the interest in yoga, meditation and esoteric philosophy may be the result of deep-rooted pain and tension resulting from imbalance in the *nadis*. He suggests that yoga offers techniques to bring about balance in our lives, to not only realise the subtle, but through a science of enhanced intelligence, intuition and creativity, and to make the subtle side of life a practical reality and experience.[8]

Feuerstein states that when the *prana* flows through the *ida nadi*, the result is an overall cooling or calming effect, while the *pingala nadi* is associated with activity. He relates this activity to the parasympathetic and the sympathetic nervous systems.[10]

According to Feuerstein, the life force normally ascends and descends along these two channels causing flux in the pranic field and, correspondingly, every 90 minutes or so, the pranic energy flow switches from one pathway to the other, so that it becomes weak in one *nadi* and strong in the other. It is interesting that depending on the predominant flow of the life force, the left or right nostril will be either more open or closed. At the time of the switch, Feuerstein explains that both nostrils are equally open for a short period, indicating that the life force flows through the central channel. This, Feuerstein claims, is the ideal condition for meditation. He states that yogis have a number of ways of effecting this even flow through the *sushumna nadi*.[10]

Feuerstein reminds us that we must not forget that the *kundalini* is goddess energy. Because of the divine nature of the *kundalini*, it cannot be coerced or controlled. Coercion and control are the favourite pastimes of the ego personality, which always seeks to predict and reshape the events of existence in order to deal with its innate insecurity and fear. In encountering the divine, the ego personality confronts the stark truth that ultimately life cannot be manipulated or controlled.[10]

Feuerstein explains that the *kundalini* is fundamental to all forms of spirituality, whether it is consciously activated or not and whether it is experienced as such or not. However, some authorities claim that *kundalini* arousal is a special process that is specific to Tantra yoga and Tantra-dependent methods such as Hatha yoga.[10]

Chakra symbology

Sturgess states that in many yoga texts the chakras are represented and visualised as luminous lotus flowers with various numbers of petals, *bija* (seed-syllable) mantras inscribed in each petal, and symbols within the centres of the lotuses. He explains that these representations of the chakras are images of the energetic experiences in symbolic form.[11]

The lotus is considered a beautiful and captivating symbol of the chakras. The lotus flower grows from the bottom of a muddy pond to rise above the water and bloom. Its roots are buried in the mud far below the water surface, but the petals are not soiled by mud. The leaves are coated with a film, upon which water forms magnificent, glittering droplets, while the flower stalk rises above the leaves, ending in large, sweet-perfumed, white or pink blossoms, which appear one at a time. Sturgess explains that symbolically the lotus flower represents the human condition, being fully grounded in earth, yet reflecting the upward aspiration of human consciousness towards the light and divine. Just like the lotus, the chakra can be closed, in bud, opening or blossoming.[11]

Satyananda states that whereas various esoteric cults and spiritual systems use different symbols to represent the chakras, in Tantra and yoga the chakras are symbolised by lotus flowers. He explains that we must pass through three stages in spiritual life, which represent our existence on three levels — ignorance, aspiration and endeavour, and illumination. The lotus also exists on three levels — mud, water and air. He explains that it sprouts in the mud (ignorance), grows up through the water in an effort to reach the surface (endeavour and aspiration) and eventually reaches the air and the direct sunlight (illumination). The lotus symbolises our growth from the lowest states of awareness to the higher states of consciousness.[8]

Each of the chakras can be visualised as a lotus flower with a specific colour and number of petals:[8]

1. *Muladhara* — four-petalled deep red lotus
2. *Svadhisthana* — six-petalled vermilion lotus
3. *Manipura* — 10-petalled bright yellow lotus

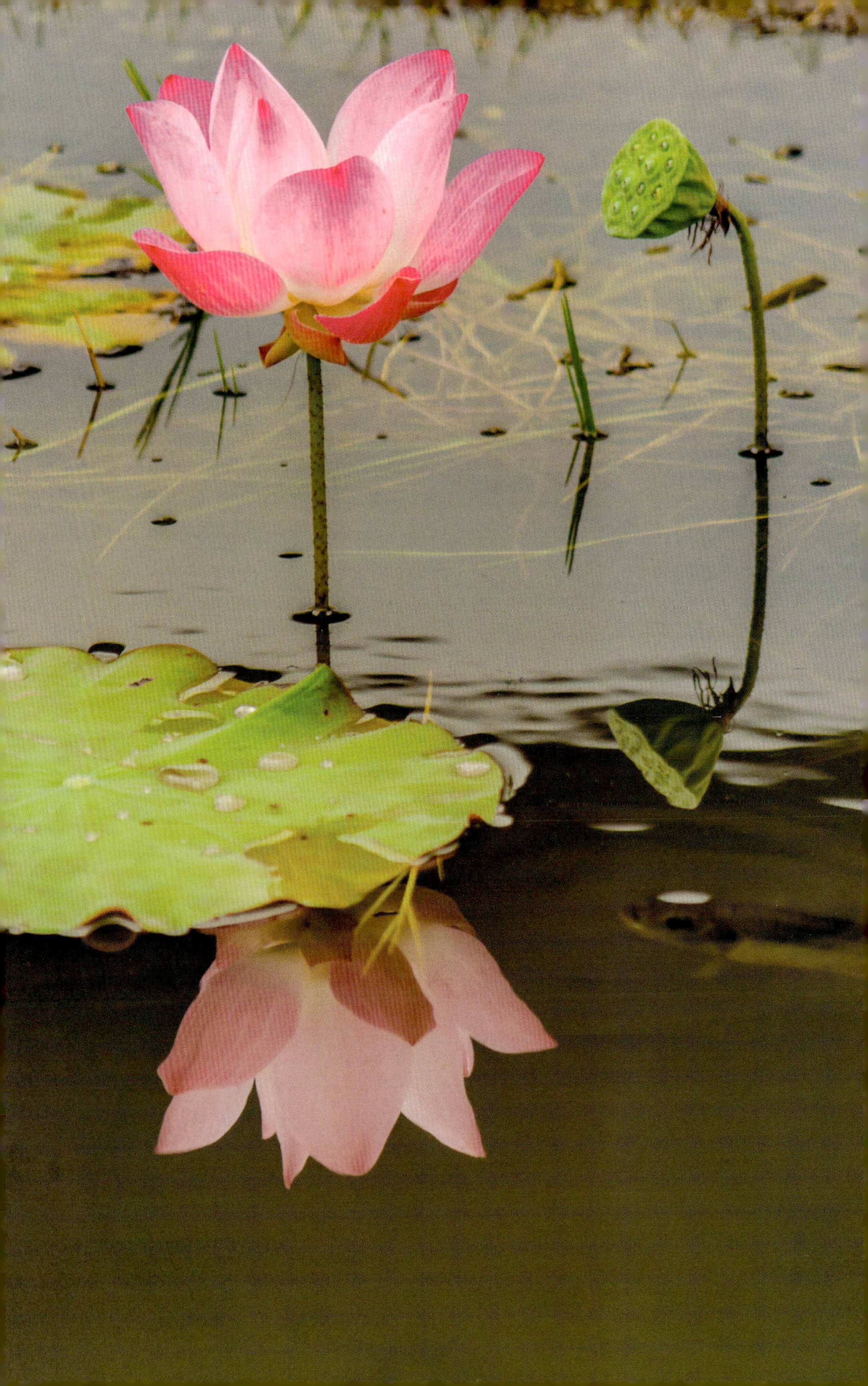

4 *Anahata* — 12-petalled blue lotus
5 *Vishuddha* — 16-petalled violet lotus
6 *Ajna* — two-petalled silver-grey lotus
7 *Sahasrara* — 1000-petalled multicoloured or red lotus.

Satyananda states that in each chakra six aspects are combined:[8]

- the chakra colour
- the petals of the lotus flower
- the yantra or geometric shape
- the *bija* mantra
- the animal symbol
- the higher or divine beings.

Satyananda explains that the animals represent your previous evolution and instincts, while the divine beings represent higher consciousness. He states that in your meditation you may visualise a different chakra colour. He states that this is okay as your experience is just as valid as his. However, he states that one thing is definite — as you move up through the chakras, the frequencies of the colours become more subtle and more powerful.[8]

I think that this is good advice when it comes to assigning essential oils to chakras. Your experience will be different from my experience. However, the energy of the essential oil will become more subtle and more powerful as we move up through the chakras. I love Satyananda's comment that there are many methods of symbolising the chakras and any attempt to describe them in detail will involve a lot of time:

> ... furthermore you are likely to become mentally constipated with facts and figures, which will confuse rather than clarify.[6]

He states that it can be very difficult to understand the original scripture.

He reminds us that chakras are subtle in nature and that any picture of them is merely symbolic.

> Don't take any pictorial representation too seriously or too literally. It is a means to an end, nothing more.[6]

8. Western Chakra System

In the 1920s, chakras were bought to the West by Woodroffe with his book, *The Serpent Power*. Chakras have come to the West also through the practice of yoga. Today they are a popular concept linking the body, the psyche and the metaphysical. Leland states that it would appear that most of what we know of the modern Western chakras comes from the Theosophical Society.[1]

The Theosophical Society

Theosophists played a significant role as early pioneers involved in the progression of the chakras. However, we also need to acknowledge the dubious origins of the Theosophical Society.

David Gordon White, Professor of Comparative Religion at the University of California, reports:

> In 1875 the Russian émigré Madame Blavatsky founded the Theosophical Society in New York together with fellow occultists

Madame Blavatsky, founder of the Theosophical Society.

> *William Quan Judge and Colonel Henry Steel Olcott ... What set Blavatsky apart from the American spiritualists were the outstanding personal contacts she had with an international cast of spirits ... she claimed to have run into the magnetosphere above Tibet, called the "Himalayan Masters" — one of whom, as she later claimed, had directly dictated Isis Unveiled to her.*[12]

White states that, as it turns out, Blavatsky's masters had been reading many of the same books that she must have read — all within a year of its publication. He explains:

> *William Emmette Coleman, a critical scholar and member of the American Oriental Society and Pali Text Society, denounced Blatvatsky for some two thousand instances of plagiarism he found in her book. The negative fallout from these and other scandals prompted Blavatsky and Olcott to decamp for India in 1878.*[12]

Once in India, White explains that Blavatsky revealed that the 'Masters' she had been channelling were in fact 'Mahatmas', a Sanskrit term meaning 'Great Souls'. In 1882, the society moved its headquarters to Adyar. Blavatsky continued her dialogue with the Mahatma; however in 1885, the British Society of Psychical Research declared Blavatsky a patent fraud, devoting 174 pages of its proceedings to argue its case against her. Under this new cloud of scandal, White explains that Blavatsky left India for Europe.[12]

White states that, despite the founder's misadventures, the Theosophical Society is credited with having projected yoga onto the magnetosphere of the late nineteenth century Indian and Western consciousness.[12]

The practice of having work telepathically dictated was very common in the early twentieth century. In 1927, the English theosophist Alice Bailey published a book titled *The Light of the Soul: Its Science and Effect*, a term paraphrased from the *Yoga Sutra*.[12]

White explains that Bailey's book drew on translations of the commentaries on Patanjali's work, even though she asserted that the sutras had been telepathically dictated to her by a 'Tibetan Brother of the Trans-Himalayan School'.[12]

Charles Leadbeater

Another book written by a theosophist in 1927 was Leadbeater's *The Chakras*. In the forward of the 2013 edition, Judith provides a modern Western interpretation of the chakras:

> *The chakra represents a map for our healing, a profound formula for wholeness and a template for transformation. They describe the soul's architecture; just as we study bones, muscles, and organs of the body's physical architecture, the chakras enable us to study the subtler energies of the soul. Like the human face, this architecture varies from person to person, yet it has elements common to all.*[13]

Leadbeater describes the meaning of the word *chakra*:

> *The word chakra is Sanskrit and signifies a wheel. It is also used in various subsidiary, derivative, and symbolic senses, just as its English equivalent; as we might speak of the wheel of fate, so does the Buddhist speak of the wheel of life and death ... The special use of the word chakra with which we are at the moment concerned is its application to a series of wheel-like vortices which exist in the surface of the etheric double of man.*[13]

He goes on to explain:

> *The chakras or force centers are points of connection at which energy flows from one vehicle or body of a man to another. Anyone who possesses a slight degree of clairvoyance may easily see them in the etheric double, where they show themselves as saucer-like depressions or vortices in its surface.*[13]

He describes the chakras as wheels that are perpetually rotating and the energy as flowing into the physical body. Here we read of the chakras being developed or underdeveloped:

> *... the centers are in operation in everyone, although in the undeveloped person they are usually in comparatively sluggish motion, just forming the necessary vortex for the force, and no more, in a more evolved man they may be glowing and pulsating with living light, so that an enormously greater amount of energy passes through them, with the result that there are additional faculties and possibilities open to the man.*[13]

Leadbeater claimed to have been clairvoyant and was able to see the chakras. Judith suggests that he was a person ahead of his time and a pioneer in the field of subtle energies.[13]

Hands of light

Brennan, author of *Hands of Light — A Guide to Healing through the Human Energy Field*, states that there are many systems that people have created from their observations to define the auric field. She explains that all these systems divide aura into layers and define the layers of location, colour, brightness, form, density, fluidity and function.[14]

Brennan observed seven layers of aura which she relates to each chakra. She describes the chakras as follows:

> *All the major chakras, minor chakras, lesser chakras and acupuncture points are openings for energy to flow in and out of the aura. We are like sponges in the energy sea around us. Since this energy is always associated with a form of consciousness, we experience the energy we exchange in terms of seeing, hearing, feeling, sensing, intuiting or direct knowing.*[14]

Brennan states that it is important to open the chakras and increase our energy flow, because the more energy we let flow, the healthier we are. She claims that illness is caused by an imbalance of energy or a blocking of the flow of energy.[14]

She explains that psychological material related to each chakra is brought to consciousness by increasing one's energy flow through that chakra.[14]

> *Too much psychological material would be released by a sudden flow of energy, and we could not process it all. We therefore work in whatever growth process we are in to open each chakra slowly, so that we have time to process the personal material that is released and integrate the new information into our life.*[14]

According to Brennan the functions of the chakras are:[14]

- to vitalise each auric body, and thus, the physical body
- to bring about the development of different aspects of self-consciousness. Each chakra is related to a specific psychological function
- to transmit energy between each of the auric levels.

Brennan also describes in detail the psychological functions of the seven major chakras. She describes the chakras in the same way that Arthur E Powell did in 1925, in his book *The Etheric Double*.

> *In the etheric double, as well, incidentally, as in each of our other vehicles, there are certain force-centres, or chakrams, as they are called in Sanskrit, this word meaning literally a wheel or revolving disc. The chakrams are situated on the surface of the double, that is about a quarter of an inch outside the skin of the body. To clairvoyant sight they appear as vortices or saucer-like depressions of rapidly rotating matter.*[15]

Powell describes the role of the chakras as follows:

> *The first is to absorb and distribute Prana, or Vitality, to the etheric and thence to the physical body, thus keeping these alive. The second function is to bring down into the physical consciousness whatever may be the quality inherent in the corresponding astral centre. It is the lack of development of the etheric centres which accounts for the failure to bring into the physical brain memory of astral experiences ... When, however, they return to their sleeping physical*

bodies, scarcely any memory of the astral life filters through the brain, simply because the necessary etheric bridge is not built. When the etheric centres are fully developed, there is full and continuous memory of astral experiences in the brain.[15]

Maslow's hierarchy of needs and chakras

Leland states that it should come as no surprise to both contemporary yoga practitioners and New Age esotericists that the Western chakra system as we know it today originates in a peculiar mix of Eastern mysticism, behavioural psychology and multiple bodywork modalities that came together at the Esalen Institute in Big Sur, California in the 1960s and 1970s. He explains that the Esalen Institute was the birthplace of the human potential movement, a mixture of 1960s counterculture, and the precursor of the New Age movement of the 1980s and beyond.[1]

Leland refers to Abraham Maslow as the godfather of Esalen. Maslow is also referred to as the father of humanistic psychology. The key elements of Maslow's contribution to American psychology are his hierarchy of needs. This hierarchy has five levels, although articles published just before Maslow's death indicate that he was suggesting a sixth level. They are as follows:[1]

1. physiological (survival) needs
2. safety needs
3. belongingness and love needs
4. esteem needs
5. self-actualisation
6. self-transcendence.

In 1979, an article appeared in the *American Theosophist* by psychotherapists Thomas B. Roberts and Robert H Hannon comparing Maslow's hierarchy of needs with the chakra system. The authors suggest that if we divide Maslow's lowest level into survival and sexual needs, we then have seven levels.[1]

They are as follows:[1]

1. root — biological needs, food, water, shelter, freedom from pain
2. sacral — sex and reproduction
3. solar plexus — security via power and control

4   heart — love, devotion, caring for others
5   throat — vocal expression, verbal knowledge
6   third eye — psychic visualisations, intuition, inner direction
7   crown — peak, transcendent, experience, unites man with infinite.

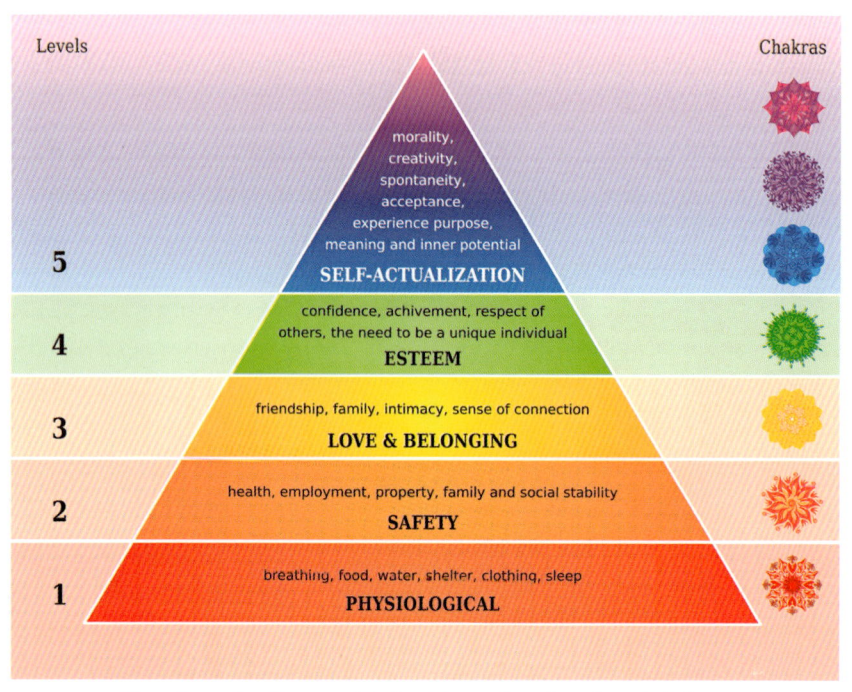

The relationship between Maslow's hierarchy of needs and chakras.

Leland suspects that Maslow may have been influenced by reading books on Eastern philosophy, especially Taoism, in the early 1940s. Leland suggests that it was Ken Dychtwald, who referred to himself as a humanistic psychotherapist, who clearly articulated the Western Chakra System we know and use today. His book, *Bodymind: A Synthesis of Eastern and Western Approaches to Self-Awareness, Health and Personal Growth,* first published in 1977, provides us with in-depth exploration of the vital body and mind connection.[1]

According to Leland, Dychtwald based his book on his experience while living at Esalen from 1970 to 1974.[1]

Nowadays, Dychtwald is better known as a specialist in psychology and sociology and the economics of aging. Dychtwald refers to his interest in *kundalini*:

> *My own interest in kundalini yoga began when I first realized that the kundalini perspective on psychosomatic structure and process is in some ways similar to some of the Western approaches, such as bioenergetics, Reichian energies, Rolfing and chiropractic.*[16]

He suggested that the chakras are a path along which an individual might travel on their personal road to optimal body–mind health and the full realisation of their human potential.[16]

9. The Relationship between Chakras and Physical Anatomy

The nerve plexus and endocrine system

Those working with subtle energies often refer to chakras as the interface of human physiology and subtle energies. However, VanSteenhuyse states that there is no broadly accepted understanding of exactly how chakras influence physiological function. It is not surprising that scientific research generally overlooks how chakras may influence physiological function.[7]

The challenge for anyone interested in explaining chakras is to demonstrate how something non-physical can interact with the physical.[7]

Roney-Dougal states that in Western terms the three *nadis* (*ida, pingala* and *sushumna*), which interweave and cross each other at the sites of the chakras, can be thought of as the central nervous system (*sushumna*) in the spinal cord. On either side of the spine runs the autonomic nervous system which has two aspects: the parasympathetic system (*ida*) and the sympathetic system (*pingala*). The sympathetic and *pingala* is the activating aspect and the parasympathetic and *ida* is the relaxing aspect. Where they cross, they form plexuses or nodes, from which nerves go out to, for example, the hearts, lungs, diaphragm, digestive system and endocrine organs.[17]

Wisneski refers to chakras as energy transducers for subtle energies. He claims that chakras convert the subtle energies to a resonance that the body can use, which means that the subtle energy band is transduced into hormones and neurotransmitters.[18]

Wow — stop right there!

Professor David Kennedy, author of *Plants and the Human Brain*, states that it is well known that a diverse range of plant secondary metabolites are able to modulate the functioning of the human brain. Most of these secondary metabolites fall into three chemical groups: the phenolics, the terpenes and the alkaloids. I was particularly interested in the chapter on terpenes, as these are the most common constituents found in essential oils. He explains that many of the neurotransmitters, neuromodulators and hormones that are integral to the functioning of our own nervous system are in fact the chemical products of metabolic processes that existed before the differentiation of plants and animals over a billion years ago. Many of these neurochemicals play key roles in the lives of plants, often sharing functional similarities with the roles they play as signalling molecules in mammals.[19]

You can understand why I believe that essential oils play such an important role in energy medicine and subtle therapies.

Gerber explains that chakras exist on the outside of the etheric body, and are points of connection through which energy flows from one being to another. Gerber also describes chakras as energy transformers, stepping down energy of one form and frequency to a lower level energy. This energy is then translated into hormonal, physiological and cellular changes throughout the body.[20]

He claims that the chakras are, in turn, connected to each other and to the portions of physical-cellular structure via fine subtle energetic channels known as *nadis*.[20]

Gerber suggests that dysfunction at the level of the chakras and *nadis* can, therefore, be associated with pathological changes of the nervous system. He suggests that there is a special alignment between the seven major chakras, glands and nerve plexuses that are necessary for optimal human functioning. He is adamant that a decreased flow of subtle energy through one of the chakras can give rise to underactivity of any of the major endocrine glands.[20]

Many state that each chakra is associated with a major nerve plexus and an endocrine gland. The seven major chakras are located in a vertical line ascending from the base of the spine to the head. Chakras appear to be involved in the flow of higher energies via specific subtle energetic channels to the cellular structure of the physical body. The flow of this energy through our chakra system is influenced by our personality and our emotions, as well as our state of spiritual development. Anatomically, each chakra is associated with a major nerve plexus and an endocrine gland.

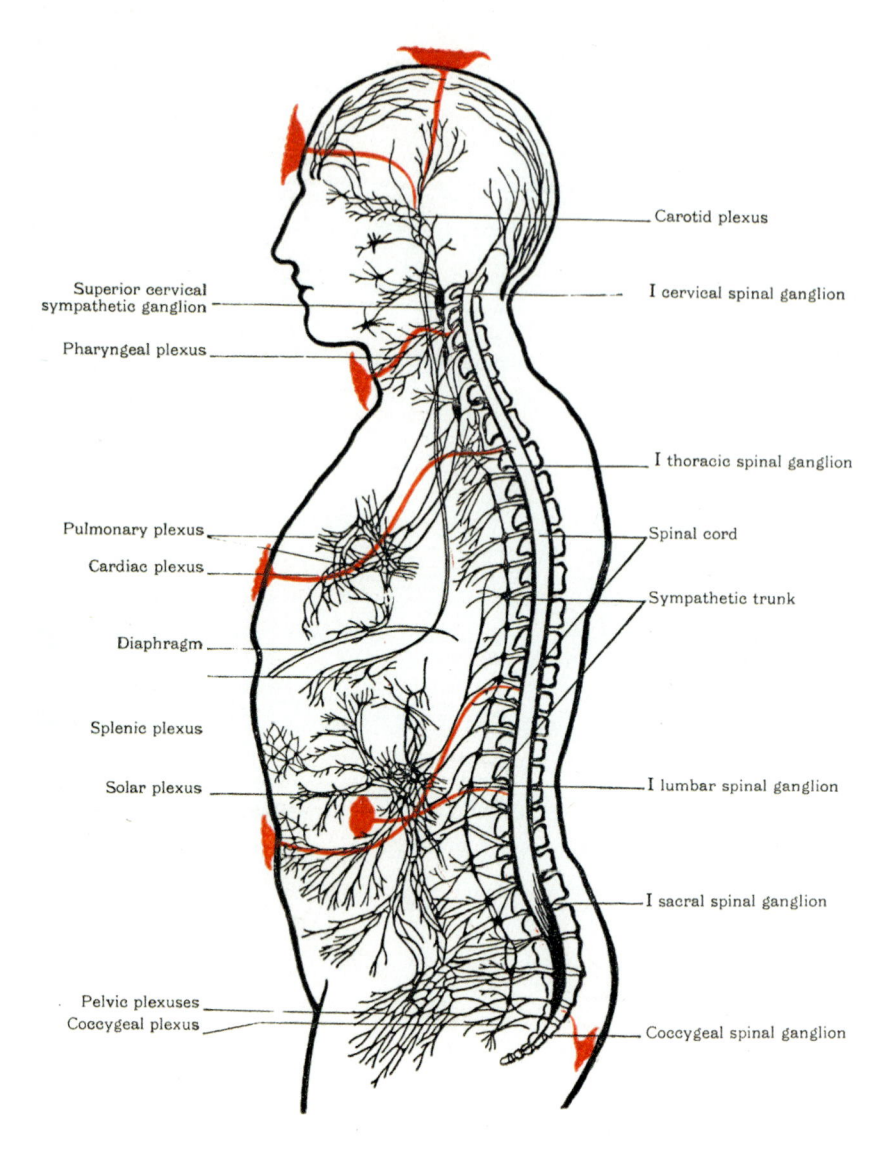

PLATE VI
THE CHAKRAS AND THE NERVOUS SYSTEM

Roney-Dougal states that there are many differing correspondences and attributes linking the chakras to the various nerve plexuses and endocrine glands. Confusion between Central Nervous System (CNS) location and other locations of chakra influence often occurs.[17]

Chakra	Endocrine gland according to Brennan	Endocrine gland according to Sturgess	Nerve plexus	Area of the body governed
Crown	Pineal	Pituitary	None	Upper brain, right eye
Third eye	Pituitary	Pineal	Medullary plexus	Lower brain, left eye, ears, nose, nervous system
Throat	Thyroid	Thyroid	Cervical plexus	Bronchial and vocal apparatus, lungs, alimentary canal
Heart	Thymus	Thymus	Cardiac plexus	Heart, blood, vagus nerve, circulatory system
Solar plexus	Pancreas	Adrenals	Solar plexus	Stomach, liver, gall bladder, nervous system
Sacral	Gonads	Testes/ovaries	Sacral plexus	Reproductive system
Base	Adrenals	Perineal body	Coccygeal plexus	Spinal column, kidneys

The relationship between the major chakras and the area of the body they nourish according to Brennan and Sturgess.

Chakras and gap junctions

Richard Maxwell, a clinical neuropsychologist and author of a fascinating paper, *The Physiological Foundation of Chakra Expression*, hypothesises that the intercellular gap junction connections may provide a physiological mechanism underlying subtle energy such as chakras and acupuncture. He argues if chakras exist and can influence physiological activity, some aspect must be accessible to objective analysis.[21]

He proposes that chakras are associated with embryological organising centres in the CNS. This is the same model used to describe the mechanisms of acupuncture.[21]

Gap junctions are hydrophilic passages between the cytoplasm of two adjacent cells created by a hexagonal array of connexin proteins, and probably a newly discovered family of pannexin proteins. Maxwell states that gap junctions have different conductance and gating properties associated with the exchange of small molecules and ions capable of electrical conductance. He states that gap junctions play an important role in synchronising endocrine secretion, in the function of the heart, in the synchronised firing of neurons, the interactions between neurons and glial cells, and in coordinating activity in many embryological processes.[21]

He states that yoga practices could stimulate increases in the number of gap junction connections. He refers to a recent study in acupuncture demonstrating increased expression of gap junction protein after acupuncture. Other studies in humans involving acupuncture have demonstrated modified limbic and subcortical brain activity. Glial functions in the brain have been related to many neurological and psychiatric disorders.[21]

He postulates that yoga practices such as chakra concentration exercises and mantra meditation could do more than the current concept of modulating frontal attention circuits, potentially also promoting fundamental changes in neural structures that allow a broader neural/glial syncytium to be established. It is suggested that as a yoga practitioner becomes more adept, subtler systems using gap junctions could be activated, changing energetic states in groups of cells, including opening connections between different compartments within the glial syncytium.[21]

Maxwell suggests that the difference between chemical and electrical communication within the CNS and the autonomic nervous system (ANS) could explain why chakras are perceived to be non-physical. Chemical synaptic activity of the CNS and the ANS may be able to be subjectively distinguished from the activity and influence of the chakras because the effect of chemically based nerve function spreads in a manner that is distinct from electrical gap junction networks. It is suggested that the physical base of the chakra may be a hub of typically dormant electrical circuitry that becomes accessible to conscious control, providing the potential for subtle influence over the activities of the CNS, ANS and endocrine system.[21]

Maxwell states that, while gap junctions are a physical structure, their functions and mechanisms of control are just beginning to be understood and it is conceivable that they offer a viable new approach to explaining the physiological effects of chakras.[21]

The third eye and the pineal gland

Roney-Dougal states that the endocrine glands are all positioned at the traditional locations of the chakras and their functions are remarkably equivalent to the traditional descriptions of the chakra functions. She proposes that the endocrine system is the physiological aspect of the chakras and the ANS can be equated with the *nadis*. She states that the pineal gland works together with the pituitary through the hypothalamus, controlling the endocrine system.[17]

Many state that the pineal gland in esoteric literature has long been associated with the third eye chakra. The *Ajna* chakra is located directly behind the centre of the forehead, which is where the pineal gland sits. Activating the *Ajna* is said to result in deep insight, intuition and psychic powers such as telepathy and clairvoyance.[17]

Rick Strassman's best-selling book, *DMT: The Spirit Molecule*, documents the role of the powerful mind-altering compound DMT (N,N-dimethyltryptamine), which is also secreted from the pineal gland. DMT is involved in out-of-body states, and is known to produce profound changes in sensory perception, mood and thought. It is an integral component of the Amazonian brew ayahuasca.[22]

Strassman's 'spirit gland' hypothesis suggests that there are similarities between the psychedelic experience and what Buddhists call *bodhicitta*, the awakening towards compassion for all sentient beings that is accompanied by a falling away of the attachment to the illusion of an independent existing self.[22]

The pineal gland is well known as a melatonin-secreting endocrine gland integral to the circadian rhythm. However, Strassman proposes that the pineal gland excretes large quantities of DMT during extremely stressful life episodes. This explains the highly visual and auditory nature of many mystical and other endogenous psychedelic experiences.[22]

St John states that techniques, such as smoking DMT, drinking ayahuasca or consuming other 'teaching plants', such as psychoactive mushrooms, may be involved in New Age practices such as channelling, where messages from sources outside of the individual's normal consciousness potentiate revelatory gnosis, or a form of guidance in which crucial information is transmitted.[22]

St John is not surprised that Blavatsky and other esotericists suggested that the pineal gland was associated with the 'third eye', and that reactivation of the pineal gland enabled lucid dreaming, out-of-body experiences, near-death experiences, astral travel, and ultimately the evolution of consciousness.[22]

Roney-Dougal reports that the pineal gland has been found to synthesise various β-carbolines and peptides, and to contain enzymes to produce psychoactive compounds such as DMT. The two precursors that are most likely to be involved are serotonin and tryptamine. It is interesting that these compounds have wide-ranging effects throughout our brain, affecting our gonads, adrenals, pancreas, thyroid and other emotional and endocrine activities.[17]

Roney-Dougal states that the β-carbolines are neuromodulators, which are MAO inhibitors preventing the breakdown of serotonin. This, she states, leads to an accumulation of physiologically active amines within the neuronal synapses that may lead to hallucinations, depression or mania depending on the amines being affected. She claims that the action of pinoline (one of the pineal β-carbolines) on serotonin triggers dreaming. It has been suggested that more than 60% of spontaneous psi experiences occur during the sleeping and dreaming state of consciousness, and pinoline has been suggested as the neurochemical that triggers this particular state of consciousness.[17]

Furthermore, Roney-Dougal points out that carbolines are the CNS inhibitors of GABA, a neurotransmitter. This action is similar to that of benzodiazepines, which are used to relieve anxiety, have anticonvulsant action, and are hypnotic and muscular relaxants. Therefore, pinoline may also act as a physiological tranquilliser and hypnotic.[17]

Roney-Dougal speculates that when the pineal gland is stimulated, as it would be in some chakra meditative practices, an individual is more likely to enter an altered state of consciousness, which is psi-conducive.[17]

Woolfe states that, long before any scientific discoveries about the pineal gland had been made, philosophers and physicians had speculated about its function. Galen postulated that the pineal gland regulated the flow of 'psychic pneuma' in the brain. Psychic pneuma was considered the vaporous substance that Galen described as 'the fine instrument of the soul'.[23]

Descartes considered the pineal gland as the principal seat of the soul. Woolfe questions Strassman's hypothesis that DMT is considered the mediator between the physical and spiritual world and that the pineal gland is responsible for its production.[23]

It is well known that the pineal gland produces and releases the hormone melatonin in a rhythmic manner. It converts tryptophan — an amino acid — into serotonin, and then into melatonin. The daily onset of melatonin secretion is associated with the onset of nocturnal sleepiness.[23]

Woolfe explains that in humans, light-sensitive nerve cells in the retina detect light, which travels to the pineal gland affecting melatonin production. He clearly explains many of the physiological responses associated with the production of melatonin in the pineal gland such as regulation of the cardiovascular system and increased immune activity. He does agree that there is recent evidence that suggests DMT might be produced in the human pineal gland; however, he points out that just because DMT can have psychedelic effects, this does not mean that it is the only function or reason for being endogenously produced.[23]

The fact is that DMT has been detected in human blood, plasma, urine, and kidney and lung tissue. It has also been detected in higher concentrations in the cerebrospinal fluid that surrounds the brain and the spinal cord. Research has found that, in the body, DMT is involved in neuro-regeneration and that it is able to protect brain cells and the immune system when it is under stress.[23]

However, when it comes to the role of DMT and human consciousness, the evidence is not so clear. He correctly points out that we do not know if a DMT-producing pineal gland is responsible for altered states of consciousness, and that we should not jump to the conclusion that the descriptions of the third eye chakra are clear evidence of a DMT-producing pineal gland. The fact is there is no evidence to disprove it and to put forward an argument based on cognitive bias* simply reinforces the evidence linking the pineal gland to the third eye chakra.[23]

---

*   Cognitive bias means that it is an inherent human tendency to find meaningful patterns where there may not be any.

10. Chakras and Consciousness

Vedic model of consciousness

Sturgess states that the human being is a soul wearing a physical body and suggests that consciousness and intelligence are attributes of the soul, not the gross body. He explains that the bodies or sheaths obstruct the true spiritual knowledge about the concealed soul. When the obstruction veils are removed, the self is realised. He describes the soul as ever-shining consciousness, perfect and complete, having no limits and without beginning or end. The light of knowledge that flows through *manas* (mind), *chitta* (field of consciousness), *buddhi* (intellect), *ahankara* (ego) and the *indriyas* (senses) is called consciousness.[11]

Swami Rama, Rudolph Ballentine and Swami Ajaya, authors of *Yoga & Psychotherapy — The Evolution of Consciousness*, state that it is problematic and difficult to compare modern psychology with yoga psychology. In modern psychology, the mental body is the most studied by making inferences about mental functioning through observed outward behaviours. In contrast, in yoga psychology, the mind is studied directly through introspection, such as meditation practices. The mind is often seen as an obstacle to that level of consciousness that a practitioner of yoga seeks.[24]

They also state that the Vedantic concept of the mind uses concepts of *manas*, *chitta*, *buddhi* and *ahankara* in order to arrive at an understanding of our mental functions. For example, the power of decisiveness in yoga psychology is called *buddhi*, which means a special kind of intelligence or wisdom. It is from this word that Buddhism takes its name.[24]

They provide us with a very good explanation about the interpretation of yoga psychology according to the various schools. For example, they state that conceptualisation of the mind according to Vedanta psychology and Jnana yoga, which includes concepts of *manas*, *chitta*, *buddhi* and *ahankara*, is relatively comparable with, and acceptable to, Western thinking. It is based, to some extent, and organised around the teachings and experiences of others. However, yoga of Pantanjali and Raja yoga are based more on personal experience. They state that Pantanjali's psychology is simple and not restricted to those who can master the complex concepts of refined psychology.[24]

Beyond the ego

In modern psychology, the term 'consciousness' often refers to 'that of which I am aware'. Consciousness is, therefore, considered an attribute of the ego. However, in yoga psychology, consciousness exists on various levels.[24]

Rama, Ballentine and Ajaya explain that, for one who has not developed or experienced higher levels of consciousness beyond the ego, their exact nature remains obscure. They explain that in yoga philosophy and psychology, a higher consciousness is assumed to exist as a potential in everyone. However, in modern psychology, everything that lies outside of the scope of the ordinary waking consciousness is considered part of the unconscious.[24]

In yoga psychology:

> *... human development is not seen as merely the elaboration of the ego. It is considered a gradual uncovering and development of consciousness. Consciousness manifests itself in such forms as the mental structures, but has the potential of freeing itself from them. With the progressive loosening of attachments, it gradually disentangles itself from the physical and mental forms, which both express it, and, at the same time, obscure and contaminate it.*[24]

At each level of consciousness, there is a diminishing degree of density of *prakriti* and an increasing degree of purity of consciousness. That is, there is an increasing correspondence between the current level of consciousness and pure consciousness. In the process of personal evolution, there is a progressive decrease in the attachments to identifications with people and objects. At each level of development, consciousness uses certain vehicles such as body, energy, mind or the higher *buddhi* to express and manifest itself. These are instruments for the consciousness to use. In yoga psychology, the ego is only one of the possible vehicles of consciousness; however, in Western psychology, the ego is the primary, and consciousness is a property of it. A psychology based on the limitations of the ego-level of consciousness can only be pessimistic about the possibility of developing beyond those narrow confines.[24]

On the other hand, yoga psychology asserts that there is an underlying consciousness which is trying to free itself from the confines of the mind. Consciousness tends towards evolution upwards, and when attachments to the denser levels of existence are broken it is permitted to follow its natural course upward toward a more serene and higher consciousness. At each level of development, giving up more attachments further expands the field of awareness and allows a higher consciousness to emerge. This leads beyond what can be imagined by ordinary waking consciousness. It brings one to the furthest reaches of one's potential — a universal awareness where there is no longer a distinction between the knower and the known. All is experienced simultaneously as part of oneself.[24]

The seven centres of consciousness

Sturgess describes chakras as a gateway to higher consciousness and that we will perceive our reality through the chakra in which our awareness is most dominant. For example:

> *If it is the first chakra (Muladhara), then our awareness and experience will resolve around insecurities and about our basic needs and instincts, such as our need for food, shelter, and procreation. If it is the second chakra (Svadhisthana) then sexual energy and pleasure can dominate our awareness. At the third chakra (Manipura) the ego can assert itself. A need for dominance or power can manifest as anger, aggression, control and intolerance.*[11]

Sturgess states that each chakra represents a higher level of human awareness and that the aim of chakra awareness and meditation is to bring the lower chakras into balance with the upper and higher chakras, so that our lives are not conditioned and governed in the mundane existence of the lower chakra consciousness. He suggests that most people in the world have lost awareness of their divine nature as a result of involvement in the world of illusions and limitations and that their consciousness is imprisoned in the lower chakras.[11]

> *... the so-called normal person is practically asleep. Some might even say it is non-existent. Only a few rare souls take the initiative to*

develop beyond conditioned living in ego-consciousness, and seek to regain their freedom by awakening and raising their consciousness to a higher level.[11]

Sturgess explains that the concept of chakras is a system of understanding our consciousness and who and what we really are. He suggests that meditation on the chakras is the means for dissolving the deep-seated and latent *samskaras* and obstacles blocking our spiritual awareness to the ultimate goal of self-actualisation.[11]

He recommends yoga meditation as a journey from the restless, emotional and distracted state of mind to a state of inner calm and stillness. He states that in a meditative state you will become aware of your own awareness, and in doing so your continuous stream of thoughts and feelings are replaced with the quiet, effortless inner awareness and attention that brings you inner joy.[11]

Drapkin et al. suggest that the chakras are a system of spiritual anatomy that suggests spirituality emerges in a developmental fashion. They investigated the psycho-spiritual development of individuals in accordance with chakra theory. They claim that chakra theory posits that spirituality emerges in a developmental monotonic fashion with increasing degrees of connection and spiritual awareness. They found that people further into the progression generally showed greater mental health and stronger character virtues, while individuals in earlier stages of development displayed greater pathology and lower levels of character virtues. They used five profiles of spiritual connection:[25]

- connection through love
- connection through sense of purpose
- connection through nature
- connection through contemplative practice
- sense of being connected to the oneness of the universe.

The study found that those who were low in all five variables were labelled the 'disconnected' class, and the participants who were high in all five variables were labelled the 'highly connected' class. The disconnected class displayed the greatest psychopathology (depression and anxiety) and the lowest levels of positive psychology traits (gratitude, grit, satisfaction with life, self-compassion and flourishing), while the highly connected class displayed the lowest psychopathology and highest level of positive psychology traits.[25]

It was suggested that, according to the chakra theory, the disconnected class, which was low in all five variables of spiritual connection and high in psychopathology, may reflect a deficit or trauma at a very early stage of development, during the formation of the first three chakras in the first four years of life.[25]

There is extensive research to confirm that there is an inverse relationship between spirituality or religiosity and symptoms of anxiety disorders. Studies have also confirmed that mindfulness-based therapy was moderately effective for improving anxiety and mood symptoms. It was suggested that the findings of this study further investigate the universal progression of spiritual development based on chakra theory.[25]

Chakras and spiritual development

Myss states that each of the chakras contains a universal spiritual life lesson that we must learn as we evolve into higher consciousness:[26]

- base chakra: lessons related to the material world
- sacral chakra: lessons related to sexuality, work and physical desire
- solar plexus chakra: lessons related to ego, personality and self-esteem
- heart chakra: lessons related to love, forgiveness and compassion
- throat chakra: lessons related to will and self-expression
- third eye chakra: lessons related to mind, intuition, insight and wisdom
- crown chakra: lessons related to spirituality.

According to Judith, the chakras are associated with different levels of consciousness and archetypes. The lower chakras, for example, are related to more practical elements of our lives — survival, movement and action. They are ruled by physical and social law. On the other hand, the upper chakras represent mental, emotional and spiritual realms and work on a more symbolic level through words, images and concepts.[27]

Judith states that each of the chakras represents a major area of human psychological health:[27]

- base — survival
- sacral — sexuality
- solar plexus — power
- heart — love
- throat — communication
- third eye — intuition
- crown — consciousness.

The chakras can also be seen as an archetypal depiction of individual maturation through seven distinct stages. At each stage, we gain more understanding of our personal and spiritual power, since each chakra represents a spiritual life lesson or challenge common to all human beings.[27]

Judith suggests that when a person masters each chakra, he or she gains power and self-knowledge that becomes integrated into their spirit, advancing them along the path of spiritual consciousness.[27]

Chakras, psychotherapy and energy healing

Hover-Kramer and Halo Shames explain that, because the psyche and soma are so closely interrelated, issues will often surface in the emotional dimension of the field before manifesting in the denser, physical body. They suggest working with the human energy field for emotional issues can be very beneficial for preventing physical disease. Working on the energy centres can also assist with psychological concerns such as self-esteem, awareness of feelings and effective self-expression.[28]

The concept of healing through the energy field is a very powerful tool for resolving deep psychological wounds. The therapeutic relationship allows for blocked energy to be released from the multidimensional field, often enabling one to spontaneously connect with some deeper part of oneself, such as enhanced creativity and the spiritual dimension.[28]

They suggest that energy healing is one of the many pathways that lead to personal transformation. An energy therapist can help a client understand their traumatic past or current conflict. The therapist can help to pinpoint the exact area in the energy field associated with the trauma. This then allows the client to identify the issues related to the affected energy centres. Working at their own pace, they can then address the energetic constriction, transform the turbulence, and fill in the gaps of missing knowledge or emotional support.[28]

For many of us, life demands an orientation towards the external world. However, when the external world overwhelms us, our coping mechanisms fail and that part of the human energy field that is most vulnerable breaks down. For some, the breakdown may be in a specific organ or physiological function that is weakest because of heredity or stress experiences. For others, the emotions may become distressed.[28]

Underlying all these dilemmas is a pervasive spiritual disease, which they describe as a sense of emptiness and discontent. Illness is seen by many depth psychologies as a loss of meaning or loss of one's soul. It is not surprising that transpersonal psychology based on the pioneering work of Jung and Maslow enhances the understanding of human nature beyond the realm of traditional psychology by exploring the psyche in relation to the collective unconscious and its quest for spiritual awareness.[28]

Hover-Kramer and Halo Shames explain that, when they speak of the spiritual dimension, they are addressing the personal quest for wholeness by aligning with the forces that are greater and beyond one's limited ego self.[28]

The spiritual dimension is understood as a natural evolution towards wholeness, which Jung called the path of individuation. It may be expressed through specific religious or meditative practices; it may be reflected by holding a deeply personal connection to the universe, nature or a sense of inner joy.[28]

When energy techniques are applied in psychotherapy, the client often experiences a rapid shift in increased inner awareness. This is often the result of the embodied presence of caring that emanates from the intentional field of the healer. In traditional 'talk therapies', 10 or more sessions might be needed to establish a similar level of trust or inner peacefulness.[28]

Heart-centred consciousness

Beshara asks us to think of the chakra system as a bio-socio-psycho-spiritual model of consciousness. He states that the reductionist scientific view is that the brain is the seat of consciousness. While he is grateful for the significant contributions of science, he does, however, claim that industrialisation has dehumanised us and that social media has disconnected us from the real world. He is not suggesting that technology is good or bad, but questions how can we create eco-friendly technologies that are harmonious with nature in the ultimate or nondual sense. He suggests a paradigm shift in the way we think that is reminiscent of the Buddhist concept of the Middle Way. The goal is individual transformation, which cannot happen unless there is balance, and the key to balance is the heart.[29]

Beshara asks us to think of understanding the chakras as an important life skill. He describes the chakra system as a multimodal approach than can ultimately lead us to nonduality — that is, if we manage to balance all our chakras. However, he states this is a difficult never-ending task that requires constant training over a lifetime. He suggests it can get easier and more enjoyable the more we do it, just like developing a new skill.[29]

Sahasrara symbolises enlightenment as a mode of consciousness — where one is no longer separate, when one is completely open to all that is, or when the concept of one is no more. He states:

> *... but I find that goal to be overly ambitious for the rest of humanity not because they are lesser individuals but because they are struggling through the first three modes of consciousness symbolized by the first three chakras: muladhara, svadisthana and manipura.*[29]

Beshara states that imbalances in the three lower chakras symbolise the highest tendency toward selfishness, with the first chakra representing the most selfish and the solar plexus chakra representing least selfish. Balancing in the higher three chakras — *Vishuddha*, *Ajna* and *Sahasrara* — primarily deal with the spiritual realm, symbolising the highest tendencies towards selflessness.[29]

The fourth chakra — the heart chakra — is special as it is situated exactly in the centre of the seven chakras. Beshara states that it symbolises the overall balance between all modes of consciousness and the ultimate potential for individual and global transformation.[29]

He suggests that, since most individuals are stuck at the lower three chakras, we should put all our efforts into opening the heart chakra and ensuring it is balanced so that there can be greater health, happiness and peace on both the individual and societal levels.[29]

Beshara introduces us to the concept of two hearts: the anatomical heart and the metaphysical heart. He reminds us that in ancient cultures, the heart was considered the seat of consciousness. He explains that the brain, or more appropriately the mind, is one of the seven modes of consciousness (*Ajna*).[29]

Beshara comments on the neurophysiology of chakras and the growing field of energy psychology and subtle energy; however, he states that his approach is to regard chakras metaphorically as modes of consciousness.[29]

He asks the question — so what are modes of consciousness?

> *Modes of consciousness are modes between which we oscillate. If all of our chakras are balanced metaphorically speaking then we can move seamlessly between the seven different modes of consciousness. These modes symbolically signify our awareness (or lack thereof) of the different levels of reality starting with the physical all the way to the spiritual.*[29]

He states that some of the qualities associated with heart-centred consciousness are direct knowing and ego-transcendence, intuition, compassion, wisdom, synchronisation and coherence, direct cognition, integration, intentionality, balance, healing and empathy, self-acceptance, universal love and transformation.[29]

The negative qualities of an overactive *Anahata* include being co-dependent, sentimental, smothering, inordinately responsible, and given to overdoing it and burning out; however, when it is underactive, we experience ourselves as being hard-hearted, stingy, uncaring, thoughtless, callous, greedy and calculating. Whenever our heart-centred consciousness is in balance we feel generous, compassionate and sensitive, and display unconditional positive regard for others, and caring for self and others.[29]

Beshara concludes that, before we can balance the world, we must first balance our heart chakra, so that we can experience health, peace and happiness, within and without.[29]

11. Chakras and Lifespan Development

Best writes an interesting article in which she examines the chakra system model of lifespan development. All humans follow a developmental sequence as they mature from infancy through to adulthood. Barring significant trauma, this sequence will follow a predictable pattern and is relatively consistent across cultures.[30]

Transpersonal psychology is based on the premise that human function potentiates along a continuum that can be divided into three sections:[30]

- pre-personal (prior to the formation of a separate ego)
- personal (ego formation)
- transpersonal (superseding a fully functional ego).

Best suggests that the chakra system may have been the source of inspiration for the model of lifespan development promoted in transpersonal psychology.[30]

While Williams James is regarded as the father of transpersonal psychology, Jung is credited with being the first Western psychologist to embrace cross-cultural perspective in the development of his theories.

Best states that traditional views of psychological development are predicated upon the construction of stable psychological structures that can support a healthy ego. Transpersonally oriented development theory states that the first major phase of development leads to the personality and the second major phase leads beyond it. This notion that healthy human functioning requires development beyond the formation and stability of the ego most clearly has its origins in Eastern philosophy.[30]

According to Best, Erikson's stages of development offer many parallels to the chakra system, including his description of the concerns that correspond to the transition to higher order chakra stages of development. According to Erikson:

> *Mid-adulthood marks a stage where the individual will either remain self-absorbed or turn his focus outward toward society and*

an interest in leaving a legacy of creativity and productivity. His corresponding stage to the throat chakra is described as a challenge of intimacy versus isolation.[30]

According to Judith, for many people, adult chakra development never occurs as they remain in dependency and powerlessness and never break from their programmed instinctual patterns.[27]

People may never have spiritual cravings and may never discover the potential of their higher selves. Once a person leaves home and begins to live independently, the chakra development begins. Some people have children before developing job skills; some begin with spirituality and have a family later, or never have a family at all. Some spend a short time establishing an economic base, a relationship, a mode of creative expression, while others spend their whole life at any one of these tasks.[27]

Base chakra: The first issue to solve is one of survival — getting a place to live, learning to care for yourself or a means of independent income. The time spent on this stage varies from person to person. For some, it is a lifetime struggle.[27]

Sacral chakra: One now forms sexual relationships. This is not to say that sexuality has not been occurring for many years, but one now has awareness of 'others' and the need for partnership becomes important. Satisfaction of emotional needs is the primary drive.[27]

Solar plexus chakra: An adult's individuation process liberates us from having to conform to the expectations of parents, friends or culture. It allows us to become true individuals living our life under our own power and will. We move from dependency, powerlessness and obedience to the creation of our own path and future. Here begins the task of making our own way in the world — developing a personal career, building skills to meet challenges and controlling our destiny. A misaligned solar plexus chakra seeks power over others; the awakened solar plexus chakra seeks power with others.[27]

Heart chakra: The focus on relationships eventually matures into true empathy, altruism and lasting partnerships. We examine ourselves in terms of the relationship with the world around us. Our relationships with colleagues, co-workers, friends and community also develop.[27]

Throat chakra: This is the stage where we wish to make our personal contribution to the community. It may mean creating a business, writing a book, building a home or seriously pursuing an artist hobby. With most people this happens around midlife. With more creative personalities, it may happen much sooner and may proceed or dominate other activities.[27]

Third eye chakra: This stage involves reflection and the exploration of mythology, religion and philosophy. There may be a period of searching in the form of travel or renewed study. This is often a time of spiritual interest and development. Such searching often intensifies when children are grown and the adult has more time and freedom for contemplation and spiritual practice.[27]

Crown chakra: This is a time of wisdom, spiritual understanding, knowledge and teaching. We bring together information gathered throughout life and pass it on to others.[27]

It must be remembered that adult development is often affected by unresolved childhood conflicts. If you realise that you have not gotten very far on some of these levels, then you will find understanding the psychospiritual aspect of your chakras very helpful.

12. Chakras, Yoga and Meditation

The book *Yoga & Psychotherapy* by Swami Rama, Rudolph Ballentine and Swami Ajaya provides us with a holistic framework for the practice of psychotherapy using the traditional teachings of yoga, which also incorporates the chakras. They claim that the primary thrust of Western psychology is to strengthen the ego, where as in yoga psychology, the ego is only a stepping stone to further evolution. They state that what is often referred to as 'higher states of consciousness' and 'mystical' is simply a completion of human development. They suggest that the chakras, which they refer to as the seven centres of consciousness, come into prominence during the process of meditation:[24]

> *They seem to constitute the structure of inner reality and their framework provides a sort of workshop within which one operates to explore oneself and evolve a higher consciousness.*

They explain that proper meditation on each successive chakra results in a new level of integration. Each level of integration is a result of a synthesis that occurs between two polarities.[24]

For example, the polarity synthesised at the level of *Ajna* chakra is that between *ida* and *pingala*, or the right and left aspects of the personality. Polarities involved at the throat chakra can be symbolised by the mother and child, that is to say, the nurtured and the nurturer. The polarity involved at the naval chakra has to do with activity and passivity in the sense of domination and submission. At the sacral chakra, the polarity is that between the male and the female. The polarities involved at the first chakra level are between the attacker and the attacked, the hunter and the prey, the devil and the divine or, simply, the 'bad' and the 'good'.[24]

The goal of yoga and meditation is to facilitate the integration between the two polarities. They explain the result of integration for each chakra.

> *At the first chakra, the integration of the good and the bad gives one the quality of solidity, or earthiness. The integration of the sacral chakra brings into awareness those aspects of one's personality*

which correspond to the opposite sex, but which one has exiled their awareness in order to create a functional sexual role for oneself. The integration of the solar plexus chakra has to do with the resolution of the issue of domination and submission. Integration of the heart chakra brings one the quality of sensitivity, empathy and the ability to experience compassion and selfless love. Integration at the throat chakra gives one the ability to be creative and to recreate oneself, to grow and to evolve. Integration at the third eye chakra results in an activation of intuition and the ability to see clearly with the inner vision. The integration of the crown chakra leads one to cosmic consciousness.[24]

Yoga practices exist to help the student free themselves of the narrow perspectives of the lower chakras and to view the world from those which are higher. Devotional practices, austerities, service to others, the study of philosophy, *pranayama* and meditation all exist to decrease attachments, allowing the unfolding of a more comprehensive awareness.[24]

When we study the higher chakras, we pass beyond the perspectives of most of modern psychology and we leave the realm of experience which they ordinarily encompass. There are many yoga practices that one can use to help awaken the state of consciousness associated with the higher centres.[24]

For example, Bhakti yoga or the yoga of devotion helps channel one's emotions towards pure love and service to one's ideals, thus bringing consciousness from the lower chakra to the heart chakra. It has an emphasis on prayer, worship, chanting and other devotional practices that focus energy on the throat chakra.[24]

On the other hand, Jnana yoga, the yoga of self-study and the study of the written wisdom, allows us to focus energy on the two higher chakra centres of consciousness. Rama, Ballentine and Ajaya suggest that the approach one takes should depend on their temperament and abilities.[24]

They state that the meditational practices of Raja yoga also help raise consciousness to the higher centres. They explain that in yoga there are traditionally two separate approaches to meditation on the chakras. One is to begin at the base chakra and concentrate on it until one has a thorough grasp of the energies and emotions that are involved with this chakra. After this process has led to a synthesis or resolution of the confusions existing at this level, you move your attention to the next highest chakra and begin to work on this centre. They explain that this process can be very difficult and time-consuming since one is attempting to find their way through the more primitive sides of oneself without having cultivated any of the advanced levels of consciousness which can be used as a tool.[24]

The other more common practice in yoga is to avoid any concentration and meditation on the lower chakras and focus on a selected higher centre.

13. Chakras and the Human Biofield

Measuring the human biofield

Rubik explains that electrical currents, along with their associated magnetic fields, can be found in the body. These electrical and magnetic fields are complex and dynamic and are associated with the dynamic processes such as heart and brain function, blood and lymph flow, ion transport across cell membranes, and many other biological processes. She explains that a broad spectrum of electromagnetic waves all emanate from the body. It is believed that the peak intensity of the electromagnetic radiation of the human biofield is the infrared region of the electromagnetic spectrum, in the range of 4 to 20 microns in wavelength. It has been suggested that this emission is from the thermal effects associated with metabolism.[31]

However, Rubik is more interested in measuring the biofield that is unrelated to thermal excitation of biomolecules, such as visible light. She states that some researchers speculate that extremely low-level visible light emissions from organisms called biophotons may communicate key electromagnetic bioinformation.[31]

No agreement has been reached in the scientific community in defining the biofield; however, Rubik suggests that the human biofield may carry important information of a diagnostic and predictive value for medicine.[31]

> *By measuring various aspects of the biofield, we may be able to recognize organ and tissue dysfunctions even in advance of diseases or symptoms and treat them appropriately so as to eradicate them. We may also be able to use biofield measurements to predict whether the effect of a particular course of therapy will be effective or ineffective.*[31]

The research into measuring biofields is still in its infancy. Rubik explains that various techniques have been developed to measure the biofield and fall into three categories:[31]

- high-voltage electrophotography
- acupuncture conductivity measurements
- biophoton measurements.

I was surprised to find an increasing amount of research not only confirming that all cells emit a weak, biophoton emission, but also examining the possible role in diagnosis and therapeutic interventions.

van Wijk & van Wijk state that detection and characterisation of biophoton emissions has led to suggestions that it has potential future applications in medicine. A review found research investigating biophoton emissions in the following fields:[32]

- influence of biological rhythms, age and gender
- intensity of emission and its left–right symmetry in health and disease
- emission from the perspective of traditional Chinese medicine
- emission in different consciousness studies.
- detection of peroxidative processes.

It was concluded that based on the initial results, further research into the field is justified.[32]

One paper, for example, examined the role of biophotons in regulating the aging process. The author of this paper concludes by stating:

> ... biophoton signals may well serve as the language of cells. Further intense research on ultraweak photon emission is needed to unravel other secrets in human life and their complex processes in aging and vital activities in general.[33]

A 2016 paper suggested that ultraweak photon emissions (UPEs) could be combined with metabolomic data* to provide a far more personalised approach to improving wellbeing. It has been reported that these UPEs originate from oxidative metabolic reactions and are therefore closely related to the rate of electronic transport in mitochondria and the generation of reactive oxygen species (ROS), reactive nitrogen (RNS), and/or lipid peroxidation. When perturbed, these reactions give rise to excessive oxidation, causing damage to lipids, nucleic acids and proteins. These damaged biomolecules can cause loss of cellular functions.[34]

---

* Metabolomics is used to measure metabolite profiles in bodily fluids, thus reflecting the complex interaction between the environment and the body.

It has been reported that a wide range of conditions are associated with changes in the UPE profile, including aging, diurnal biological rhythms and conscious activities.[34]

High-voltage electrophotography: gas discharge visualisation (GDV) camera

Scientific acceptance of Kirlian photography has been limited because the type of equipment used in earlier years varied significantly and from investigator to investigator, and there is a wide range of parameters that needs to be controlled to successfully photograph the biofield. Russia has been one of the most active countries in developing new scientific applications for bioelectrography.[35]

GDV, developed by Dr Korotkov, is one of the best-known systems for contemporary high-voltage electrophotography based on the Kirlian effect that was first discovered in Russia in 1948. The GDV equipment is certified as a medical device by the Russian Ministry of Health. According to Rubik, Kirlian photography was not introduced to the West until the 1970s because of the Cold War. Rubik reminds us that the Kirlian technique was used clinically in Germany for decades.[31]

The GDV camera uses pulses (10-microseconds) of high-frequency (1024 Hz), high-voltage electricity (10-15 kv) that is selectable from various ranges. The subject sits or stands in front of the camera and places their fingertips, one at a time, on an electrified glass plate of the camera. When the camera is activated, the computer sends a pulsed electric field to the plate. When the fingertip is electrified, it emits a corona discharge of light that is then captured by the GDV. This information is then sent to a computer for analysis. The GDV camera takes a digital photo of an individual's ten fingertips, while the software maps the biofield, chakra energy and meridian energy.[31]

Capturing the natural biophoton emission of the human body allows one to identify the functional state of an individual in real time. It is stated that in cases of imbalances and dysfunctions, or an abnormality of the microcapillary blood circulation, the transfer of electrons to the tissue is altered or inhibited, and therefore the electron flow is not full and the stimulated current is either very small or very irregular. Therefore, the gaps in the biophoton emission are indicators of the impeded transfer of electron density to the body's tissues and an abnormality in the energy supply of organs and systems.[36]

My first encounter with GDV

At an integrative medicine conference in Japan where I was speaking and launching the Japanese edition of *The Complete Guide to Aromatherapy*, I met an interesting person who had a big queue of people lining up to have their energy field photographed using a GDV device.

Maeba san was so busy, so I never had a chance to have my GDV energy field measured at the conference. We exchanged business cards and he kindly invited me to his office as he was also very interested in essential oils and wanted to do some research into the effects of essential oils upon our energy field.

I was so excited to meet with Maeba san in his office. He briefly explained that the GDV was based on Kirlian photography, using the latest digital technology and software to map the entire body energy field.

We did not waste any time having my energy field measured. The process involved each of the 10 fingertips being photographed. Through a process of complex algorithms, the entire body energy can then be determined to create an image of the entire aura. He described my aura below as being very healthy and strong.

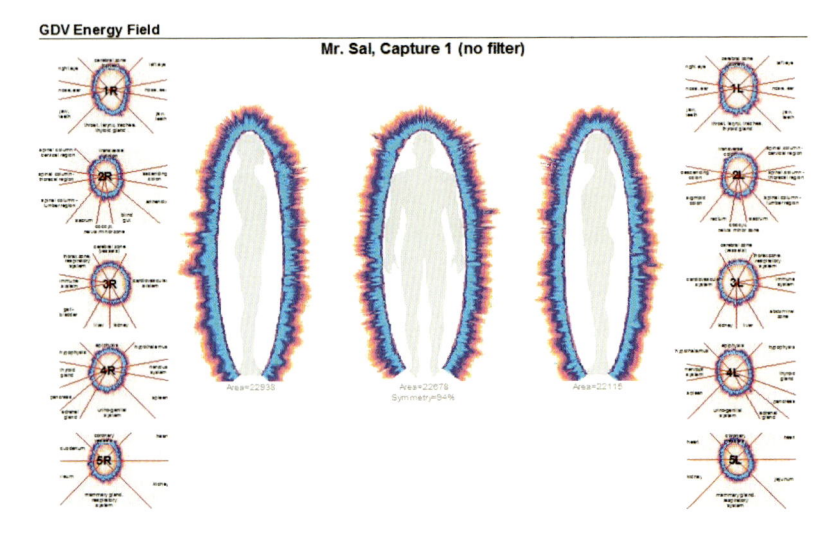

Sal's GDV energy field.

The GDV software can make a quantitative estimate of the chakra energy centres and graphically display the level of activation of each chakra. Ideally the chakra centres should be centrally aligned along the centre line and of even size, as can be seen below.

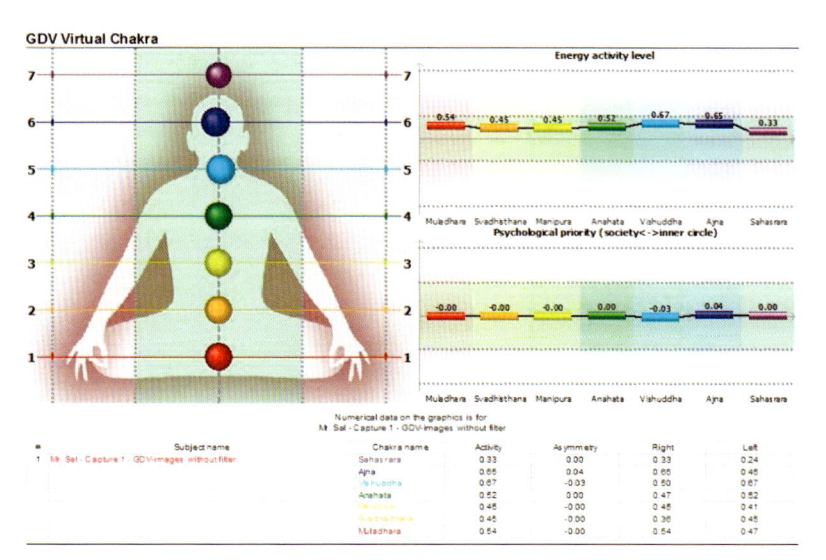

Sal's GDV chakra energy levels.

He pointed out that my energy field was uniform, without any breaks, holes or strong outbursts. This, he also explained, indicated a healthy individual in a good emotional state.

On the day, I had a friend with me who also volunteered to have her biofield and level of chakra activation measured.

In the GDV image on the next page (above), the field is very uneven, erratic and you can see lots of holes and energy outbursts.

The GDV chakra image on the next page (below) indicated that many of the chakras were misaligned and their size too small or enlarged. When people have strong stress, depression or are emotionally upset, the chakras may be totally out of alignment.

On this particular day, my friend had just received some very upsetting news and I have no doubt that this contributed to many of the chakra centres being out of alignment.

We then asked my friend to inhale her favourite oil, which happened to a special blend of 23 essential oils called *Green Goddess* blend. After a few

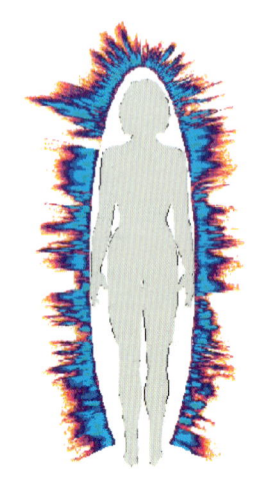

106 Aromatherapy and Chakras

Before inhaling Green Goddess blend. 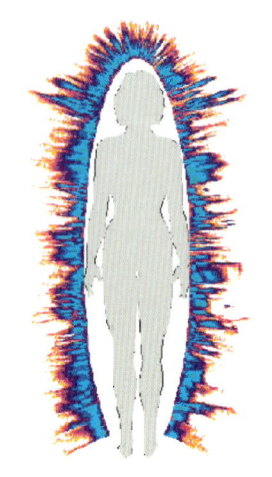   After inhaling Green goddess blend.

My friend's GDV field.

minutes the GDV was done again, and we were so surprised to see how the chakra energy centres had become much more balanced. See the chakra image on the next page.

Not surprisingly my friend was feeling calmer after inhaling the blend, but what was so amazing was how her chakra energy centres became more balanced and more aligned.

One of the obvious questions that I asked is — how long does this last? My friend did feel more relaxed and calmer for the rest of the day. However, I think more studies need to be done using GDV to thoroughly investigate how long the essential oils can influence the energy field and the chakra

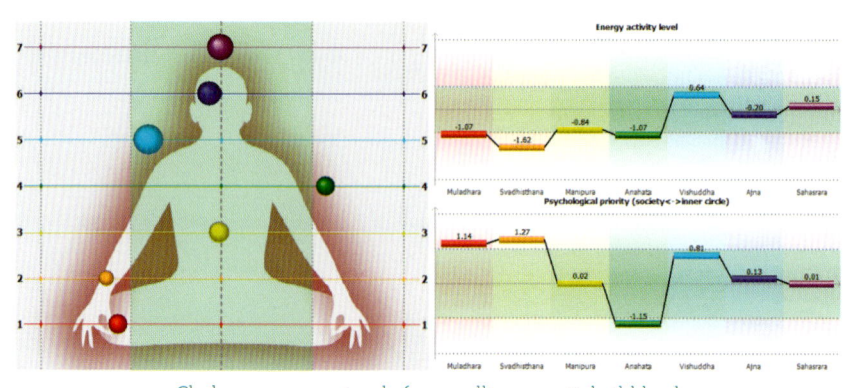

Chakra energy centres before smelling essential oil blend.

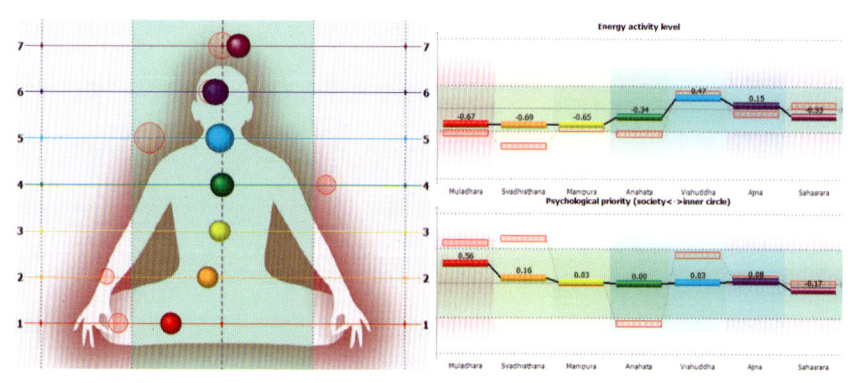

Chakra energy centres a few minutes after inhaling Green Goddess blend.

energy centres. GDV is one of the few techniques that can be used to identify the energetic impact of essential oils on our energy field. Using GDV analysis, we can become better aware of our emotional states and how they influence our energy centres.

It is so exciting to know that inhaling essential oils can have such a powerful effect on our biophoton field and can indeed play a role in balancing our chakras.

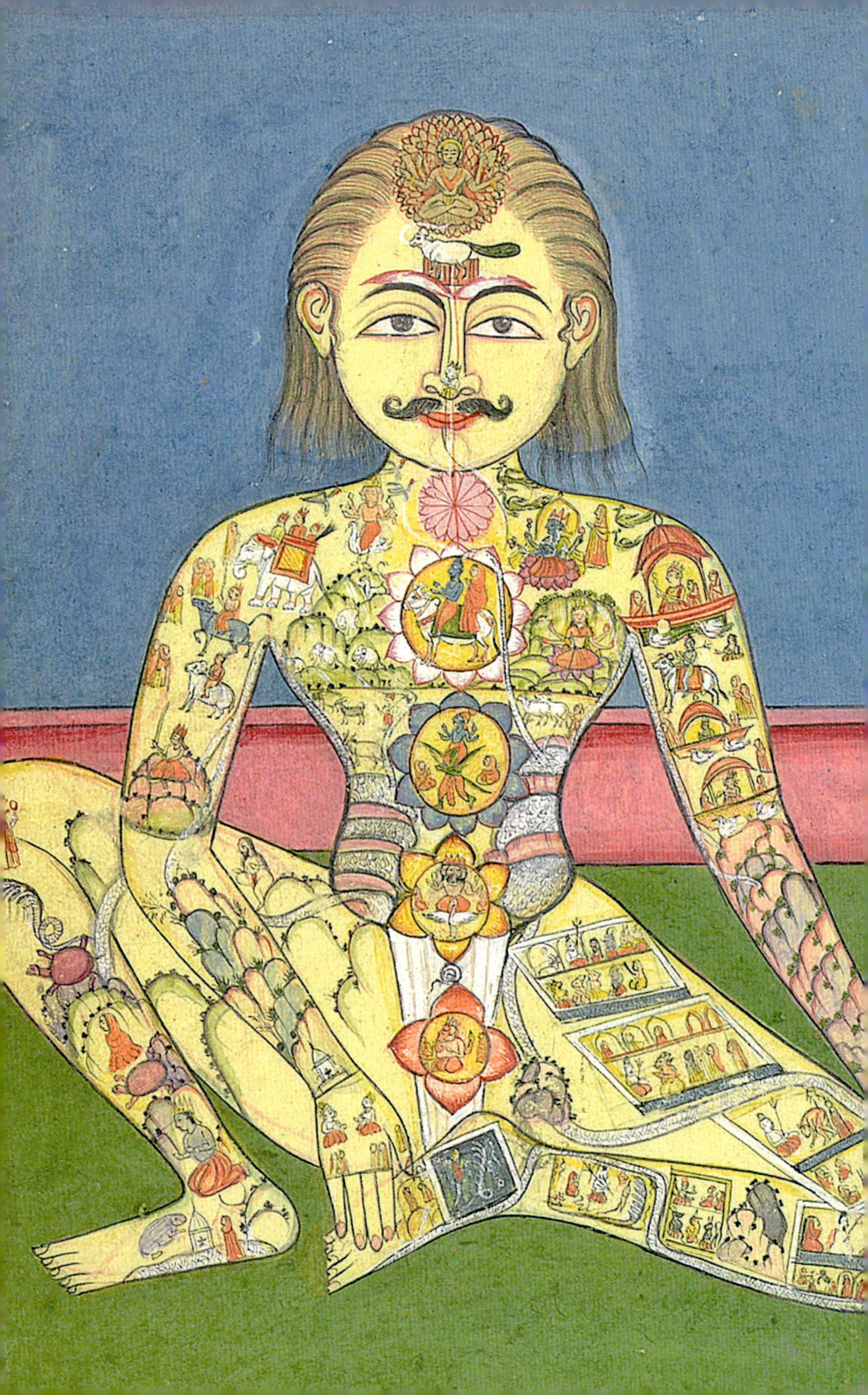

Part [3]
The Chakras

14. Base Chakra

15. Sacral Chakra

16. Solar Plexus Chakra

17. Heart Chakra

18. Throat Chakra

19. Third Eye Chakra

20. Crown Chakra

14. Base Chakra

It's a miracle
I was born
I don't need another reason
To deserve
To take the space
There's a room for us all
I am safe
I belong
I can express myself
Freely
Or simply be
Grounded
Nurtured
Nourished
Standing tall
In my centre
To share my light
And participate
In the game called life
Connected to Mother Earth
And all
In love.

Marzena Skowronska

Name

The base chakra is also known as the root or coccygeal chakra. Its Sanskrit name, *Muladhara*, also spelt *Mooladhara*, means 'root' or 'support'.

Purpose

Brennan states that the base chakra is related to the quantity of physical energy and will to live in the physical reality.[1]

Judith explains that the root chakra is concerned with physical needs and basic human survival.[2]

Myss states that the base chakra is the foundation of emotional and mental health. She explains that the base chakra energy manifests in our need for logic, order and structure.[3]

King states that the root chakra is the resting place of the *kundalini*. She explains that before this energy can awaken, the base chakra must be opened and cleared.[4]

Sturgess explains that the base chakra corresponds to the physical earth plane. He states that it provides the instinctual drives and energy necessary for basic survival needs of security, food and shelter. It represents the primitive instinctive drive and will to survive, with its associated feelings of fear, defensiveness, aggression, gratification of the senses, and the instinct to have sex and reproduce.[5]

Nardi describes the root chakra is like a seed in soil; however, he also explains that while we need soil to grow, we cannot remain in the soil or it will smother us.[6]

Colour

Red

Location

The base chakra is located at the base of the spine, between the anus and genitals.

Element

Earth

Physical association

The base chakra is associated with the adrenal glands, bowel and large intestines.

Psychospiritual

Judith explains that the base chakra reflects the degree to which we feel connected to the earth or are grounded in our activities. The amount of energy flow through the base chakra is the reflection of one's ability to link with the earth and to function effectively upon the earth plane from day to day. On a practical level, this refers to the ability to keep one's feet firmly upon the ground.[2]

Judith states that disconnection from the body has become a cultural epidemic. She explains that we have become alienated from the very roots of our existence and when this occurs, we lose the joy that arises from the dynamic connection with our lives — for example, living in an urban landscape that has no connection with nature, or a mundane routine job.[2]

The base chakra provides us with the ability to provide for life's necessities, the ability to stand up for ourselves and a sense of security. The base chakra helps us to grasp the importance of a fit, healthy body as we travel upward through higher and higher levels of consciousness.[2]

Gerber explains that the root chakra is the seat of *kundalini*:

> *The kundalini is symbolized as a coiled serpent within the sacral/coccygeal region. The coiled serpent represents a powerful subtle energy that is poised and waiting to spring into action. Only when the proper meditative and attitudinal changes have occurred does this force become directed upwards through the appropriate spinal pathway and activate each of the major chakras during the ascent to the crown. The kundalini is the creative force of manifestation which assists in the alignment of the chakras, the release of stored stress from the bodily centers, and the lifting of consciousness into higher spiritual levels.*[7]

Myss states that the base chakra is our connection to traditional family beliefs that support the formation of identity and a sense of belonging to a group of people in a geographic location. She states that the term tribal reflects the archetype of the base chakra.[3]

Satyananda explains that the awakening of the base chakra is very important because it is the seat of *kundalini* and the seat of great *tamas*. He explains all our passions, all our guilts and all agonies have their roots here, and warns us that when awakening takes place in the base chakra as a result of yoga practice or other spiritual disciplines, many things may explode into conscious awareness in the same way that an erupting volcano pushes to the surface things that were hidden beneath the earth. He advises us that it is important that the awakening of the *Ajna* chakra should accompany the awakening of the base chakra. He explains that the mental faculties of the *Ajna* chakra will give us the ability to witness the events of the base chakra awakening objectively and with greater understanding. This will make the experience less disturbing and traumatic.[8]

Traditional symbology

Muladhara is traditionally represented by a lotus flower with four deep crimson petals. In the pericarp is a yellow square, the symbol of the earth element. The golden yellow square, yantra of the earth element, is supported by an elephant with seven trunks. The elephant is the largest of all the land animals and possesses great strength and solidity, attributes of the *Muladhara*.[8]

The seven trunks represent the seven main constituents that are vital to physical functioning or the seven tissues of the body according to Ayurveda. In the centre of the yellow square is a deep red inverted triangle symbolising the creative energy or *Shakti*. Within the triangle there is a smoke-coloured *sivalinga*, which represents an astral body. Around this linga, which represents the astral body, the *kundalini* is coiled three and a half times. Three represents the three *gunas* or qualities of nature in an individual. Satyananda explains that as long as the three *gunas* are operating, individuality is functioning within the confines of ego. The half represents transcendence.[8]

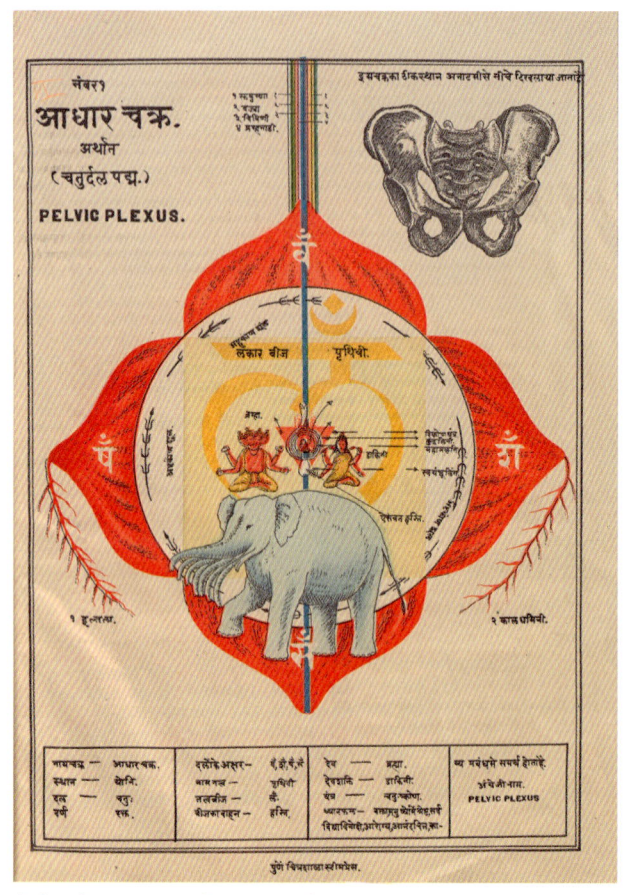

Base chakra from MS Sanskrit 391. Authored by Swami Hamsasvarupa, 1900s.

Archetype

King explains that the positive archetype for the base chakra is the Earth Mother, representing our ability to be in charge of our life force. The Earth Mother is a strong source of nourishment as she is rooted in the energy of the earth. The dysfunctional archetype is the victim. The victim has a low level of consciousness and energy. The victim will always assume that someone or something external is the cause of what happens in their life and that they have no control over their fate.[4]

Tubali describes the personality type of the base chakra as the builder. They are lovers of detail and structure, and they like to be in charge of the material and earthly plane.[9]

According to Tubali, builders represent 40% of the world population. They are typically drawn toward work as police, lawmakers, accountants, doctors, programmers, technicians and in construction. Builders do not like being eccentric or standing outside accepted structures. They tend to be conformists and feel better when they are affiliated with established systems. They are usually not interested in the abstract. They are fascinated by the deep intelligence of matter and the beauty of material things; however, builders do not like change. Tubali explains it is as if they simply do not understand why the Divine would create a changing world when it could have created something stable that lasts forever. They feel safest when they are dealing with details.[9]

In the presence of builders, we often feel calm and secure. Builders help us see the beauty in all the small detail and appreciate the joy of routine, which can connect us to the rhythm of nature. One of the biggest gifts of builders is that they show us the importance of community and virtues such as respect, justice, honour and righteousness. Tubali also explains that they remind us to honour our roots and teach us to respect our family, our community and the land that gives us sustenance and support.[9]

Challenges

Judith states that the challenges associated with the base chakra include body, foundation, survival, grounding, nourishing, trust, health, home, family and prosperity.[2]

Judith explains that when survival is threatened, we feel afraid. Fear heightens our awareness; it energises our body and mind and prepares us for action. Fear brings our attention into the here and now to address the threat, but focuses the attention outward and upward to the chakras of perception and mental activity. To work through fear is to learn to relax and feel the subtle energies of the body. When we combat fear, we strengthen the base chakra, when we live in fear, we weaken it.[2]

King explains that the base chakra's biggest obstacle is when you do not feel secure — when you are disconnected from your physical body and the natural world. Fear is considered the biggest obstacle to the flow of energy in the base chakra. Fear about your personal safety, fear about not fitting in with your family or friends, or where you live, about your job and money issues, about being alone, even about death.[4]

Behavioural characteristics

Sturgess states that the positive attributes of the base chakra are vitality and growth, while the negative qualities are inertia, laziness, self-centerdness, greed, rigidity and intolerance.[5]

Nardi states that if an activity becomes routine or habitual, we are feeding this chakra. If we are borrowing or transmitting an idea given to us by someone else without investigating it or trying it out for ourselves in some way, we are likely to be strongly influenced by this chakra.[6]

Johari explains that a person who is dominated by *Muladhara* chakra is obsessed by the desire to find security. He compares the behaviour of base chakra people to the behaviour of ants that are faithfully working for the queen.[10]

Balanced

Judith states that a balanced base chakra is represented by good health, vitality, well-groundedness, comfort in body, sense of trust in the world, feeling of safety and security, ability to relax and be still, stability and prosperity.[2]

Nardi states that when our base chakra is balanced, we have a healthy pride in our heritage, experience harmony with parents, are comfortable with a place to call home, enjoy being in nature, attend to factual practicalities and are aligned with life's cycles and seasons.[6]

Excess

Judith states that an excessive base chakra may result in obesity and overeating, hoarding, greed, sluggishness, laziness, fear of change, addiction to security and rigid boundaries. An excessive chakra feels heavy and sluggish. The body is usually large and dense, with excessive weight distributed around the hips, thighs and buttocks. If there is no weight problem, often the muscles are hard and rigid.[2]

Deficiency

Judith explains that a deficient base chakra may result in disconnection from the body, underweight, being fearless, anxious or restless, poor focus, financial difficulties, poor boundaries and being disorganised. A person with a deficient base chakra does not recognise the body's importance. Grooming and hygiene are poor, and dressing is sloppy. Details about life are not important, whereas fantasy, dreams, knowledge and spirituality are very important.[2]

Judith states that when we are disconnected from our body, our actions become compulsive. She is concerned that disconnection from the body is a cultural epidemic and considers it the most alarming as it separates us from the very roots of existence.[2]

Prendergast states that when the base chakra is contracted, we are prone to feel terror or generalised anxiety.[11]

Health issues

Judith states that physical issues associated with imbalances of the base chakra include:[2]

- disorders of the bowel and large intestine
- disorders of the bones
- issues with legs, feet, knees, base of spine
- eating disorders
- frequent illnesses.

Myss states that the base chakra energy connection to the physical body is the spinal column, rectum, legs, bones, feet and immune system.[3]

Sturgess states that it is not surprising that the adrenals are associated with the base chakra. He explains that the adrenals produce hormones that influence the body's metabolism and are involved in the 'fight-or-flight' response that is triggered by stress.[5]

King explains that physical problems in the base chakra show up at the base of your spine, in your legs and feet, in your bones, or in your immune system. It may also manifest as eating disorders, adrenal insufficiency, or rectal or colon cancer.[4]

Essential oils for the base chakra

Essential oils that balance the base chakra are generally those oils from roots, woods and resins. They are grounding, strengthening and centring.

Typical essential oils that have the greatest affinity with the base chakra include:

Angelica root — grounding.[12]

Benzoin — grounding and comforting, especially during psychological 'releasing' experiences.[12]

Bergamot — supports love for one's physical body.[12]

Buddha wood — grounding and connects us with the earth.

Cedarwood, Atlas — connects us with the earth forces.[12,13]

Coriander seed — promotes feelings of security and earthly connections.[12,13]

Frankincense — grounds, calms and centres. Links base with the crown.[12,13,14]

Ginger — promotes feelings of security and is grounding.

Myrrh — strengthens, energises and supports the base chakra.[12,13,14]

Oakmoss absolute — grounding, increases sense of prosperity and security.[12,13]

Patchouli — strengthens and grounds, excellent for people who are overthinking. Promotes the connection of the physical body and the subtle body.[12,13]

Peru balsam — promotes feelings of safety and comfort.[12,13]

Sandalwood — promotes inner unity, realigning body, mind and spirit. Grounds and connects us with our sense of being.[12,13,14]

Vetiver — balances, grounds and protects. Promotes strength and a deep sense of belonging.[12,13,14]

Aromatherapy blends

Use these blends in a diffuser or add to 10ml of jojoba oil to use as a massage oil or an anointing oil.

Balance

Feel grounded and connected to nature with *Balance* chakra blend. *Balance* is a synergy of black pepper, Atlas cedarwood, lavender, sweet orange, patchouli and vetiver essential oils.

Grounding

This blend connects and grounds us with the energy of the earth.

>2 drops coriander seed
>2 drops sweet orange
>2 drops patchouli

Integrate the body and spirit

This blend integrates body and spirit, allowing our *kundalini* to awaken.

>2 drops frankincense
>2 drops myrrh
>2 drops sandalwood

Promote prosperity

This blend strengthens and nurtures a feeling of prosperity and security.

>2 drops Atlas cedarwood
>2 drops ginger
>2 drops oakmoss absolute

Questions for self-examination

Myss asks the following questions for self-examination:[3]

- What belief patterns did you inherit from your family?
- Do any of them still have authority over you?
- What superstitions do you have? Which have more authority over you than your own reasoning ability?
- Do you have a personal code of honour? What is it?
- Have you ever compromised your sense of honour? If so, have you taken steps to heal it?
- Do you have any unfinished business with your family members? If yes, what prevents you from healing your family relationships?
- List all the blessings that you feel come from your family.
- If you are a parent, what qualities would you like your children to learn from you?
- What tribal traditions and rituals do you continue?

- What tribal characteristics within yourself would you like to strengthen and develop?

King states that if you answer yes to three or more of the questions below, the chances are you need to balance your base chakra:[4]

- Do you have a hard time staying focused?
- Are you excessively fearful?
- Do you have any phobias?
- Are you taking medication for anxiety?
- Are your desk, household or finances disorganised?
- Do you feel too weak for sustained physical activity?
- Are you very uncomfortable when things change?
- Are you often doing one thing while thinking of another?

Activities to strengthen your base chakra

Judith recommends the following activities to strengthen the base chakra:[2]

- physical activities such as an exercise program or yoga
- lots of touch, regular massage
- bioenergetic grounding
- Hatha yoga
- doing work that you love
- developing a conscious relationship with money
- listening to stimulating music with deep beats such as drums or music that makes your body move like Latin American music.

King suggests simple ways to strengthen your base chakra such as walking barefoot, hiking in the park or in the mountains, dancing, belly breathing, gardening, creating order and structure in your house, wearing the colour red.[4]

Tubali suggests several lifestyle activities to keep the base chakra balanced:[9]

- Avoid resting too much.
- Incorporate some form of dynamic physical activity into each day.
- Develop a sense of detachment that will help you realise that life's structures do not serve as the purpose of life itself.

- Learn to step outside your core group — home, family, community or nation.
- Every now and then, go on an intentional adventure that breaks your routine or evokes excitement.

Nardi suggests the following activities to cultivate the base chakra:[6]

- Question assumptions. If you engage in a daily habit or follow a belief that you have not yet examined, consider researching it and reflecting on its tangible impact.
- Shed excess possessions. Sort through what you have accumulated and donate or sell excess material goods.
- Live in healthy spaces. No matter how small or large, find a personal space for yourself that is free of stressors.
- Put down your roots. Make a place you can call home, a family nest, where you have roots and feel safe and comfortable.
- During meditation or yoga, connect to the earth, breathe in deeply down to the belly and focus on the earth as your support.
- Give thanks each day for your meals and other material benefits. Focus on what you have rather than what you lack.

Affirmations for the base chakra

Judith recommends the following affirmations to strengthen the base chakra:[2]

- It is safe for me to be here.
- The earth supports me and meets my needs.
- My body is becoming more important to me. I nurture it constantly.
- I am responsible for my life. I can cope with any situation.
- I deserve the best that life has to offer. My needs are always met.

15. Sacral Chakra

The mystery of life
Is to remember to have fun
Through play we meditate
Become fully present
Forget there are limits
Tap straight to the Source
Enable the space
For magic to take place
When we get lost
In what is giving us joy
We get inspired
Create with the spirit
Totally immersed
Connected to the flow of the Universe
Miracles happen
We find our purpose
Life becomes meaningful
We don't have to be so serious
To achieve big things
Quite the opposite
We need to let go
Relax
And move our hips
Into the music of our soul.

Marzena Skowronska

Name

The sacral chakra is also known as the navel chakra, gonadal chakra or splenic chakra. The Sanskrit name for the sacral chakra is *Svadhisthana*, meaning 'sweetness', and its associations are indeed what makes life sweet — pleasure, sexuality, nurturing, movement and change.

Purpose

Brennan states that the sacral chakra relates to the quantity of sexual energy of a person. When this centre is open, a person feels their sexual power, if it is blocked, whatever sexual force and potency a person has will be weak and disappointing. They will probably not have much sexual drive, tend to avoid sex and disclaim its importance and pleasure, resulting in undernourishment in that area.[1]

Judith states that the purpose of the sacral chakra is movement and connection.[2]

King explains that the sacral chakra is the centre of our pleasure principle. It is also about our relation with others, about attraction and desire.[4]

Sturgess states that the sacral chakra corresponds to the astral plane. It is the seat of the subconscious mind and where all our life experiences and impressions from the past are formed. He explains that the association of this chakra with the water element is to do with 'flow'.[5]

Colour

Orange

Location

The sacral chakra is located at the base of the spinal column, at the level of the coccyx. It is in the front of the body at the level of the pubic bone, between the navel and genitals.

Element

Water

Physical association

The sacral chakra is associated with the urinary system and reproductive system.

Psychospiritual

Gerber describes the sacral chakra as the subtle energy seat of sexuality. From a psycho-energetic standpoint, the sacral chakra is associated with the expression of sensual emotion and sexuality.[7]

Judith states that many cultures frown upon people expressing their emotions and consider emotional reactions as a sign of weakness; however, she states that passion is an essential motivating force for vitality, power and creativity. When passion is suppressed, our feelings become dull.[2]

Judith claims that sexuality and spirituality have long had a conflicted relationship, explaining that many people see them as polarised rivals for consciousness. Such philosophies tell us that to become spiritual we need to overcome desire, to renounce sexuality and to rise above our feelings. However, in Tantra practice, sexuality and spirituality are an invisible whole — each enhancing the other.[2]

Judith explains that in balancing the sacral chakra, we must reclaim our right to feel. We must reclaim passion and pleasure. The sacral chakra leads us from basic existence to help us embrace what makes life worth living.[2]

Sturgess states that the sacral chakra corresponds with the astral plane. It is the seat of the subconscious mind where all our life experiences and impressions from the past are formed. He explains that the sacral chakra is concerned with creativity in all forms, and with procreation and the life-sustaining energy behind the sexual impulse. The sacral chakra is also referred to as the centre of self-expression and joy.[5]

Prendergast states that the sacral chakra deals with themes of sensual and sexual pleasure and gratification, play, movement, creativity and physical power.[11]

Traditional symbology

Satyananda explains that *Svadhisthana* can be experienced as black in colour, as it is the seat of primary ignorance. However, traditionally, it is depicted as a six-petalled vermilion or orange-red lotus.[8]

Sturgess states that the six petals represent the flow of energy from six *nadis*. He explains that six passions are associated with the six petals: lust, anger, greed, deceit, pride and envy.[5]

The element of this chakra is Water, symbolised by a white crescent moon within the pericarp of the lotus. The crescent moon is formed by two circles that engender two further yantras. The larger has outward turned petals and represents the conscious dimension of existence. On the inside of the crescent moon is a similar petalled but smaller circle with petals facing inwards. This is the unconscious dimension, the store of formless

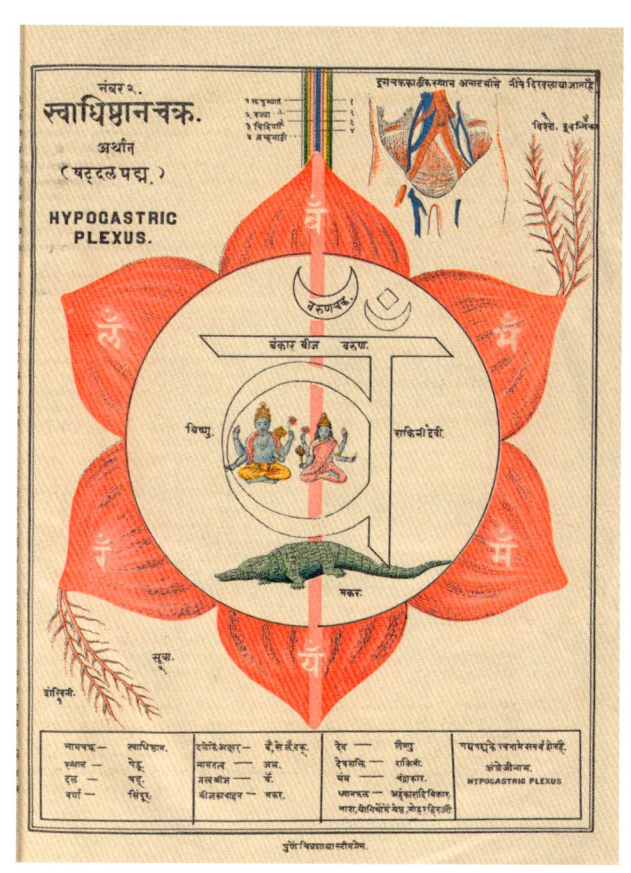

Sacral chakra from MS Sanskrit 391. Authored by Swami Hamsasvarupa, 1900s.

karma. These two yantras are separated by the white crocodile in the crescent moon. The crocodile is the vehicle that carries the whole phantom of unconscious life. It symbolises the subterranean movement of the karmas.[8]

Sturgess states the crocodile is associated with laziness, insensitivity and sensuality, depicting the sensuous nature of a person who is stuck at this level.[5]

Archetype

King explains that the positive archetype of the sacral chakra is the monarch. The monarch enjoys abundance, is happy and feels good about themselves. They trust their body and understand what they hunger for, but they do not overindulge or become addicted to anything.[4]

The dysfunctional archetype is the martyr who sacrifices and suffers. Martyrs devote themselves to making sure that their children, parents, partner or boss are okay, even if that diminishes their own chance to be creative and happy. King states that they harbour a deep sense of guilt and feel like they deserve to suffer. They never express their own feelings or desires, and they can make you feel bad if you do.[4]

Tubali describes the personality type of the sacral chakra as the artist. Artists live in the moment, with no purpose, no future and no worries. They live for the sheer pleasure found in the here and now. According to Tubali, artists represent around 7% of the world population. They are typically drawn towards work as musicians, artists, comedians, stage performers, dancers and fashion designers. They have a tendency to be surprising and to do the unexpected. Tubali refers to them as the most colourful of all the seven chakra personality types.[9]

Artists desire heightened feelings and experiences. They seek to understand life by experiencing it. Tubali states that many of us were sacral chakra types as teenagers and in our early twenties. We may have been adventurous and took risks, we were extremely romantic. Everything seemed so magnified. When they were in love, the entire world was illuminated, when love faded, it seemed as if the entire world would fall apart.[9]

The sacral chakra personality is constantly excited. They constantly need to feel excited. They can react strongly to situations, and this is why all experiences are either horrible or wonderful. They are not content with any middle ground and love being moody. Artists know how to enjoy, but they also know how to be depressed. They commonly experience depression, melancholy and moodiness.[9]

They can also be quite egotistical and, to a certain degree, even narcissistic. Tubali states:

> *As far as they're concerned, everything, including other people, revolves around their feelings. How they feel is all-important, and the people around them are but an extension of their own excitement.*

Tubali states that appreciation is a beautiful quality of the sacral chakra types. They have the gift of eternal youth. Sacral chakra types are able to teach us how to embrace our natural energies and the joy of the physical body. They help us realise our sexual potential, telling us we should not be too moral and rigid. They encourage us to appreciate beauty and elegance in the simple, most taken-for-granted things in life.[9]

Challenges

Judith states that the issues associated with the sacral chakra include movement, sensation, emotions, sexuality, desire, need and pleasure.[2]

According to Judith, many cultures frown upon emotional expression or consider emotional sensitivity a weakness. This infringes our basic right to feel. For example, the following terms all affect our basic rights to feel — 'you have no right to feel angry', 'boys do not cry', 'you should be ashamed of yourself?'. Feeling is a very important way of obtaining information about our wellbeing. When our right to feel is affected, we become out of touch with ourselves and disconnected.[2]

Judith explains that when we reclaim our right to feel, we also reclaim passion and pleasure and our sensate connection to both inner and outer reality.[2]

> *We free the flow of dynamic energy that is essential for growth, change, and transformation and release the armor that separates us.*[2]

Judith explains that pleasure invites us to pay attention to our senses, to live fully in the present and to enjoy the experience of being alive. She suggests that our culture often equates maturity with the ability to deny pleasure.[2]

> *We are often told to put our pleasures away as we grow older — to sit, work hard, deny or control our feelings. Pleasures we once knew become regulated by guilt, held inside by rigidity in the body and rigidity in our thinking.*[2]

She explains that when primary health pleasures are denied, secondary pleasures take over. She refers to secondary pleasures as the pleasure of drinking, drugs, avoiding responsibility, sexually acting out or overeating. According to Judith, this can become the basis of addictions:

> *Since secondary pleasures cannot really satisfy our longing for primary pleasures, our lack of satisfaction makes us crave more, forming the basis of addictions.*[2]

Judith also states that sexual abuse can have long-lasting effects on all aspects of the sacral chakra such as the free flow of energy within the body, the ability to have intimacy, pleasure and healthy sexuality as an adult, comfort with emotions, a healthy sense of boundaries and a positive relationship with one's own body.[2]

She describes sexual abuse as anything that does not respect the natural development of a child's sexuality. She explains that being consciously aware of the abuse, learning about its effects, and engaging in the healing process will promote profound changes in every aspect of one's life; however, she does wisely recommend the help of professionally trained therapists to assist with the healing process.[2]

King states that one of the biggest challenges of the sacral chakra is addiction — addiction to alcohol, drugs, food, shopping, exercise, sex and gambling, just to name a few.[4]

Behavioural characteristics

Johari states that the expansion of personality starts with the sacral chakra. In the base chakra, the basic goal is the pursuit of financial security, whereas in the sacral chakra, one's attention is diverted to desires, fantasies of a sexual nature and creativity. Art, music and poetry are attractive and meaningful. In the sacral chakra, the desire for the highest enjoyment, the bliss attained in *samadhi*, takes the form of a longing for marital pleasure.[10]

Balanced

Judith states that a balanced sacral chakra is reflected by graceful movements, emotional intelligence, ability to experience pleasure, nurturing oneself and others, ability to change and healthy boundaries. A balanced second chakra has a deep emotional core that is grounded enough to be contained and open enough to flow and connect. Healing our wounds in this chakra creates the necessary emotional depth for developing true power, compassion, creativity, insight and awareness — all aspects that lie ahead on the chakra journey.[2]

Nardi states when the sacral chakra is healthy, we are able to tap into our creativity and talents, we are physically fit and have a healthy lifestyle, we are emotionally mature with few hang-ups and know how to deal with baggage.[6]

Prendergast states that when the sacral chakra is balanced there are feelings of physical potency, playfulness, creative flow and sensuality.[11]

Excess

Judith states that an excessive sacral chakra results in sexual addiction, pleasure addiction, excessively strong emotions, being ruled by emotions, oversensitivity, seductive manipulation, emotional dependency and obsessive attachment.[2]

Judith explains that when someone has an excessive sacral chakra, they feel most alive when they experience intense emotional states. For example, when one says 'I am angry', it implies that they are that emotion rather than merely having a momentary feeling. For some people, the only time they feel they are anything is when they are feeling some kind of intense emotion.[2]

Deficiency

Judith states that a deficient sacral chakra may cause rigidity in the body and attitudes, frigidity, fear of sex, poor social skills, denial of pleasure, excessive boundaries, fear of change and lack of desire.[2]

Prendergast states that when the sacral chakra is closed there are often feelings of body shame, disgust with sexuality, guilt, impotence and physical powerlessness.[11]

Health issues

Judith states that physical issues associated with imbalances of the sacral chakra include:[2]

- disorders of the reproductive organs, spleen, urinary system
- menstrual difficulties
- sexual dysfunction — impotence, premature ejaculation, frigidity, non-orgasmic
- lower back pain
- dull senses — loss of appetite for food, sex or life.

According to King, health issues associated with the sacral chakra include problems with the male and female reproductive organs, sexual dysfunction, inflammatory bowel disease, appendicitis, chronic lower back pain or sciatic nerve pain, and bladder or urinary problems.[4]

Gerber states that other illnesses resulting from dysfunction of the sacral chakra include colitis, irritable bowel syndrome, bladder tumours, malabsorption diseases of the small intestine, various types of sexual dysfunction, prostatitis and lower back pain.[7]

Essential oils for the sacral chakra

The essential oils that balance the sacral chakra are typically rich and sweet floral oils, the sweet resin and sweet citrus oils. Typical essential oils that have the greatest affinity with the sacral chakra include:

Cardamom — stimulates sexual energy.[13]

Coriander seed — increases creativity and passion.[12,13]

Geranium — nourishes feminine creativity and promotes relaxed spontaneity.[12,13]

Ginger — increases sexual desire.[12]

Jasmine absolute — connects our spirituality and sexuality. Promotes creativity and artistic development.[12,13]

Mandarin — promotes creativity and our ability to enjoy life.

Neroli — connects spirituality and sensuality. Promotes sensual comfort.[12,13]

Orange, sweet — promotes joy in sexuality and creativity.[12,13]

Patchouli — spiritualises sexuality. Facilitates enjoyment of the senses and awakening of creativity.[12,13,14]

Peru balsam — promotes sensuality and confidence.[13]

Rose absolute and otto — connects sexuality with the heart. Promotes creativity and love of beauty.[12,13]

Sandalwood — connects sensuality with spirituality.[12,13,14]

Ylang ylang — promotes sexuality, helps unite our emotional and sexual natures.[12,13]

Aromatherapy blends

Use these blends in a diffuser or add to 10ml of jojoba oil to use as a massage oil or an anointing oil.

Allure

Allure chakra blend is a blend of jasmine absolute, mandarin, sandalwood, cardamom, ylang ylang and patchouli pure essential oils. *Allure* is sensual and warming in nature. It connects us with our sexual and reproductive energy and with the great love of beauty.

Promote passion and sensuality

This blend nurtures love and integrates our spirituality and sexuality.

    1 drop coriander seed
    2 drops jasmine absolute
    3 drops sweet orange

Support our right to feel

This blend creates an emotionally safe place, allowing us to accept love.

>   2 drops patchouli
>   1 drop rose otto
>   2 drops sandalwood

Nurture the artist

This blend nurtures our creative energy and artist archetype.

>   1 drop jasmine absolute
>   2 drops mandarin
>   1 drop Peru balsam
>   1 drop sandalwood

Questions for self-examination

Myss asks the following questions for self-examination:[3]

- How do you define creativity?
- Do you consider yourself a creative person?
- Do you follow through on your creative ideas?
- Do you often direct your creative energies into negative paths of expression?
- Do you exaggerate or embellish 'facts' to support your point of view?
- Are you comfortable with your sexuality? If not, are you working toward healing your sexual imbalances?
- Do you use people for sexual pleasure, or have you felt used? Do you respect your own sexual boundaries?
- Do you have an impression of the Divine as a force that exerts justice in your life?
- Are you a controlling person?
- Do you engage in power plays?
- Are you able to see yourself clearly in circumstances related to power and money?
- Does money have authority over you? Do you make compromises that violate your inner self for the sake of financial security?

- How often do survival fears dictate your choices?
- Can you master your fears about finances and physical survival, or do they control you and your attitudes?
- What goals do you have for yourself that you have yet to pursue? What stands in the way of acting upon those goals?

King states that if you answer yes to three or more of the questions below, the chances are you need to balance your sacral chakra:[4]

- Are you generally pessimistic, and do you say things such as: 'I'm never going to find a life partner' or 'I cannot lose weight' or 'I cannot earn enough money'?
- Are you unable to both give and receive pleasure?
- Are you unable to both give and receive money?
- Do you have a crushing sense of somehow failing in life?
- Have you ignored your ethics in exchange for money, power or sex?
- Do you care too much about what others think about you?
- Do you put aside your own dreams?
- Do you frequently feel like you are all alone in the world?
- Are you unable to release what has happened in the past?
- Do you always feel the need to buck authority?

Activities to strengthen your sacral chakra

Judith recommends the following activities to strengthen the sacral chakra:[2]

- hot aromatic baths
- deep tissue massage
- experience balanced sexuality
- listening to music with a bounce or that flows
- emotional release or containment
- movement therapy.

King suggests simple ways of clearing sacral chakra blockages such as finding a hobby or activity you enjoy that allows you to express your creativity and to surround yourself with beauty such as art and flowers.[4]

Tubali suggests several lifestyle activities to keep the sacral chakra balanced:[9]

- Keep your body active.
- Use beautiful music and dance to channel your energy.
- Be careful not to submit yourself to a life of commitments and routines that can dry up the spirit.
- Choose a career that ensures you have independence and gives you space to be creative.
- Look for opportunities in any field of art.
- Maintain a sense of drama in your life and your spiritual practices.

Affirmations for the sacral chakra

Judith recommends the following affirmations to strengthen the sacral chakra:[2]

- I am moving towards a time when I am totally happy and fulfilled. Life offers me everything I need for that journey.
- I am worthy of love and sexual pleasure.
- My sexuality is sacred.
- I absorb information from my feelings.
- I am prepared to honour my body and feel good about my sexuality.
- Life is pleasurable.

16. Solar Plexus Chakra

I have the power
It's all within me
I don't have to look for support
Externally
Rather tend
To the inner flame
And in turn
It will light up my way
Wisdom
Courage
It's all sitting here
Waiting for me
To be revealed
By engaging navel
I move the energy
To awaken my strengths
And remember the gifts
I came here to share
We all have a role to play
On this earthly plane
So I turn on
My internal sun
Allowing it
To shine bright.

Marzena Skowronska

Name

The Sanskrit name for the solar plexus chakra is *Manipura* — 'lustrous gem'. The literal meaning of *Manipura* is the 'city of jewels'.[5,8]

Purpose

Brennan explains that the solar plexus chakra is associated with the great pleasure that comes from deeply knowing one's unique and connected place within the universe:

> *A person with an open solar plexus chakra can look up to the starry heavens at night and feel that he belongs. He is firmly grounded in his place within the universe. He is the center of his own unique aspect of expression of the manifest universe and from this he derives spiritual wisdom.*[1]

She states that when this chakra is open and functioning harmoniously, a person will have a deeply fulfilling emotional life that is not overwhelming. However, she claims that when this centre is open but the 'protective membrane' over it is torn, they will have great uncontrolled extremes of emotions.[1]

Brennan suggests that the solar plexus chakra serves as a block between the heart and sexuality. She suggests that the solar plexus is a very important centre with regard to human connectedness. She refers to psychic or etheric cords that are created whenever we develop relationships with another human being. When a relationship comes to an end, these cords are slowly disconnected.[1] She states:

> *The nature of the chakra cords that you build in your first family will be repeated in all the following relationships that you create later ... As you move through life, and mature, you gradually transform the child/mother cords into adult/adult cords.*[1]

Judith explains that the purpose of the solar plexus chakra is to transform the inertia of matter and movement into conscious direction of willed activity. She explains:

> *Earth and Water are passive and dense. They move downwards. Chakras one and two are instinctual. They follow the paths of least*

resistance. The fire of chakra three is dynamic and light, rising upward, moving away from gravity. This change is necessary to reach the upper chakras and complete our journey.[2]

The process of individuation begins in the solar plexus chakra:

Here we break away from internalized parents, peers, and culture, and begin to define ourselves. It is about daring to be unique, risking disapproval for the integrity of your own truth. Individuation is the unfolding of our unique destiny, the unfolding of the soul. We cannot change the world if we have not yet individuated from the way the world expects us to be. We cannot truly claim our power without the willingness to individuate.[2]

Myss explains that the solar plexus chakra relates to our connection with others, but without the root chakra's reliance on the 'tribe' or the sacral chakra's emphasis on partnerships. It is about the power of being an individual to be unique, while celebrating our continuing connection with all humanity.[3]

Satyananda explains that *Manipura* radiates and distributes pranic energy, regulating and energising the entire body.[8]

Colour

Yellow

Location

Solar plexus

Element

Fire

Physical association

Gerber states that the solar plexus chakra supplies nutritive subtle energy to most of the major organs of digestion and purification. These include the stomach, pancreas, liver, gall bladder, spleen, adrenal glands, lumbar vertebrae and the general digestive system.[7]

Psychospiritual

Judith states that, from an emotional and spiritual standpoint, the solar plexus chakra is linked to the issue of personal power. Personal power can be described as a feeling of control over one's life. Personal power also relates to how people view themselves in relation to others in their lives. Individuals with a so-called 'victim consciousness', who have no sense of control over their lives, will often manifest an imbalance in the solar plexus chakra. Domination, anger and abuse of others can also be associated with abnormal function of the solar plexus.[2]

Autonomy is necessary for achieving balance of the solar plexus chakra. Without autonomy, we cannot get to the heart, for our love comes from need rather than strength. A balanced relationship allows the people involved to be separate beings, retaining their individuality, to follow their own personal growth and to come together by choice and by will. Autonomy is essential for personal responsibility. Lack of autonomy is often characterised by blaming. If we blame others for our problems, we have not yet individuated. By strengthening and stimulating the solar plexus chakra, you will attain a state in which you can shake off the fears of rejection, criticism and standing apart from the group and create your own unique identity.[2]

Sturgess states that *Manipura* contains many precious jewels with the qualities of self-confidence and self-assurance, and provides us with the ability to make the right decisions with clarity, wisdom and knowledge. *Manipura* is the centre of willpower, energy and vitality. It generates and distributes pranic energy throughout the whole body, controlling our energy balance, vitality and strength.[5]

Satyananda states that when the consciousness evolves to *Manipura*, one acquires a spiritual perspective. The powers gained through the awakening of *Manipura* are the ability to create and destroy, knowledge of one's own body, freedom from disease and the ability to withdraw the energy to *Sahasrara*.[8]

Prendergast states that the solar plexus chakra governs a complex set of emotional issues including interpersonal boundaries and connectedness, interpersonal power dynamics, dependency and commitment, emotional vulnerability and authenticity, individual initiative, over-control of self and others, interpersonal trust, sensitivity to criticism and one's sense of belonging in the world.[11]

Johari explains that the root cause of consumerism is the ego. The ego is not very active in the base and sacral chakras. The ego develops in the solar plexus chakra with the desire to be somebody who is recognised by others as special and the desire to be powerful and authoritative.[10]

Traditional symbology

Manipura is symbolised by a 10-petalled bright yellow lotus. Satyananda states that some Tantric texts state that the lotus petals are the colour of heavily laden rain clouds.[8]

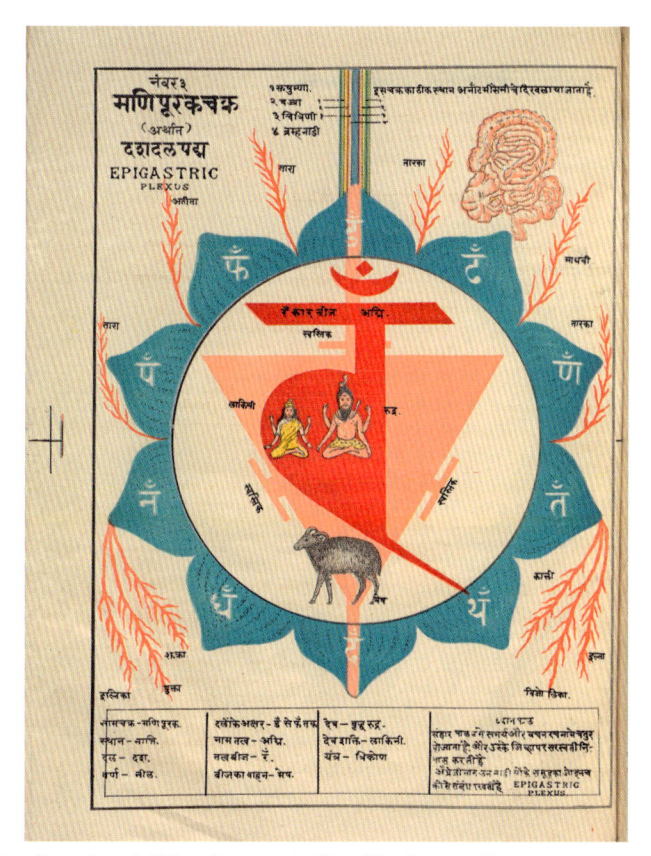

Solar plexus from MS Sanskrit 391. Authored by Swami Hamsasvarupa, 1900s.

He states that the centre of the lotus is the region of fire, symbolised by an inverted fiery red triangle, representing the fire element and the spreading of energy.[8]

Johari explains that each of the 10 petals represents one aspect of Braddha Rudra, the deity of this chakra. They are 1) spiritual ignorance, 2) thirst, 3) jealousy, 4) treachery, 5) shame, 6) fear, 7) disgust, 8) delusion, 9) foolishness and 10) sadness. The 10 petals also depict the 10 *pranas*.[10]

The triangle has a swastika in the shape of a T on each of its three sides. Satyananda explains that this represents the formative forces of fire. In the lower apex is a ram, symbolising dynamism and invisible endurance.[8]

Archetype

King states that the solar plexus chakra's dysfunctional archetype is the servant, who is not aware of their own worth. They do not take responsibility for their own self-esteem, relying on others for acknowledgement. King also explains that the third chakra generates a lot of power. She explains that when you recognise this power as your own, you exemplify the positive archetype of the solar plexus chakra, the warrior.[4]

Tubali describes the personality type of the solar plexus chakra as the achiever. They are intensely fiery, energetic, restless and ambitious. One of the greatest strengths of the achievers is their exceptional determination. Achievers are known for their invincible determination and their ability to overcome challenges and obstacles. They are able to handle crises and are effective decision-makers. However, achievers can be impatient and are often control freaks.[9]

According to Tubali, achievers represent around 25% of the world population. The main challenge for achievers is that they are always trying to become 'someone' and what they fear most is failure. They always must be busy, doing something. This is what gives them a sense of worth. They need to fill their lives with stress and overload their schedules, making sure they always have something to do. The biggest challenge for the solar plexus chakra archetype is to learn to face emptiness. They must learn to stop being proud of doing so much and being busy.[9]

Tubali states that solar plexus chakra types are here to teach everyone else how to believe in their own capacity for success. He explains that they teach us the value and power of our own will.[9]

Challenges

Judith states that the issues associated with the solar plexus chakra include energy, activity, autonomy, individuation, will, self-esteem and power. Traumas and abuses associated with the solar plexus chakra include shaming, authority, volatile situations, physical abuse, age-inappropriate responsibilities and inherited shame from parents.[2]

Part of healing the solar plexus chakra must involve reclaiming the right to act. Many cultures clearly define acceptable behaviours and expect blind obedience. Many people follow in the footsteps of others, afraid to innovate, afraid to be free. When our right to act is restricted, our willpower is weakened and our vitality decreases.[2]

Behavioural characteristics

According to Judith, when one has a healthy solar plexus chakra, they have vitality and energy and are very enthusiastic about life. She explains that autonomy is necessary for a healthy solar plexus chakra. Without autonomy, we cannot get to the heart chakra, because our love comes from need rather than strength.[2]

Judith explains that autonomy is essential for personal responsibility. If we cannot see ourselves as individuals, we cannot take responsibility for our actions and will remain passive and irresponsible, often complaining about our state of affairs and blaming others.[2]

Johari states that the solar plexus chakra is the seat of the Fire element, which manifests as anger and fiery temperament. The motivation of a solar plexus chakra person is the desire for identification, recognition, power and better living conditions.[10]

Prendergast states that, when the solar plexus chakra is open and balanced, one feels trusting of others, feels socially at ease, and is able to express appropriate anger. When it is contracted or distorted, one becomes distrustful, oversensitive to criticism, inappropriately angry, emotionally overdependent or aloof, volatile or emotionally dumb. A great deal of anger, fear, and shame is often found stored in the solar plexus chakra.[11]

Judith states that people with either excessive or deficient solar plexus chakras may be attracted to stimulants such as caffeine, amphetamines or cocaine.[2]

Balanced

Judith states that a balanced solar plexus chakra is reflected by responsibility, being reliable, balanced, good self-esteem, balanced healthy ego, confidence, spontaneity, self-discipline and being able to meet challenges. A healthy balanced solar plexus chakra exhibits energetic vitality, enjoyment and enthusiasm for life. We do not lose our direction when challenged, but go forth with strength and will. We enjoy engaging in activities, tackling challenges and grappling with the world.[2]

Sturgess explains when the solar plexus chakra is in balance and functions in the right and positive way, reason and emotions are balanced, and our personal power is used to cooperate and help others rather than competing, dominating or trying to control others.[5]

Nardi states that when the solar plexus chakra is balanced, we know our identity and values, we are energised to take action, life holds meaning and purpose, we confidently move towards our goals and we stand firm for what matters to us.[6]

Excess

Judith states that an excessive solar plexus chakra leads to overt aggression, dominating and controlling, need to be right, need to have last word, manipulative attitude, attraction to sedatives, temper tantrums, stubbornness, competitiveness, arrogance and hyperactivity.[2]

Judith explains that a person with an excessive solar plexus chakra is ruled by a rigid will. She explains that an excessive will is not necessarily strong for it lacks flexibility and may become brittle and fragile. An excessive will may flare in anger or retreat in fear when challenged. An excessive will has a constant need to be in control of oneself, of others and of situations. In extreme situations, such a person will become a bully — dominating, aggressive and angry. Sometimes an excessive will can be seen in the control of one's body. Dancers, athletes, weight trainers, runners and even yoga practitioners sometimes push their bodies like machines, pushing them against their will.[2]

Sturgess states that the fire of *Manipura* fuels the ego, which can often manifest as anger, rage, aggression, intolerance, lack of consideration or disregard for others. He explains that in this chakra we have both the fire of desire and the power of the emotions to deal with.[5]

Deficiency

Judith explains that people with a deficient solar plexus chakra may have low energy, low self-esteem and poor digestion, and be emotionally cold.[2]

Health issues

According to Gerber, imbalances of the solar plexus chakra can affect any one of the digestive organs of the body that receive energy from this centre. The adrenal glands are linked to the solar plexus chakra. The adrenal glands play an important role in hormonal activation of the body systems during times of stress. He explains that when there is a blockage of the solar plexus chakra, diseases may occur, which can cause degeneration of the adrenal gland and lead to fatigue and weakness. Gerber explains that the solar plexus chakra is an important energy centre of the body, which contributes to the outward vitality of the personality. Other physical disorders may include eating disorders, diabetes, chronic fatigue and hypertension.[7]

Judith states that imbalances of the solar plexus chakra can lead to eating disorders, digestive disorders, disorders of the stomach, pancreas, gall bladder and liver, hypoglycaemia, diabetes, muscle spasms, muscular disorders, chronic fatigue and hypertension.[2]

Judith states that people suffering from chronic fatigue syndrome manifest a depletion of the solar plexus chakra energy, which leads to conditions associated with candida overgrowth, Epstein-Barr syndrome, Lyme disease and food allergies. She explains that the body is calling for rest and recharging, for contacting the deeper sources of energy.[2]

Essential oils for the solar plexus chakra

The warm, spicy oils such as aniseed, black pepper, cardamom, cinnamon bark, clove bud, sweet fennel and ginger strengthen our solar plexus chakra. Other essential oils that strengthen the solar plexus chakra include essential oils with a sharp zesty citrus aroma such as lemon, lime and yuzu, which are energising, and essential oils with a strong leafy scent such as basil, peppermint, pine, rosemary or thyme, which promote self-confidence. Also, use essential oils that help protect us against negative influences such as cypress or juniper berry. Typical essential oils that have the greatest affinity with the solar plexus chakra include:

Black pepper — strengthens courage and willpower.[12]

Cardamom — strengthens courage and willpower, promotes creativity.

Cedarwood, Atlas — strengthens confidence and willpower.[12,13]

Roman chamomile — encourages calm acceptance of our own limitations.[12,13]

Cinnamon bark — strengthens courage and willpower.

Coriander seed — strengthens courage and willpower, promotes creativity.[13]

Cypress — promotes confidence and patience.[12,13]

Fennel, sweet — increases courage, confidence and motivation.[12,13]

Geranium — helps us gain control over our lives.[12,13]

Ginger — promotes courage and confidence.[12,13]

Juniper berry — strengthens willpower, protects against negative influences, restores confidence.[12,13,14]

Lemon — promotes a healthy self-esteem and protects against negative influences and energises.

Peppermint — helps overcome feelings of inferiority.[12]

Petitgrain — promotes a healthy self-esteem.[12]

Pine — energises, clarifies personal will, restores self-confidence and strength of will.[12,13,14]

Rosemary — protects from external influences. Boosts self-confidence and energises.[12,13,14]

Sandalwood — promotes positive self-esteem.[12]

Spruce, black — energises, restores self-confidence and willpower.

Tea tree — purifies and restores self-confidence and willpower.[12]

Thyme — promotes self-confidence.[13]

Ylang ylang — promotes self-confidence and enthusiasm.[12]

Aromatherapy blends

Use these blends in a diffuser or add to 10ml of jojoba oil to use as a massage oil or an anointing oil.

Harmony

Harmony chakra blend is a synergy of vetiver, juniper berry, lemon, frankincense, Roman chamomile and aniseed pure essential oils. These oils promote self-esteem, restore self-confidence and protect us from negative external influences.

Promote courage and willpower

This blend boosts confidence, supports courage and strengthens willpower.

    1 drop black pepper
    2 drops Atlas cedarwood
    2 drops lemon

Adrenal tonic

This blend supports the adrenals during times of stress.

    1 drop ginger
    2 drops rosemary
    2 drops spruce

Soothe anger and arrogance

This blend soothes anger and arrogance.

>   1 drop Roman chamomile
>   2 drops geranium
>   2 drops petitgrain

Questions for self-examination

Myss asks the following questions for self-examination:[3]

- Do you like yourself? What don't you like and why? Are you actively working to change the things about yourself you don't like?
- Are you critical of others? Do you blame others as a way of protecting yourself?
- Are you able to admit when you are wrong? Are you open to feedback from other people about yourself?
- Do you need the approval of others? If so, why?
- Do you consider yourself strong or weak? Are you afraid of taking care of yourself?
- Have you been in a relationship with a person you didn't really love, but it seemed better than being alone?
- Do you respect yourself? Can you decide to make changes in your life and then stick to your commitment?
- Are you afraid of responsibility? Or do you feel responsible for everything and everyone?
- Are you continually wishing your life were different? If so, are you doing anything to change it, or have you resigned yourself to the situation?

King states that if you answer yes to three or more of the questions below, the chances are you need to balance your solar plexus chakra:[4]

- Do you have a lot of suppressed anger, fear or grief?
- Do you hold on to your resentments?
- Do you tend to blame others for your problems?
- Are you jealous of others? Do you think the grass is greener somewhere else?
- Do you feel like you never have enough time?

- Are you a control freak?
- Do you worry that others will overpower you?
- Do you have to win?
- Do you feel good about yourself only when you receive external approval?

Activities to strengthen your solar plexus chakra

Judith recommends the following activities to strengthen the solar plexus chakra:[2]

- risk-taking (for deficiency)
- deep relaxation therapy (for excess)
- vigorous exercise
- detoxifcation
- psychotherapy — to build ego strength, release or manage anger, work on shame issues, and encourage autonomy
- listening to music that is mentally stimulating such as chimes or horn instruments.

King suggests simple ways to clear solar plexus chakra blockages such as spending some time in the sun in the early morning, doing physical activities outdoors or taking a walk by the ocean or any other body of water. She also states it is important that you accept personal responsibility, self-discipline, confidence and energy.[4]

Tubali suggests several lifestyle activities to keep the solar plexus chakra balanced:[9]

- Try to channel some of your energy of conquest inwards. Strive for self-mastery, rather than constantly trying to be 'number one' in the world.
- Find ways to transform your intense search for power into a quest for inner power.
- Learn to listen to your heart and cultivate the qualities of sensitivity, caring and service.
- Pay attention to your friends and family. Life is more than just achieving and moving forward.
- Avoid forcing your energy on others, whether that energy takes the shape of anger, rage, or even violence.

- Remain humble and connect to some higher will in life.
- Don't skip vacations, and don't fall into the trap of 'working vacations'.

Affirmations for the solar plexus chakra

Judith recommends the following affirmations to strengthen the solar plexus chakra:[2]

- I accept and value myself exactly as I am.
- My personal power is becoming stronger each day.
- I accomplish tasks easily and effortlessly.
- I can do whatever I will to do.
- I am my own person. I choose how to think and behave.

17. Heart Chakra

If you ever felt a pain
So deep it made your heart break
And now you are afraid to trust again
As you don't want to be hurt
Open heart feels like too much risk
But a closed one won't bring true happiness
You will be pleased to find out
That our hearts have the strength
To transform the grief
And open ourselves to endless possibilities
If only we can forgive
And find it within
To offer ourselves the love
That we are yearning for
Do what nourishes our souls
Slowly the armour will dissolve
We will find the courage to trust again
Vulnerability will be our friend
And compassion will prevail.

Marzena Skowronska

Name

The Sanskrit name for the heart chakra is *Anahata*. *Anahata* means 'sound made by two things striking' or 'unstuck', describing the co-existence of body and spirit.

Purpose

Brennan states that the heart chakra is the most important chakra used in the healing process.

> *All energies metabolized through the chakra travel up the vertical power current through the roots of the chakra and into the heart chakra before moving out of the hands or eyes of the healer. In the healing process, the heart transmutes the earth plane energies to spiritual energies and the spiritual plane energies into earth plane energies to be used by the patient.*[1]

Judith states that the purpose of the heart chakra is concerned with forgiveness and compassion — unconditional love through which we accept another for doing their best. We thus begin to develop true self-acceptance.[2]

Mastering the heart chakra helps us to enhance our emotional development and recognise the potency of that powerful energy we call 'love'. The basic right of the heart chakra is — to love and be loved.

Colour

Green

Location

Chest, heart, cardiac plexus

Element

Air

Physical association

The heart chakra is associated with the circulatory system, heart, lungs, arms, breasts and upper back. Gerber states that the most important link between the heart chakra and the physical organ is seen in the association of the heart chakra and the thymus gland. He claims that researchers in the developing field of psychoneuroimmunology have yet to examine the subtle energetic links between emotion and immunological function. He states they have only examined the physiological links between human emotions and illness, but there is a deeper esoteric aspect of immunology that has yet to be fully grasped.[7]

Gerber suggests that a significant energy factor contributing to a strong immune response is a healthy flow of energy through the heart chakra to support the thymus gland. He also explains that many heart diseases have their roots in the emotional nature or astral body. He suggests that strong emotion is an exacerbating factor in many types of angina pains.[7]

Psychospiritual

Sturgess explains that the heart chakra is the seat of the emotional heart-mind that stores our emotions and experiences. It represents pure and unconditional love. He states that through the heart chakra we can reach beyond the ego and connect and commune with the hearts and minds of others.[5]

Judith states that the heart chakra is integral to an individual's ability to express love. She states that love may manifest as brotherly love towards neighbours and friends, as emotional love in a relationship between lovers and also as spiritual love. The highest form of spiritual love is unconditional love towards others.[2]

Judith explains that the most common block in the heart chakra is the absence of self-love. She asks:[2]

- How can we have intimacy with others if we are distanced from our self?
- How can we reach out to others when we are drowning in shame and criticism?
- How can we treat another with respect if we treat ourselves abusively?

Often when we fall in love, we strip ourselves of our defences. When we open to another, we expand and grow. When we are hurt in matters of love, we are hurt in our most vulnerable, trusting aspects. The purest form of self is wounded. It no longer seems safe to be authentic. We often not only lose our lover, but ourselves as well. This is the deepest loss.[2]

Sadly, the heart chakra is easily damaged, diminished or wounded.[2] As Judith explains:[2]

> *Nothing is quite so uplifting as the flowering of love; nothing so devastating as its loss.*[2]

Sturgess explains that the heart chakra is a pivotal point of transition between the three lower chakras which are related to the world of body, mind and senses and associated with survival, security, sensuality, sex and power — and the higher chakras which are related to a higher and more evolved consciousness.[5]

Johari states that the heart chakra individual has overcome the preoccupations of the lower chakras such as security of the base chakra; sensuality and sexuality of the sacral chakra; and fame, authority, social status, power and physical immortality of the solar plexus chakra. Johari describes a spiritually inspired heart chakra person as saintly.[10]

Traditional symbology

Satyananda states that the *Anahata* chakra is a shining crimson colour, like that of the bandhuka flower.[8] It has 12 petals, representing the expansion of energy in 12 directions and the divine qualities of the heart, such as love, peace, harmony, bliss, understanding, empathy, compassion, unity, clarity, purity, kindness and forgiveness.[5]

The inner region is hexagon in shape, representing the Air element. It is made up of two interlaced triangles, symbolising the union of *Shiva* and *Shakti*. The inverted triangle is the symbol of creativity or *Shakti* and the upright triangle represents consciousness or *Shiva*. The vehicle, located within the hexagon, is a black antelope, which is known for its alertness and fleetness or foot.[8] Sturgess explains that the antelope symbolises alertness, attentiveness and the lightness of the Air element.[5]

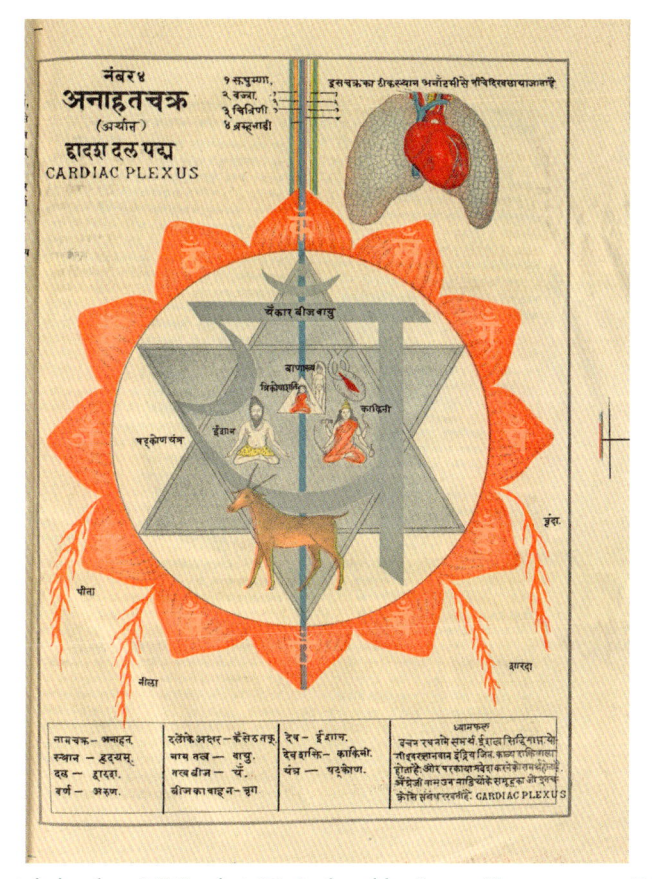

Heart chakra from MS Sanskrit 391. Authored by Swami Hamsasvarupa, 1900s.

Archetype

King states that the performer is the dysfunctional archetype of the heart chakra. These are people who hide their dark side while playing at love. She states that performers make it look like everything is fine, but cannot accept the responsibility that comes with real intimacy. On the other hand, the lover is the positive archetype of the heart chakra. King explains that lovers love all of humanity and all life forms on the planet, as well as themselves. They understand the importance of forgiving others and themselves. They feel worthy of receiving love, and they allow it to flow through their open heart and expand in all directions.[4]

Tubali describes the personality type of the heart chakra as the caretaker. They express and demonstrate the power of love and emotion. Their main passion is to bring people together and promote harmony. They are typically drawn towards work as therapists, healers, mediators, activists, volunteers, religious devotees and family people. Caretakers represent around 15% of the world's population.[9]

Caretakers are commonly found among those who strive to form loving families, raise children, cultivate friendships and create opportunities for intimacy. Tubali states that in their most radiant form, caretakers demonstrate an unwillingness to sacrifice themselves for higher principles or for others in trouble.[9]

Caretakers communicate with the world through their emotions. If they feel strongly about something, it must be true, and this influences the way they make decisions. Tubali states that caretakers can be innocent to the point of being naive. They generally believe in the inherent goodness of others. They usually approach life with an optimistic spirit. In relationships, caretakers are very devoted; however, they can also become so demanding. They can also become intensely jealous and possessive towards their loved ones. They can have difficulty thinking logically because they are guided by their heart and their emotional centre.[9]

Caretakers always need to love and be loved. To avoid rejection, they will simply give, give, give all the time. This is what often motivates their sacrifice and their focus on others. The most unbearable experience for this chakra type is to be unloved and rejected. When they are rejected, they feel as they are as good as dead. Heart chakra types need to acknowledge that they are often motivated by dependency, insecurity and addiction and that they must learn to accept the feeling of rejection and know that, even when someone appears to reject them, they are still alive and breathing.[9]

Tubali explains that heart chakra personality types are our greatest teachers when it comes to matters of the heart:

> *Blessed with the intuition that, without an overflowing heart, nothing makes sense, they help us to complete our picture of the meaning of life. They teach us that devotion is the key to filling our heart with meaning ... They also teach us that, as long as we do not open ourselves to love, we miss out, not only on an essential component of genuine self-fulfilment, but also on our connection to a meaningful life.*[9]

Challenges

Judith states that issues associated with the heart chakra include love, balance, self-love, relationship, intimacy, devotion, reaching out and taking in. Part of healing the heart chakra must involve reclaiming the right to love and be loved. In a family, this can be damaged by any dysfunction in the parents' ability to love and care for their child.[2]

Traumas and abuses associated with the heart chakra include rejection, abandonment, loss, shaming, constant criticism, unacknowledged grief, divorce, death of a loved one, lovelessness, conditional love, and sexual or physical abuse. She explains that when grief is denied, we become numb to our feelings and our aliveness. We become hard and cold, rigid and distant. We may feel dead inside. When grief is acknowledged and expressed, we find a vital key to opening the heart. Tears are shed, truth is expressed and the heart lightens. A sense of spaciousness emerges, allowing more room inside for our spirit. Coming to terms with our own grief leads us toward compassion for others.[2]

King explains that the heart chakra's biggest obstacle is heartbreak. She explains that certain life situations can wreak havoc on your heart chakra, such as rejection, emotional or physical neglect and abuse, chronic depression, co-dependency, the betrayal of a cheating partner or the loss of a loved one. Any of these can cause heartbreak, which may cause your heart chakra to close.[4]

Behavioural characteristics

Nardi states that the heart chakra keeps us in touch with our humanity and conscience. He explains that when the heart chakra is healthy, we give our full loving attention to our work, which becomes our vocation rather than a job.[6]

When the heart centre is open, Prendergast explains, we feel love of self and others, joy, compassion, gratitude, empathy and grief. When it is contracted, we may feel self-hatred, shame, falseness, bitterness, rage, alienation and isolation.[11]

Balanced

Judith states that a balanced heart chakra is reflected by compassion, love, empathy, peace, balance and a strong immune system.[2]

Sturgess explains that when this chakra is open and balanced, we have the ability to give and receive selflessly, and love and compassion become a natural expression of feeling from the heart. He explains that the path towards higher consciousness begins at this chakra.[5]

Nardi states that when the heart chakra is balanced, we are able to give practical care to others, we are willing to be vulnerable, we enjoy a long-term romantic coupling, we are emotionally honest and we treat others as unique human beings.[6]

Excess

Judith explains that excess energy of the heart chakra may lead to co-dependency, poor boundaries, being demanding, clinging behaviour, jealousy and overly sacrificing. She explains that an excess in the heart chakra is not an excess of actual love. It is an excessive use of love for one's own needs. This often occurs when we overcompensate for our own wounds. She warns us that excessive love is desperate in its requirement for constant reassurance, and does not allow another's freedom to be who they are.[2]

Deficiency

Judith states that a person with deficient heart chakra may be antisocial, withdrawn, cold, critical, judgemental, intolerant of others, lonely, isolated, depressed, and show fear of intimacy, fear of relationships and lack of empathy. She explains that the deficient heart chakra responds to wounds of love by withdrawing. The heart chakra closes down and love becomes conditional.[2]

Judith explains that individuals with deficient heart chakra may lack compassion and be critical and judgemental, which in turn may hurt the people that care for them. She explains that being judgemental is a way of justifying distance from others and ensuring that one does not become too close to them. This reduces the risk of getting hurt again.[2]

Health issues

According to Judith and Gerber, health issues associated with imbalances of the heart chakra may include:

- disorders of the heart, lungs, thymus, breasts, arms
- shortness of breath
- sunken chest
- asthma
- immune system deficiency
- tension between shoulder blades, pain in chest.[2,7]

Gerber links heart disease with the heart chakra:

> ... it is ironic that most doctors and patients fail to recognize the significance of the energetic link between heart disease, the heart chakra, and one's ability to express love. Patients' awareness of this important psycho-energetic relationship could assist physicians in healing the attitudes and consciousness that helped to create the energy imbalances which predisposed them towards heart disease in the first place.[7]

Essential oils for the heart chakra

Floral and uplifting citrus oils have often been assigned to the heart. It is interesting that essential oils such as bergamot, lavender, may chang, melissa, neroli, palmarosa and ylang ylang are often used to alleviate conditions such as high blood pressure and rapid heartbeat. Typical essential oils that have the greatest affinity with the heart chakra include:

Benzoin — comforts and soothes the heart and encourages self-compassion.[12]

Bergamot — supports self-love. Opens the heart and allows love to radiate. Especially good for grief.[12]

Eucalyptus — promotes room to breathe when feeling disheartened and suffocated by responsibility.[12]

Everlasting — promotes compassion for self and others. Integrates compassion and spirituality.[12,13]

Lavender — calms and soothes the emotions of the heart. Promotes compassion.[12,13,14]

Marjoram, sweet — helps us to accept deep, emotional loss. Promotes ability to give.[13]

Melissa — relieves emotional blocks from grief. Promotes understanding and acceptance.[12,13]

Neroli — eases grief, helps us experience joyful love and opens the heart.[12]

Orange, sweet — promotes joyful love.[12]

Palmarosa — comforts the heart and relieves emotional clinging.[12,13,14]

Rose otto — promotes love, especially when the heart is wounded by grief. Soothing and harmonising.[12,13,14]

Sandalwood — opens the heart to trust and unconditional love.[12]

Spikenard — comforts and balances the heart, especially for people who take on the cares of the world.[12,13]

Valerian — comforts a wounded heart.[13]

Yarrow — promotes healthy love of self and others.[13]

Aromatherapy blends

Use these blends in a diffuser or add to 10ml of jojoba oil to use as a massage oil or an anointing oil.

Compassion

Open your heart to unconditional love with *Compassion* chakra blend. *Compassion* is a blend of bergamot, lavender, may chang, neroli, rose absolute and ylang ylang.

Comfort a wounded heart

This blend comforts and nurtures the heart chakra.

    2 drops everlasting
    2 drops lavender
    2 drops rose otto

Promote compassion

This blend promotes healthy love of self and others.

    2 drops bergamot
    2 drops sweet orange
    2 drops rose otto

Fear of intimacy

This blend opens our heart to trust unconditional love.

>2 drops lavender
>2 drops neroli
>2 drops rose otto

Questions for self-examination

Myss asks the following questions for self-examination:[3]

- What emotional memories do you still need to heal?
- What relationships in your life require healing?
- Do you ever use your emotional wounds to control people or situations? If so, describe them.
- Have you allowed yourself to be controlled by the wounds of another? Will you let that happen again? What steps are you prepared to take to prevent yourself from being controlled that way again?
- What fears do you have about becoming emotionally healthy?
- Do you associate emotional health with no longer needing an intimate relationship?
- What is your understanding of forgiveness?
- Who are the people you need to forgive, and what prevents you from letting go of the pain you associate with them?
- What have you done that needs forgiving? Who is working to forgive you?
- What is your understanding of a healthy, intimate relationship? Are you willing to release the use of your wounds in order to open yourself to such a relationship?

King states that if you answer yes to three or more of the questions below, the chances are you need to balance your heart chakra:[4]

- Is love scary to you?
- Do you give and receive love easily?
- Have you ever felt betrayed or rejected?
- Are you unable to forgive yourself and others for past mistakes?
- Are you overly critical or judgemental of others?

- Do you need to develop attributes such as altruism, compassion, forgiveness, hope, trust or harmony?

Activities to strengthen your heart chakra

Judith recommends the following activities to strengthen the heart chakra:[2]

- breathing exercises
- spending time with family or friends
- giving love and compassion unconditionally
- being patient with yourself and others
- surrounding yourself with plants
- listening to music that has the sounds of nature
- psychotherapy — may involve emotional release of grief, forgiveness where appropriate and self-acceptance.

King states that it is important to open your heart chakra; however, this can be difficult when you are experiencing or holding on to grief. She suggests breath work will allow positive energy to flow and remove any blockage of the heart. She also claims another great way to open your heart is by caring for a pet.[4]

Tubali suggests several lifestyle activities to keep your heart chakra balanced:[9]

- The most important balancing work for a caretaker is to balance your emotional excess.
- Understand that love is action and not just a feeling, as powerful as that feeling may be.
- Do not spend all your energy on intense interpersonal engagements and exchanges.
- Be careful not to force your own expectation for emotional exchange on others. Not everyone shares your intense sentiments.
- Learn to let go. There can be a tendency to cling on to relationships too strongly.
- Resist the temptation to sacrifice yourself for others or for a cause.
- Learn to love yourself.

- Avoid building a protective wall around your heart to deal with your strong emotions and disappointments.

Nardi suggests activities to cultivate the heart chakra:[6]

- Cherish your life and gifts. Appreciate your life's purposes and accept life's ups and downs.
- Know your loved ones. Take stock of those you trust with your heart, that you care about deeply, and they you.
- Be gentle with loved ones. Be thoughtful in your words and deeds with your loved ones.
- Flex your heart. An open heart has room for infinite compassion, but do not let your care for others slip into emotional overreach.
- Practise loving kindness.
- During meditation or yoga, focus on your heartbeat.

Affirmations for the heart chakra

Judith recommends the following affirmations to strengthen the heart chakra:[2]

- I am worthy of love.
- I send my love to everyone I know; all hearts are open to receive my love.
- I love myself for who I am and the potential within me.
- I am grateful for all the love that is in my life.

18. Throat Chakra

The ability to express
The truth of our heart
Is the key to live
a soul led life.
What good comes
From hearing the whispers
if we fail
to act on them
Let's stop choking on our dreams
and holding back
but rather trust
in the wisdom of our heart
It's a seat of courage
Because in its essence
It is unstruck
cannot be hurt
Let's capitalize on that
not be afraid
to find our voice
and paint the world
with the longing of our souls.

Marzena Skowronska

Name

The Sanskrit name for the throat chakra is *Vishuddha*. *Vishuddha* means 'purification'. Developing the throat chakra means choosing words that bring value to communication.

Purpose

Brennan states that the throat chakra is associated with taking responsibility for one's personal needs.[1]

> *As the person matures, the fulfillment of his needs rests more and more upon himself. Maturity is reached and this chakra functions properly when one ceases to blame others for one's lack in life and goes out to create what one needs and desires.*[1]

The purpose of the throat chakra is associated with communication, self-expression and creativity through sound.[2]

Judith explains that in the first four chakras we concern ourselves with form, movement, activity and relationships — things that can be easily observed; however, in the throat chakra our attention moves to vibrations, as subtle, rhythmic pulsations that move through all things.[2]

The throat chakra is associated with the sense of hearing and listening. Sturgess refers to it as the centre of communication, creativity, self-expression, non-attachment and learning to accept and receive.[5]

Sturgess explains that sound is important to the throat chakra. He explains that the state of the throat chakra is expressed by the quality of our speech and that learning to develop and express the voice brings the throat chakra into full expression. The voice, he claims, is the reflection of our personality, our thoughts, feelings and emotions.[5]

The inner qualities of the throat chakra are calmness and expansion. When we quieten mental restlessness by directing energy inward and upward in meditation, we reach a deep level of inner calm and an expansion of consciousness. Sturgess suggests that until we learn to think, talk and act with calmness and an even-minded attitude, we cannot make our life productive.[5]

Sturgess states that the practice of silence helps us attain calmness and evenness of mind. All spiritual vision and deeper understanding are unfolding in silence, meditation and contemplation. The practice of silence, however, does not mean merely refraining from speech. It means stilling the vital energies so that there is a cessation of all inner and outer activities. In silence, we are able to think clearly and concentrate and we are able to express our ideas through our outer actions more effectively.[5]

Satyananda explains that the throat chakra represents a state of openness in which life is regarded as the provider of experiences that lead to a greater understanding. He states that one ceases to avoid the unpleasant aspects of life and seek the pleasant. Instead, he claims that life flows in the way that allows things to happen in the way they must.[8]

> *Both poison and nectar are consumed in vishuddhi chakra, and they are understood to be but parts of this equal acceptance of dualities and polarities of life.*[8]

Colour

Bright blue

Location

The throat chakra has influence over the major glands and structures in the neck region. These include the thyroid and parathyroid glands, the mouth, vocal cords and trachea.

Element

Akasha (ether, space)[10]

Judith states that sound is the element associated with the throat chakra.[2]

Physical association

There is an association between the throat chakra and the parasympathetic nervous system.[7] Gerber explains that the greater part of the parasympathetic division of the autonomic nervous system originates in the tenth cranial nerve, also known as the vagus nerve. The vagus nerve leaves the brainstem and travels down the neck to innervate the hearts, lungs and abdominal organs. The parathyroid gland, which is energised by the throat chakra, regulates calcium metabolism in the bones via the secretion of parathyroid hormone. The thyroid gland also regulates the general metabolic activity of cells in the body and produces thyrocalcitonin, a hormone that affects calcium and bone metabolism in a manner opposite to that of the parathyroid hormone.[7]

Gerber explains that, because the throat chakra energises both the thyroid and parathyroid glands, each of which is involved in regulating calcium metabolism in bone cells, the throat chakra also affects skeletal activity.[7]

Psychospiritual

The throat chakra is the centre of higher creativity, such as the creation of word and song. Speech and sound are means by which we can vibrationally communicate with one another and verbally express new ideas.[2]

Judith states that communication is the essential function of the throat chakra. She explains that self-expression is the gateway between the inner world and the outer. Only through self-expression does the outer world know what's inside of us:

> *Self-expression in the fifth chakra is a counterpart to the sensate reception coming in through the second chakra. In the second chakra, we opened a gate that allowed the world in through our senses. In the fifth chakra, we open a gate that allows our inner self to get out into the world. These two chakras are often linked, such that problems in one will often be reflected in the other.*[2]

The throat chakra is described as the internal gateway between mind and body. Judith explains that mastering the throat chakra helps us grasp the importance of purifying ourselves by honestly recognising how we feel, following our dream, using personal power to create and having the confidence to communicate our emotions to others.[2]

Gerber states that the throat chakra is the first of the spiritual triad of higher centres and is associated with the ability to hear things at a subtle energetic level. He claims that it is considered the centre of religious devotion and the mystical instinct because of its association with the energies of the causal body.[7]

Johari states that meditation on the throat chakra brings calmness, serenity, purity, a melodious voice, the command of speech and mantras, and the ability to compose poetry. He states that it makes one youthful and capable of understanding the hidden messages in dreams.[10]

Traditional symbology

According to Satyananda, *Vishuddha* is represented by a dark grey coloured lotus; however, it is commonly perceived as a purple lotus of 16 petals. These 16 petals correspond to the number of *nadis* associated with this centre. In the pericarp of this lotus is a circle which is white like the full moon, representing the element ether or *akasha*. This is the gateway to

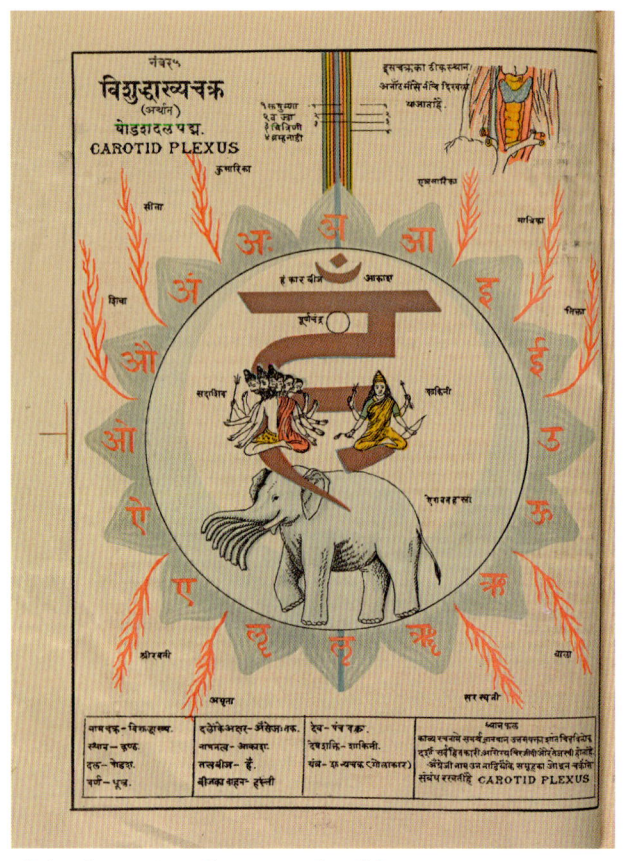

Throat chakra from MS Sanskrit 391. Authored by Swami Hamsasvarupa, 1900s.

liberation for one whose senses are pure and controlled. Within this moon shape is the snow-white elephant, also symbolic of the *akasha* element.[8]

Archetype

King states that the silent child is the dysfunctional archetype of the throat chakra. She explains that the silent child feels safest when silent and has a difficult time to express anger and frustration. The silent child may suppress frightful or painful feelings.[4]

On the other hand, she explains that the broadcaster is the positive archetype of the throat chakra. The broadcaster expresses their feelings and desires in life by speaking out. They know how important and powerful the spoken word is. They deliver their messages clearly, with respect, and follow their words up with right action. King explains that broadcasters do not lie, and that they speak from the heart, so you can always trust them.[4]

Tubali describes the throat chakra personality type as the speaker. He explains that their central passion in life is the act of communication. According to Tubali, speakers represent around 7% of the world population. They are typically drawn towards work as journalists, authors, teachers, politicians, lawyers and judges, and singers.[9]

Speakers will find happiness in those moments in life that provide an opportunity to give voice to a natural flow of expression. They also find happiness when they succeed in gathering a group of unique individuals and connecting them by making them understand and appreciate each other.[9]

Tubali explains that, because speakers are mostly interested in the grand vision, they may not be very grounded or practical. They may have their heads in the clouds. He explains that, driven by their wish to express ideas and influence people and events, throat chakra types are not very emotional and may even be perceived as uncaring. They are very enthusiastic and passionate individuals. They have a strong ability to understand people and they know how to build bridges and make people transcend differences and connect with one another.[9]

Throat chakra personality types can appear as stimulating, inspiring and awakening forces that encourage us to change. They can lead us out of our comfort zone. They give us something to believe in and remind us that there is always a reason to dream, to think big and to pursue an ideal.[9]

Challenges

According to Judith and Gerber, the issues associated with the throat chakra include communication, creativity, listening and finding one's own voice.[2,7]

Part of healing the throat chakra must involve reclaiming the right to speak and hear the truth. This right is damaged when we are not allowed to speak truthfully. When our parents, culture or government lie to us, there is an abuse of this right. Learning good communication is essential to reclaiming this right.[2]

Judith states that traumas and abuses associated with the throat chakra include lies, verbal abuses, excessive criticism (blocks creativity), secrets (threats for telling), authoritarian parents (don't talk back) and alcoholic, chemical-dependent family (don't talk, don't trust and don't feel).[2]

She explains that being told we have no right to feel a certain way when in fact that is how we feel makes a lie of our experience:

> *Hearing the words "I love you" while having the experience of being abused, neglected, or shamed makes a lie of love. Being asked to apologize for something we do not feel sorry about, to be nice to someone we clearly dislike, or to be thankful for something we didn't want are all experiences that teach us to lie. They teach us to lie to ourselves, to each other, and to our bodies. They create dissonance within the basic vibration of the self.*[2]

Judith explains that to fully express our individuality is to express our truth; however, she explains that a non-individuated person will express what people want to hear. A fearful person will be afraid to speak their truth. Negative experiences often teach us to deny and withhold the truth.[2]

King explains that the throat chakra is concerned with speaking the truth and expressing your creativity and true emotions. Dealing with controlling or abusive parents, partners or bosses; listening to excessive conversation or gossip; being fearful of speaking in groups or in public; and bottling up anger and frustration until you are almost ready to explode are some of the challenges that can negatively affect the throat chakra.[4]

Behavioural characteristics

Sturgess states that when the energy of the throat chakra is out of balance, it influences the communication between the heart and the mind, blocking the feelings of the heart.[5]

Balanced

Judith states that a balanced throat chakra is reflected by a resonant voice, being a good listener, having a good sense of timing and rhythm, having clear communication and living creatively.[2]

King states that if our throat chakra is balanced, creativity flows and we have wonderful communications.[4]

Sturgess states that when our throat chakra is balanced, we feel harmony with our goals, and will be able to translate them effectively into reality. We acquire good listening and communication skills, receptiveness, attentiveness, patience and discernment.[5]

Nardi explains that when the throat chakra works well, we communicate clearly, we persuade and inspire with honest words, we listen patiently to what others say, we look at a situation from several views and we let models and data guide decisions.[6]

Excess

Judith explains that an excessive throat chakra often leads to too much talking, inability to listen, gossiping and a dominating voice. The excessive talking is a defence that is used as a way of staying in control. A person with an excessive throat chakra wants to control the conversation and the subject matter so that they remain the centre of attention.[2]

Deficiency

Judith states that a deficient throat chakra may lead to a fear of speaking, a weak voice and shyness. A person with a deficient throat chakra cannot get their words together. They may be extremely self-conscious and shy and there is a fear of humiliation. Since this chakra is about self-expression of one's truth, we judge its openness by how well we can speak about the things closest to the heart.[2]

Health issues

According to Judith, health issues associated with the throat chakra include:[2]

- disorders of the throat, ears, voice and neck
- tightness of the jaw
- toxicity
- mouth ulcers and gum problems
- laryngitis
- swollen glands and thyroid problems.

According to King, health issues associated with the throat chakra typically show up in the shoulders, throat, neck, ears, mouth, jaws, teeth, vocal cords, nasal sinuses, cervical vertebrae, trachea and oesophagus. Common health concerns often include tight neck, chronic childhood tonsillitis, chronic sinus problems, TMJ (temporomandibular) disorder, hypo- and hyperthyroidism, thyroid cancer, and Hashimoto's or Graves' diseases.[4]

Essential oils for the throat chakra

Essential oils that balance the throat chakra generally have a herbaceous aroma. Use essential oils that promote a sense of calm and strength and enable the truth to be spoken without anger. These oils resonate with the throat chakra and encourage the expression of spiritual truth. Typical essential oils that have the greatest affinity with the throat chakra include:

Basil — promotes clarity of communication.[12]

Chamomile, German — allows one to express truth calmly and without anger.[12,13]

Chamomile, Roman — helps one to express spiritual truth.[12,13]

Sweet fennel — promotes uninhibited communication.[12,13,14]

Geranium — increases capacity to listen and communicate intimately.[12,13]

Mandarin — promotes communication of the inner child.[12]

Myrrh — provides support for confident communication.[12,13]

Orange, sweet — promotes uninhibited communication.

Peppermint — promotes clarity in communication.[13]

Sandalwood — helps one to express spiritual truth.[14]

Aromatherapy blends

Use these blends in a diffuser or add to 10ml of jojoba oil to use as a massage oil or an anointing oil.

Expressive

Speak your truth with *Expressive* chakra blend. *Expressive* is a blend of basil, German chamomile, sweet orange and sandalwood pure essential oils.

Speak truthfully

This blend helps promote a safe space to speak honestly and openly.

    2 drops geranium
    2 drops myrrh
    2 drops sandalwood

Finding your creative voice

This blend will help you find your creative outlet.

    2 drops sweet fennel
    2 drops mandarin
    2 drops sandalwood

Speak confidently

This blend gives you the courage to speak with confidence in front of large crowds.

    2 drops German chamomile
    2 drops basil
    2 drops peppermint

Questions for self-examination

Myss asks the following questions for self-examination:[3]

- What is your definition of being strong-willed?
- Who are the people that have control over your willpower, and why?
- Do you seek to control others? If so, who are they, and why do you need to control them?
- Can you express yourself honestly and openly when you need to? If not, why not?
- Are you able to sense when you are receiving guidance to act upon?
- Do you trust guidance that has no 'proof' of the outcome attached to it?
- What fears do you have about divine guidance?
- Do you pray for assistance with your personal plans, or are you able to say, 'I will do what heaven directs me to do'?
- What makes you lose control of your own willpower?
- Do you know you need to change but continually postpone taking action? If so, identify those situations and your reasons for not acting?

King states that if you answer yes to three or more of the questions below, the chances are you need to balance your throat chakra:[4]

- Are you unable to ask for what you need?
- Are you always self-editing what you say?
- Do you frequently bite your tongue and fail to speak your mind?
- Are you unable to act on inner guidance?
- Do you have a weak sense of timing and rhythm?
- Are you chronically hoarse?
- Are you honest with yourself?
- Do you often have chronic sore throat or sinus problems?
- Do you often experience pain in the neck, cervical vertebrae or shoulders?
- Do you talk too much or too loudly or stutter, or are reluctant to speak?
- Are you tone deaf?
- Are you overly shy?

Activities to strengthen your throat chakra

Judith recommends the following activities to strengthen the throat chakra:[2]

- loosen neck and shoulders
- release the voice
- singing, chanting and toning
- storytelling
- journal writing
- practise silence (if excess)
- non-goal-oriented creativity
- participate in meaningful conversations
- listen to music that is repetitive, such as echoes or sounds of ocean waves.

King explains that living your truth is an important element for the health of the throat chakra. This means expressing who you are through your feelings, thoughts and beliefs, and through speaking, writing, singing or any other artistic creation, or through your work and your hobbies. She suggests that journal writing is important to help you get in touch with your true self. Your notes can safely hold all your thoughts, feelings and insights. It can become a powerful way of expressing your truth.[4]

Tubali suggests several lifestyle activities to keep the throat chakra balanced:[9]

- Avoid immersing yourself in dreams that are too big to fulfil. He suggests that it is okay to dream wildly, but then take a deep breath, return to reality and ask yourself what part of your dream is close to your reality and keep moving, step by step and do not become paralysed by the scale of your own vision.
- Avoid emotional traps such as the need for social recognition and admiration, or past frustrations, disappointments and self-doubt.
- Resist your tendency to immerse yourself in unrealistic visions and be content to do what you can.
- Cultivate a belief in yourself and trust your abilities.
- Obey that nagging voice inside you that urges you to make a difference.
- Do not allow yourself to be limited by your own fears or others' influence.

- Engage in activities that transmit ideas such as lecturing or writing to improve your ability to explain things to others. He explains that throat chakra types are educators by nature, so they find ways to make things clear to others.

Nardi suggests the following activities to cultivate the throat chakra:[6]

- Listen objectively by stepping back to listen to yourself and others as if you were a third-party observer.
- Think systematically. Follow processes that ensure consistent thinking based on evidence.
- Speak effectively. Get comfortable speaking up and communicating clearly with relevance and honesty.
- Seek feedback. On any project or idea, seek feedback from others.
- Map your growth. Articulate a system of personal enlightenment using words to describe and understand your life experiences as a way to identify where you've been and where you could go.
- During meditation or yoga, focus on flexing your neck, keeping your throat clear, and chanting with clarity.

Affirmations for the throat chakra

Judith recommends the following affirmations to strengthen the throat chakra:[2]

- I am starting to speak up for myself.
- What I have to say is worthy of being listened to.
- I delight in my self-expression and all my creative pursuits.
- I always speak from the heart.

19. Third Eye Chakra

Intuition
Inner tuition
In to me I see
To be guided
As all the answers
Are already within me
This is the gift
Third Eye Chakra
Is presenting me with
In-sight
Access
To infinite knowledge
That is available to all of us
We just need to quiet the noise
Still the fluctuation of our minds
Find the gap between the thoughts
For the inner knowing to come out
It will show directions
To protect and enable us
To fulfil our potential
And live a conscious
Full of meaning life.

Marzena Skowronska

Name

Also referred to as the 'brow chakra', the third eye chakra, known as *Ajna* in Sanskrit, means 'to perceive' or 'to know'.

Purpose

Judith states that mastering the third eye chakra will help you to keep your mind focused on related issues, including the awareness of the benefits to be gained from transcending the purely physical world and opening yourself up to intuitive sight and wisdom: the ability to learn from experience and emotional intelligence.[2]

Judith explains that since the upper two chakras are associated with the realm of transcendent consciousness, they transcend the limitations of time and space.[2]

Sturgess explains that *Ajna* is the chakra of the mind and the seat of concentration. It represents a higher level of awareness. It is considered the centre of extrasensory perception, intuition, clarity and wisdom, and it forms the boundary between human and divine consciousness.[5]

Nardi refers to the third eye chakra as the seat of higher conscience, also called integrity of wisdom.[6]

Gerber states that our physical eyes are the tools with which we perceive tangibles, while the 'third eye', above and between the eyebrows, offers us the ability to see and understand all things. He describes it as the seat of intuition and the subtle organ involved in clairvoyance. The third eye chakra is the connection with the higher functions of consciousness; it is a psychic tool reminding us that everything we see, smell, touch or taste started as an inner vision or 'in-sight'.[7]

The development of the third eye chakra is usually referred to as a spiritual awakening. Judith claims we suddenly see with new eyes, experience profound insight, change perspective and attitude, or receive a vision.[2]

Colour

Indigo

Location

Forehead, brow, third eye

Element

Judith states that the element associated with the third eye chakra is light.[2] According to Johari, the element is *mahatattva* (supreme or great element) in which all other elements are present in their pure essence.[10]

Physical association

Physically, the brow chakra is associated with the pineal gland, the pituitary gland and the spinal cord, as well as the eyes, ears, nose and sinuses.

Psychospiritual

Gerber states that the third eye chakra is one of the psychic centres that gradually develops with meditation. An individual who has a highly developed third eye chakra has the ability to 'see within', an aspect of consciousness also related to introspection.[7]

Dreams link the conscious and unconscious mind. Judith states that dreams help link the lower and upper chakras. She explains that dreams unlock the mystery that unites the soul and spirit. Dreams can become powerful spiritual teachers because they bring us answers to problems that our conscious mind could not solve.[2]

Dreams are the psyche's way of maintaining homoeostasis — of compensating for the lack of balance as we adjust our lives to external realities. Dreams communicate essential information to the conscious mind about our health, relationships, work and personal growth.[2]

Judith explains that the development of intuition enhances our psychic abilities and is a central function of the third eye chakra. If we are shut off from our unconscious process and live almost entirely in our conscious mind, then our intuition will be underdeveloped.[2]

Prendergast states that the third eye chakra governs all beliefs and identifications, insight, intellectual understanding, clarity, vision, observation, symbols, archetypes, imagination, intuition, psychic abilities and the actualisation of one's vision.[11]

Traditional symbology

Satyananda states that our reflection of the psychic centres should begin with the *Ajna* chakra. He states that traditionally the *Muladhara* chakra is generally designated as the first chakra since it is the seat of *kundalini shakti*; however, he states there is another system in which the study of the chakras commences with *Ajna*.[8]

Ajna is the point of confluence where the three main *nadis* or forces merge into one stream of consciousness and flow up to *sahasrara*, the crown chakra. In mythology, these three nadis are represented by three great rivers — Ganga (*ida*), Jamuna (*pingala*) and Saraswati (a subterranean current which represents *sushumna*). They converge at a place called Prayag or Triveni, which is near present-day Allahabad. Indians believe that every 12 years, when the sun is in Aquarius, if one takes a dip at the point of confluence, he or she will be purified. This place of confluence corresponds symbolically to the *Ajna* chakra.[8]

Ajna is symbolised by a two-petalled lotus. Some say it is white like the moon, or silver, but Satyananda states that it is an intangible colour. Within the lotus is a perfectly formed circle which symbolises *shoonya*, the

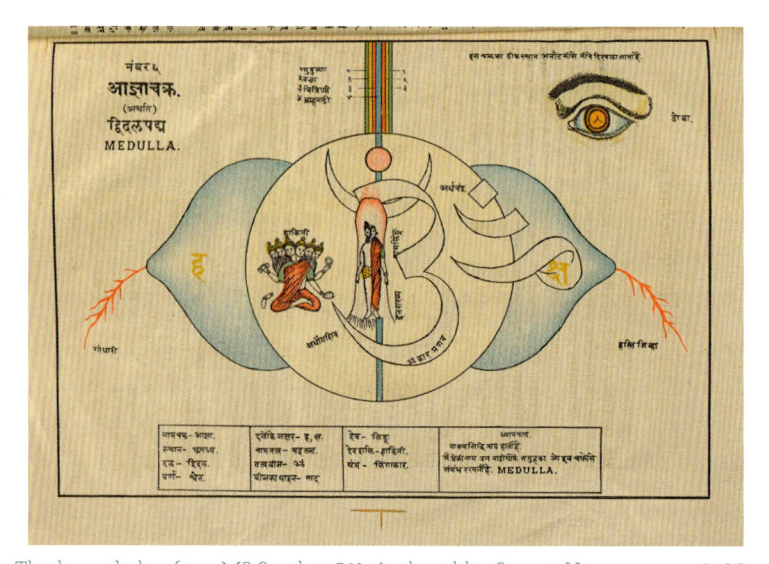

Third eye chakra from MS Sanskrit 391. Authored by Swami Hamsasvarupa, 1900s.

void. Within the circle is an inverted triangle which represents *Shakti* — creativity and manifestation. Above the triangle is a black *shivalingam*, which is a symbol of your astral body. He claims that according to Tantra, the astral body is the attribute of your personality.[8]

Archetype

According to King, the thinker is the dysfunctional archetype of the third eye chakra. She explains that the thinker lives from the rationality of the left brain and believes that emotions are highly irrational, so they rarely confront their feelings and fears. Thinkers often have an overstimulated mind, which may lead to anxiety and worry.[4]

King describes the positive archetype of the third eye chakra as the seer. The seer is the wise elder who has deep inner vision. The true seer is gifted with inner sight, and has learned to trust their inner guidance.[4]

Tubali describes the personality type of the third eye chakra as the thinker. Thinkers are great observers of life and humanity. According to Tubali, thinkers represent around 5% of the world population. They are typically drawn toward work as philosophers, scientists, researchers, inventors, non-fiction writers and critics.[9]

They can be very opinionated and hate thinking like everyone else. They appear to be aloof. This gravitates them to the academic world; however, as individuals they seek their own pathway of thinking. They need to understand everything. Understanding just a part of something cannot make them feel content; they want to reach complete wisdom.[9]

Thinkers are intense, freethinking individuals who are driven to interpret everything. Tubali explains that when most other types experience a strong emotion, they are taken by it; however, thinkers immediately want to investigate it. According to Tubali, thinkers possess highly systematic scientific minds and are usually highly intelligent. They are inventive and gifted with individualistic and unconventional ways of thinking that make them choose uncharted and daring mental pathways.[9]

However, because they live only in their head, thinkers tend to forget all about the real world. The most obvious worldly element they tend to forget about is their own body, from which they can become easily detached. Tubali explains that this is why they need grounded people around them. They can be proudly judgemental and critical. They often look down on all other types and see everyone else as wrong.[9]

Tubali refers to third eye chakra types as the greatest teachers in the world, he explains that they remind us that it is beautiful to inquire, to contemplate, to observe and to study. He also states that they are the representatives of truth:

> *They tell us that if we engage our minds, hearts, and bodies in a desire for a complete understanding of something, sooner or later the flower of life's mystery will open up before our mind's eye.*[9]

Challenges

According to Judith, issues associated with the third eye chakra include intuition, imagination, visualisation, insight, dream and vision.[2]

Judith states that each of the chakras reflects a basic right. Loss of these rights will block a chakra. Part of healing the third eye chakra must involve reclaiming the right to see. This right is damaged when we are told that what we perceive is not real, when things are deliberately hidden or denied. For example, when children see things beyond their scope of understanding, or when angry or frightening scenes occur frequently, they will diminish their own ability to see.[2]

King explains that overthinking is one of the biggest obstacles to crown chakra health. She states that:

> *Overthinking can cut off access to your inner voice and preoccupy you with highly irrational left-brain fears and emotions. By rationalizing and theorizing, you can stay stuck in the realm of the mind while your vital energy stagnates. Not only that, but you can lose out on the creativity, intuition, and wisdom that is available when your sixth chakra is in balance.*[4]

Behavioural characteristics

Balanced

Judith states that a person with a balanced third eye chakra will have intuition, perception, imagination, good memory, good dream recall and ability to visualise. She states that a balanced third eye chakra is able to calm the mind and see clearly, without any personal issues.[2]

King explains that when the third eye chakra is balanced you have immediate access to your deepest wisdom, you have the gift of inner sight and you trust your inner guidance. She explains that intuitive guidance often comes in your dreams. Your dreams give your psyche a way to communicate, telling you what is going on in your unconscious.[4]

Nardi states that when our third eye chakra is balanced, we act with integrity and we stay tuned with our conscience.[6]

Prendergast explains that, because so many feelings are influenced by thinking, when the third eye chakra is balanced, we will have a rich and balanced emotional life.[11]

Excess

According to Judith, a person with an excessive third eye chakra may experience hallucinations, delusional obsessions, difficulty concentrating and nightmares.[2]

Deficiency

Judith states that a person with a deficient third eye chakra may experience insensitivity, poor vision, poor memory, difficulty seeing the future, lack of imagination, poor dream recall and denial. She explains that people with third eye chakra deficiency have difficulty visualising or imaging things differently.[2]

Health issues

Judith states that the health issues associated with the third eye chakra include:

- headaches
- vision problems.[2]

King states that physical problems with the third eye chakra show up in the eyes and head. It may manifest as eye problems such as poor eyesight, glaucoma, cataracts, macular degeneration and blindness. Conditions of the upper or frontal sinuses, headaches, stroke, neurological disturbances and brain tumours are also associated with the third eye chakra.[4]

Gerber suggests that diseases caused by a dysfunction of the third eye chakra may be caused by an individual's not wanting to see something that is important to their soul growth. He states that difficulties associated with energy blockages at the third eye chakra can physically manifest in the form of illnesses as divergent as sinus problems, cataracts and major endocrine imbalances.[7]

Essential oils for the third eye chakra

Use essential oils that help us to connect with the higher levels of the mind and bring clarity to our understanding of spiritual truths. Essential oils that balance the third eye chakra are usually herbaceous oils such as bay laurel, basil, rosemary or sage, or floral herbaceous oils such as clary sage or everlasting. Typical essential oils that have the greatest affinity with the third eye chakra include:

Basil — clears the mind.[13]

Bay laurel — promotes psychic awareness and intuition. Releases mental blocks and outmoded beliefs.[12,13]

Cedarwood, Atlas — clears and calms the mind. Promotes a calm meditative state.[12,13]

Clary sage — increases dreaming, strengthens our intuition, inspires.[12,13]

Coriander seed — improves memory.[12]

Cypress — promotes wisdom.[12]

Eucalyptus — promotes concentration.[12]

Everlasting — activates the intuitive right side of the brain and promotes understanding.[12,13,14]

Fir — increases intuition.[12,13]

Fragonia — promotes and activates our consciousness.

Frankincense — quiets and clarifies the mind. Promotes a meditative state.[12,13]

Grapefruit — promotes mental clarity, focuses consciousness, opens and strengthens intuition.[13]

Juniper berry — assists clairvoyance, but only if used for altruistic reasons. Dispels mental stagnation.[12,13]

Lemon — promotes mental clarity, focuses consciousness, opens and strengthens intuition.[12,13]

Lemongrass — stimulates psychic awareness.[13]

Myrtle — promotes mental clarity and develops wisdom.

Neroli — reunites the conscious and subconscious mind.[12,13]

Palmarosa — clears the mind to help with decision-making, develops wisdom.[12,13]

Peppermint — promotes inspiration and insights. Stimulates the conscious mind.[13]

Petitgrain — stimulates the conscious mind and clears perception.[13]

Rosemary — promotes clear thoughts, insights and understanding.[12,13]

Sage — promotes mental clarity, strengthens our intuition and understanding.

Sandalwood — quiets the mind, promotes meditation.[12,13]

Aromatherapy blends

Use these blends in a diffuser or add to 10ml of jojoba oil to use as a massage oil or an anointing oil.

Insight

Trust your intuition with *Insight* chakra blend. *Insight* is a blend of bergamot, clary sage, fragonia, lavender, rosemary and sage pure essential oils.

Psychic

This blend helps you to develop and trust your intuition and psychic awareness.

>   2 drops clary sage
>   2 drops fragonia
>   2 drops sandalwood

Dream recall

This blend helps you to activate and enhance your dream activity.

> 2 drops everlasting
> 2 drops clary sage
> 2 drops petitgrain

Mental clarity

This blend promotes mental clarity.

> 2 drops basil
> 2 drops lemon
> 2 drops peppermint

Questions for self-examination

Myss asks the following questions for self-examination:[3]

- Do you often interpret the actions of others in a negative way? If so, why?
- What negative patterns continually surface in your relationships with others?
- What attitudes do you have that disempower you?
- What beliefs do you continue to accept that you know are not true?
- Are you judgemental? If so, what situations or relationships bring out that tendency?
- Do you make excuses for behaving in negative ways?
- Recall instances in which a more profound level of truth than you were used to hearing was revealed. Was the experience intimidating?
- What beliefs and attitudes in yourself would you like to change? Can you commit to making those changes?
- Are you comfortable thinking about your life in impersonal terms?
- Do you know you need to change but continually postpone taking action? If so, identify those situations and your reasons for not acting.

King states that if you answer yes to three or more of the questions below, the chances are you need to balance your third eye chakra:[4]

- Do you have any health conditions related to the eyes, nose, brain or neurological system?
- Do you usually forget your dreams?
- Do you tend to be close-minded?
- Do you typically only see one way to address an issue?
- Do you deny or ignore the truth of a situation?
- Do you shut off or ignore inner guidance?
- Do you behave in a way that is against your own ethics and morality?
- Do you expect negative results from most situations?
- Do you have a difficult time concentrating or focusing on tasks at hand?
- Do you often forget things you need to do?
- Do you overreact to situations rather than rationally try to deal with them?

Activities to strengthen your third eye chakra

Judith recommends the following activities to strengthen the third eye chakra:[2]

- creative visual art
- visual stimulation
- it's okay to daydream
- closing your eyes and feel the sun entering the third eye's centre
- keeping a dream diary
- meditation — this will help to develop your intuition and psychic abilities
- listening to music by Mozart or Bach.

Tubali suggests several lifestyle activities to keep the third eye chakra balanced:[9]

- Make sure you live around at least one grounded and settled person. It helps to have a base chakra type as a partner or friend.
- Try to moderate your tendency towards mental burnout. Pay attention to mental balance and make sure that you leave enough time for non-thinking activities.

- Stay in touch with nature. Appreciate the perfect order and harmony that nature represents.
- Try to experience things without interpreting or understanding them.
- Your greatest challenge is arrogance. Cultivate humility.
- Do not take pleasure in being misunderstood. Admit that everything you say can be explained simply.
- Practise being nonjudgemental. Resist the temptation to be critical all the time.

Nardi suggests the following activities to cultivate your third eye chakra:[6]

- Inspire growth by attending workshops and retreats.
- Engage in creative projects.
- Explore altered states.

Affirmations for the third eye chakra

Judith recommends the following affirmations to strengthen the third eye chakra:[2]

- The answers to all my questions lie within me.
- I trust my inner self to guide and protect me.
- Making mistakes enables me to learn, grow and develop.

20. Crown Chakra

Through meditation
I find expansion
Connect with my soul
The gateway to God
I tap into self-realization.
Knowing myself is knowing God
As I extend my crown to the sky
I am reminded that my body and mind
Are connected to something higher
A universal power
Consciousness
Vastness of spirit
Boundlessness
Pure love
That is greater
But also part of me
Which gives me trust
In the flow of life.

Marzena Skowronska

Name

The crown chakra is known in Sanskrit as *Sahasrara*, meaning 'thousandfold'.

Purpose

Judith explains that the crown chakra is about merging the divine consciousness and realising our true nature.[2]

Sturgess explains that strictly speaking, the crown chakra is not actually a chakra, as it does not belong to the planes of consciousness of the mind and body.[5]

> It is an extended field of consciousness that is experienced above the head as the highest centre of pure consciousness.[5]

Developing the other chakras was like walking on stepping stones taking us toward this ultimate goal — understanding, enlightenment, self-realisation, fulfilment and divine self.

Gerber states that the crown chakra is considered one of the highest vibrational centres in the subtle body and it is associated with deep inner searching: the so-called spiritual quest. He claims that this chakra is most active when individuals are involved in a religious and spiritual quest for the meaning of life and in the inner search of their origins as conscious evolving beings:[7]

> The opening of the crown chakra allows one to enter into the higher states of consciousness. The conscious activation of this center represents the beginning of ascension into a state of spiritual perfection.

King states the more your crown chakra opens, the more you evolve as a conscious being. When this chakra is open and in balance and resonating with all the other chakras, we can become one with the entire universe.[4]

Colour

Violet

Location

Top of the cranium

Element

Judith and King state that the element of this chakra is thought.[2,4]

Physical association

Gerber explains that at a physical level the crown chakra is associated with the activity of the cerebral cortex and general nervous system functioning. In addition, the proper activation of the crown chakra influences the synchronisation between the left and right hemispheres of the brain. The crown chakra is also closely linked with the pineal gland. For the crown chakra to be fully awakened, there must be a balance of the body, mind and spirit.[7]

Psychospiritual

When we awaken the crown chakra, we open to the possibilities of infinity of space and time and have divine wisdom and understanding of humanity, selflessness, spirituality and devotion. Judith states that the crown chakra is about merging with divine consciousness and realising our true nature.[2]

What is it that drew you to this book, your partner or the work that you do? What is it that sees, hears, remembers, feels, thinks and moves your body — our consciousness. Judith provides us with a wonderful explanation of consciousness and the crown chakra:[2]

> *We think of consciousness as our thoughts, but thoughts are what consciousness creates, not what it is. We think of consciousness as our perceptions, but there is a faculty that not only perceives, but also remembers, discriminates and integrates our perceptions. Who or what does this? We feel the pull of consciousness on our emotions, but who or what feels these emotions and how do we experience feeling. This is the mystery that we embrace in the crown chakra — a mystery that can only be experienced, not explained.*

The crown chakra strengthens our intellect; it helps establish our belief system and our understanding of the world. We also have the ability to question and think for ourselves. We are able to learn — by learning we expand our horizons, master our relationships to objects and people, and grow toward understanding and wisdom.[2]

Prendergast states that the crown chakra governs themes of transcendence, freedom, divine guidance, the soul's path and teleology.[11]

Traditional symbology

Sturgess describes the *Sahasrara* chakra as a shining moonlike white lotus of one thousand petals. It lies about 8 cm above the crown of the head with its petals pointing downwards.

The *Sahasrara* lotus has one thousand *nadis* symbolised as petals emanating from it. The thousand petals of *Sahasrara* carry the total sound-potential represented by all 50 letters of the Sanskrit alphabet. The 50 letters are repeated 20 times, 50 in each layer.

Sturgess states that *Sahasrara* is not associated with any element, colour or sound as the other six chakras are. He states that it synchronises all colours, encompassing all the senses and all the functions, and is all pervading in its power. He refers to it as the centre of quintessential consciousness.[5]

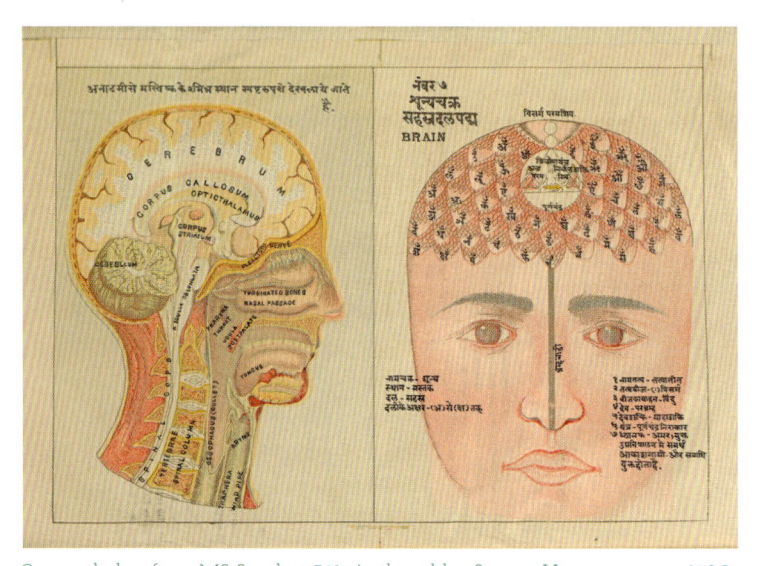

Crown chakra from MS Sanskrit 391. Authored by Swami Hamsasvarupa, 1900s.

Satyananda best explains *Sahasrara*:[8]

> *Whatever we say about sahasrara will immediately limit and categorize it, even if we say it is infinite. It transcends logic, for logic compares one thing with another. Sahasrara is the totality, so what is there to compare it with? It transcends all concepts and yet it is the source of all concepts. It is the merging of consciousness and prana.*

Satyananda explains that the union of *Shiva* and *Shakti* occurs when *kundalini* reaches *Sahasrara*. This represents the moment of self-realisation.[8]

Archetype

King states that the dysfunctional archetype for the crown chakra is the egotist or the narcissist. She states that the egotist is so full of pride and feels so important that there cannot possibly be any higher power than them. They are only interested in their own achievements, dramas and ego. On the other hand, the sage is the positive archetype of the crown chakra. The sage is a spiritual master — the embodiment of awareness, compassion and unconditional love.[4]

King states that attachment is the main obstacle standing between who you are now and becoming the sage.[4]

Tubali describes the personality type of the crown chakra as the yogi. According to Tubali, the yogi represents around 1% of the world's population. They tend to be typically found among mystics, saints, priests, monks, ascetics, sadhus, sorcerers and spiritual masters. What really matters to the yogi is the unchanging truth. The yogi considers our only purpose in life is to free ourselves from it by withdrawing from it and devoting our energy to the Divine.[9]

Happiness for the yogi is:

> *... samadhi, deep self-immersion, in which we get in touch with the supreme bliss of our innermost being. The expansion of consciousness, the loss of all limitation, and the rising of the life-force towards infinity are our only true sources of joy. Yogis are happiest when they feel they no longer belong to the earth's forms, but rather have reached*

the end of human endeavor within the world of objects and transcend all pleasures, pains, and earthly attachments.[9]

Tubali states that some of us become crown chakra types when we are immersed in deep meditation or any other kind of profound spiritual concentration. To others, crown chakra types may appear introverted, dreamy, spacey and almost transparent. However, they are deeply engaged in the rich experience of an inner world. They are able to meditate for hours without getting bored and can spend long solitary periods in nature in their timeless space. Silence comes naturally to them. They do not speak much and use only a few words to express themselves. They are gifted with a deep silence and need very little to cultivate it through spiritual practice and meditation. They demonstrate a high spiritual intelligence and intuitively grasp what others struggle to understand. Their ability to let go of possessions and attachments means that they are able to rapidly move along the path of self-transcendence.[9]

In materialistic and secular culture, yogis may be considered antisocial, unfit and unwilling to contribute to the general good. Tubali stresses that yogis must learn to admit that a certain part of their meditative life is nothing more than a wish to avoid problems and deny that they exist.[9]

They need to feel more grounded and stop resisting and denying their feelings. They have to accept that, as long as they breathe, they are on earth, not in heaven. They teach us that delving into the invisible domain of our own consciousness is an invaluable and complementary experience of human life. They teach us that what really counts in the end is divine reality. Tubali states that in our stress-ridden society, it is easy for us to appreciate the presence of the crown chakra type.[9]

Challenges

According to Judith, the challenges associated with the crown chakra include transcendence, belief systems, consciousness, higher power, divinity, union and vision.[2]

Part of healing the crown chakra must involve reclaiming the right to know. This includes the right to accurate information, the right to truth, the right to knowledge and the right to know what is going on. Equally important is one's spiritual rights — the right to connect with the divine in whatever way we find most appropriate. To force on another a spiritual dogma infringes upon our crown chakra personal and spiritual rights.[2]

Traumas and abuses associated with the crown chakra include:[2]
- withheld information
- education that thwarts curiosity
- forced religiosity
- invalidation of one's beliefs
- blind obedience (no right to question or think for oneself)
- spiritual abuse.

Judith states that the demon of the crown chakra is attachment. While attachment is necessary for maintaining and making commitments that are essential to the lower chakras, it inhibits our ability to expand into the crown chakra. She explains that for some of us, letting go of attachment means letting go of responsibility. This becomes a means of escape. When the going gets tough, we simply let go of our connection rather than resolving the challenges. In doing so we may experience freedom, but we sacrifice growth.[2]

Judith explains that letting go of attachment is about how we direct our psychic energy. She says that to let go of attachment is to release our fixation upon something external, to let go of our need to control, our desire for a certain outcome. Attachment is our way of not trusting the wisdom of the universe while it tries to teach us something. Another word for attachment is addiction. We become attached because it serves our purpose to do so — not because we are right, or because something or someone is necessarily right for us, but because we are unconsciously using that attachment to avoid some aspect of our growth.[2]

Judith suggests that religion negates spirituality when it becomes a structure for denying our feelings, avoiding the challenges of life, controlling others, or for ego-inflating righteousness. However, on the positive side, religion provides structure, and more importantly, a practice whereby one can let go and become receptive to deeper states of experience, awareness and understanding. It provides us with community and the support that comes from friends on a similar path.[2]

Behavioural characteristics

Balanced

According to Judith, the characteristics of a balanced crown chakra are:[2]

- ability to perceive, analyse and assimilate
- intelligent, thoughtful
- open-minded, able to question
- spiritually connected
- wisdom and mastery, broad understanding.

King explains that when our crown chakra is open and balanced, we have faith in the transcendent realms and we have a sense of purpose in life. She explains that when our crown chakra is open, we do not judge or criticise others as we embody love, compassion and awareness.[4]

When the crown chakra is healthy you acknowledge your spiritual need; you renounce worldly distractions, false identifications and harmful habits; you focus on your core life mission; you are fully present with a quiet mind; you are open and aligned with all other chakras and you act as a spiritual guide.[6]

Excess

According to Judith, the characteristics of an excess crown chakra are:[2]

- over-intellectualisation
- spiritual addiction
- confusion
- disassociation from body.

Deficiency

According to Judith, the characteristics of a deficient crown chakra are:[2]

- spiritual cynicism
- learning difficulties
- rigid belief systems
- apathy.

When our crown chakra is closed, we do not understand the meaning of a spiritual experience. King explains that when our crown chakra is deficient in energy, there may be an excess of energy in the lower chakras. This may create greed, materialism and the desire to control others.[4]

Health issues

According to Judith, health issues associated with imbalances of the crown chakra include coma, migraines, brain tumours, amnesia and cognitive delusions.[2]

Gerber suggests that abnormalities in energy flow at the level of the crown chakra may manifest as various types of cerebral dysfunction, including psychosis.[7]

Physical dysfunctions associated with the crown chakra include energetic disorders, mystical depression, and extreme sensitivities to light, sound and other environmental factors.[7]

King explains that physical problems associated with the crown chakra include anxiety, depression, insomnia, bipolar disorder, amnesia, headaches, strokes, brain tumours, epilepsy, multiple sclerosis, Parkinson's disease, attention deficit disorder and hyperactivity, mental illness, dementia and Alzheimer's disease.[4]

Essential oils for the crown chakra

In reality, if one were to truly attain *Sahasrara*, then there would not be any need or use for essential oils; however, we may consider using those essential oils that are woody, resiny or light florals. These essential oils have the ability to connect us with the divine within and without. Typical essential oils that have the greatest affinity with the crown chakra include:

Angelica root — connects us with angelic guidance and aligns us with our higher selves.[12]

Benzoin — calms the emotions and mind for meditation.[13]

Cajeput — supports and encourages devotion to spirit.[12]

Cedarwood, Atlas — restores a sense of spiritual certainty. Strengthens connection with the divine.[12,13]

Chamomile, Roman — connects throat and crown chakra to facilitate hearing and communication.[12]

Frankincense — connects us with the eternal and divine. Strengthens spiritual consciousness and aspirations.[12,13]

Galbanum — helps connect us with the divine.[13]

Juniper berry — helps us to connect with and act from our highest ideals, enlightens.[12]

Lavender — helps to integrate spirituality into everyday life.[12,13]

Lime — promotes spiritual growth.

Melissa — promotes spiritual growth.[12]

Myrrh — strengthens spirituality.[12,13]

Neroli — promotes direct communication with spiritual guides.[12,13]

Rose otto — promotes a sense of spiritual connection.[12,13]

Rosemary — helps us to strengthen our spiritual path.[12,13]

Sandalwood — promotes deep meditation. Encourages states of higher consciousness.[12,13]

Spikenard — increases love and devotion for the divine.[12,13]

Aromatherapy blends

Use these blends in a diffuser or add to 10ml of jojoba oil to use as a massage oil or an anointing oil.

Cosmic

Create sacred space for divine wisdom with *Cosmic* chakra blend. *Cosmic* is a blend of frankincense, lavender, cold-pressed lime and sandalwood essential oils.

Divine

This blend helps heighten our spiritual awareness and connects us with the Divine.

    1 drop sandalwood
    2 drops neroli
    2 drops rose otto

Mindfulness

This blend promotes meditation and helps us find our purpose in life.

>   1 drop frankincense
>   1 drop myrrh
>   1 drop sandalwood

Integrating spirituality into our daily life

This blend helps to integrate spirituality into everyday life.

>   2 drops Atlas cedarwood
>   2 drops lavender
>   2 drops myrrh

Questions for self-examination

Myss asks the following questions for self-examination:[3]

- What guidance have you sought during meditation or praying?
- What type of guidance do you fear the most?
- Do you bargain with the Divine? Do you complain to the Divine more than you express gratitude?
- Are you devoted to a particular spiritual path? If not, do you feel a need to find one?
- Do you believe that your God is more authentic than the Divine in other spiritual traditions?
- Are you waiting for the Divine to send you an explanation for your painful experiences? If so, list them.
- How would your life change if the Divine answered your questions by saying: 'I have no intention of giving you insight at this point in your life?' What would you do then?
- Have you started and stopped a meditation practice? If so, what are the reasons that you failed to maintain it?
- What spiritual truths are you aware of that you do not live by? List them.
- Are you afraid of a closer relationship with the Divine because of changes it might trigger in your life?

King states that if you answer yes to three or more of the questions below, the chances are you need to balance your crown chakra:[4]

- Do you distrust or not believe in your higher power?
- Do you feel like you've been abandoned?
- Do you feel unsupported by the universe?
- Do you feel alone and isolated?
- Do you feel as though your mind is foggy?
- Do you regularly feel overtired and like you are not getting enough sleep?

Activities to strengthen your crown chakra

Judith recommends the following activities to strengthen the crown chakra:[2]

- seeing the Divine in everybody, everywhere, look inside for answers
- focusing on dreams and writing down one's visions and inventions
- learning and studying
- spiritual discipline
- enjoying quiet contemplation, meditation and yoga
- silence as the crown chakra's inspiration music.

Judith explains that of all the methods for healing and nurturing the crown chakra, meditation is perhaps the most potent tool available. She explains the benefits of meditation:

> *Meditation is a technique for energizing, calming, and clarifying the mind. Its purpose is to train the mind to enter subtler states of consciousness and transcend the petty concerns that usually occupy the mind, allowing us to access a deeper, grander state of awareness.*[2]

Judith suggests that there are many techniques one can use to obtain a meditative state. The technique that works best for you depends on your basic character and needs at the time. For example, if you are trying to calm your thoughts in a time of crisis, it may help to count your breaths, as even regular breaths will calm the body. If it is difficult for you to sit still, you may try a moving or walking meditation. If your mind has a lot of mental chatter, you may try a mantra meditation, which helps to set up a rhythmic entrainment in your mind that brings harmony to your thoughts and actions. On the other hand, Judith suggests that if you are trying to cleanse yourself of the stress you bring home from work, it may be helpful to run energy through the body, as if taking a shower in sensation and light.[2]

Judith explains that meditation can have profound results:

> *As our thoughts often keep us engaged in repetitive patterns and limited beliefs, meditation can yield a mental silence that allows us to access a deeper wisdom, a deeper state of consciousness. As we quiet the mind, we have the option to disengage our habitual responses — anger or judgement, fear or desire — and free ourselves from these patterns. As we disengage, we become lighter, emptier, and more able to access the transcendental states of universal consciousness.*
>
> *Meditation can bring previously buried unconscious material from the lower chakras into consciousness. Thus meditation also serves the ascending, liberating currents as it refines our vibrations chakra by chakra, yielding deeper understanding and self-knowledge. Once we allow the constant chatter of the mind to subside, the deeper whispering underneath emerges, just as dreams do when our conscious mind is asleep.*[2]

According to King, the main way to cultivate the crown chakra is by being mindful. Therefore, the best practice to open your crown chakra is through regular practice of meditation and prayer to strengthen your connection to the universal field of consciousness.[4]

Tubali suggests several lifestyle activities to keep the crown chakra balanced:[9]

- Learn to accept that there is a point in being in a body and experiencing human life.
- Try to experience life from an objective point of view and realise that there is more than one possible perspective.
- Learn to value and act from your heart centre. The heart bridges deep spirituality and life in the world.
- Make sure you are in contact with other aspects of your being. It is important not to ignore life's fiery passion represented by the sacral chakra; not to ignore the ambition and will of the solar plexus chakra;

not to ignore the wish for manifestation of the throat and not to ignore the discriminating wisdom of the third eye chakra.
- Take responsibility for something or someone, even if it is just a pet.
- Honour your need for meditation, retreats and periods of silence.
- Since you are not interested in money or in a 'career', look for easy, undemanding jobs that can fill your needs, or find a profession that suits your spiritual framework.

Nardi suggests some activities to cultivate the crown chakra:[6]

- Engage in a spiritual practice.
- Renounce worldly distractions.
- Stay responsible.
- Act as a spiritual guide.

Affirmations for the crown chakra

Judith recommends the following affirmations to strengthen the crown chakra:[2]

- I cease to limit myself intellectually and creatively and connect my spirit to the source of all knowledge.
- I release all limited thoughts and lift myself up to ever higher levels of awareness.
- I tune into the union with my higher power.

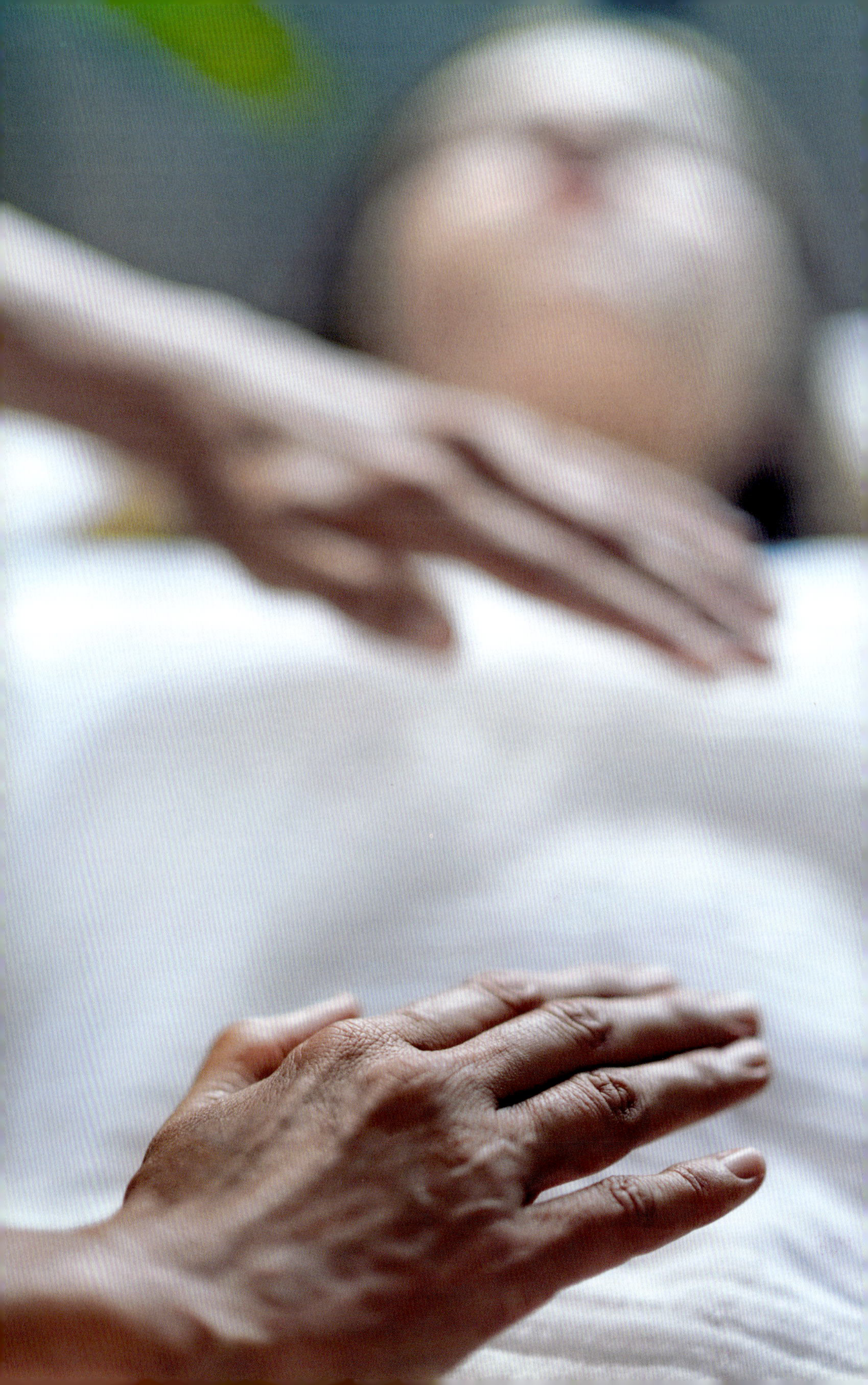

Part [4]
Chakra Healing

21. Chakra Imbalances

22. How to Balance Your Chakras

23. How to Use Essential Oils to Balance the Chakras

24. Afterword

21. Chakra Imbalances

How to become more aware of the state your chakras?

Judith states that first and foremost, focus your attention on learning to interpret your life's challenges symbolically — find meaning in them. Think and feel how they connect to your health. Bring attention every day to the challenges you face and to how your mind and spirit respond to them. Observe what causes you to lose power, and where you feel the loss. Evaluate the spiritual and biological activity that occurs as a consequence.[1]

Secondly, think of yourself at all times as an energy being as well as a physical one. The energy part of your self is the transmitter and recorder of all your thoughts and interactions. Develop the habit of evaluating the people, experiences and information you allow into your life. Consciously and regularly evaluate your interactions and their influence on your emotional and physical power.[1]

Reflect on the *Questions for self-examination* in each chakra section. These questions will assist you in understanding the state of each chakra. Each chakra is associated with particular functions within the body and with specific life issues and the way we handle them, both inside ourselves and in our interactions with the world.

Visualise the chakras as sites where we receive, absorb, and distribute life energies. Through external situations and internal habits, such as long-held physical tension and limiting self-concepts, a chakra can become either deficient or excessive and therefore imbalanced. These imbalances may develop temporarily with situational challenges, or they may be chronic. A chronic imbalance can come from childhood experiences, past pain or stress, and internalised cultural values.

Chakra imbalances

A deficient chakra neither receives appropriate energy nor easily manifests that chakra's energy in the world. There's a sense of being physically and emotionally closed down in the area of a deficient chakra. Think of the slumped shoulders of someone who is depressed and lonely, their heart chakra receding into their chest. The deficient chakra needs to open.[1]

When a chakra is excessive, it is too overloaded to operate in a healthy way and becomes a dominating force in a person's life. Someone with an excessive throat chakra, for example, might talk too much and be unable to listen well. If the chakra were deficient, he or she might experience restraint and difficulty when communicating.[1]

Henderson, author of *Emotion and Healing in the Energy Body*, explains that chakra imbalances may be of three types: empty, depleted and excessive. If the chakra has been starved of much of its environmental energetic needs during its stage of development, it is described as empty. A chakra becomes depleted when its store of energy is overused. He explains that this applies mostly to the sacral and solar plexus chakras. When we physically overwork, the energy of the sacral chakra becomes depleted; however, restoring energy to a depleted chakra usually involves rest and proper nutrition. TCM is also an effective way of restoring depleted energies of chakras.[2]

On the other hand, Henderson explains that if a chakra is overfed with environmental energies during the stages of development, that chakra is said to be excessive. A chakra also becomes excessive when it is unable to dissipate energy into the adjacent chakras. This situation mostly applies to the sacral, solar plexus and heart chakras.[2]

Chakra blockages

We have all experienced times when the free flow of energy seems blocked. For example, if our physical health or personal finances are in constant crisis, then we may have an energy blockage in the base chakra.

According to Judith, childhood traumas, cultural conditioning, limited belief systems, restrictive or exhausting habits, physical or emotional injuries can all contribute to a chakra blockage. Life is full of challenges and difficulties and each one of us develops different coping strategies. However, when the challenges persist, our coping strategies become chronic patterns, anchored in the body and psyche as defence structures.[1]

Judith states to unblock a chakra requires us to address the problem on multiple levels:[1]

- *Understand the dynamics of that particular chakra* — this means knowing the chakra system well enough to understand the nature of each chakra and its influence on us.
- *Examine the personal history related to that chakra's history* — each chakra has a developmental stage, with traumas and abuses that may affect its functioning. Understanding the relationship between these traumas and the chakras will give you vital information about the nature of the blockage.
- *Apply exercises and techniques* — there are meditations, yoga practices, physical activities, essential oils and visualisation techniques that can help to influence change in the chakra.
- *Balance excess and deficiency* — if a chakra is blocked, we must learn to let go. If it is blocked by perpetual avoidance, we must learn to focus on that area in both our bodies and our lives.

Chakra excess and deficiency

Judith explains that we have two ways of coping with stress, negative experiences or trauma. We may increase our energy and attention in order to fight the stress or we may decrease it in order to avoid the situation. This results in an excessive or deficient coping strategy. Avoidance leads to chakra deficiency and overcompensation leads to chakra excess. For example, a bully who compensates for insecurity by dominating others exhibits an excess solar plexus chakra. A person who constantly talks may have excessive throat chakra while an overweight person may have an excessive base chakra to feel protected and grounded.[1]

Excessive and deficient chakras are both the result of coping strategies to deal with stress, trauma and unpleasant situations. They both restrict the energy flow through the chakras and they both result in dysfunctional behaviour and health problems.[1]

Judith states that in theory, healing chakra imbalances should be simple. An excessive chakra needs to discharge energy and a deficient chakra needs to receive energy. However, she explains that it may be difficult to open a chakra that has been closed for 40 years due to trauma.[1]

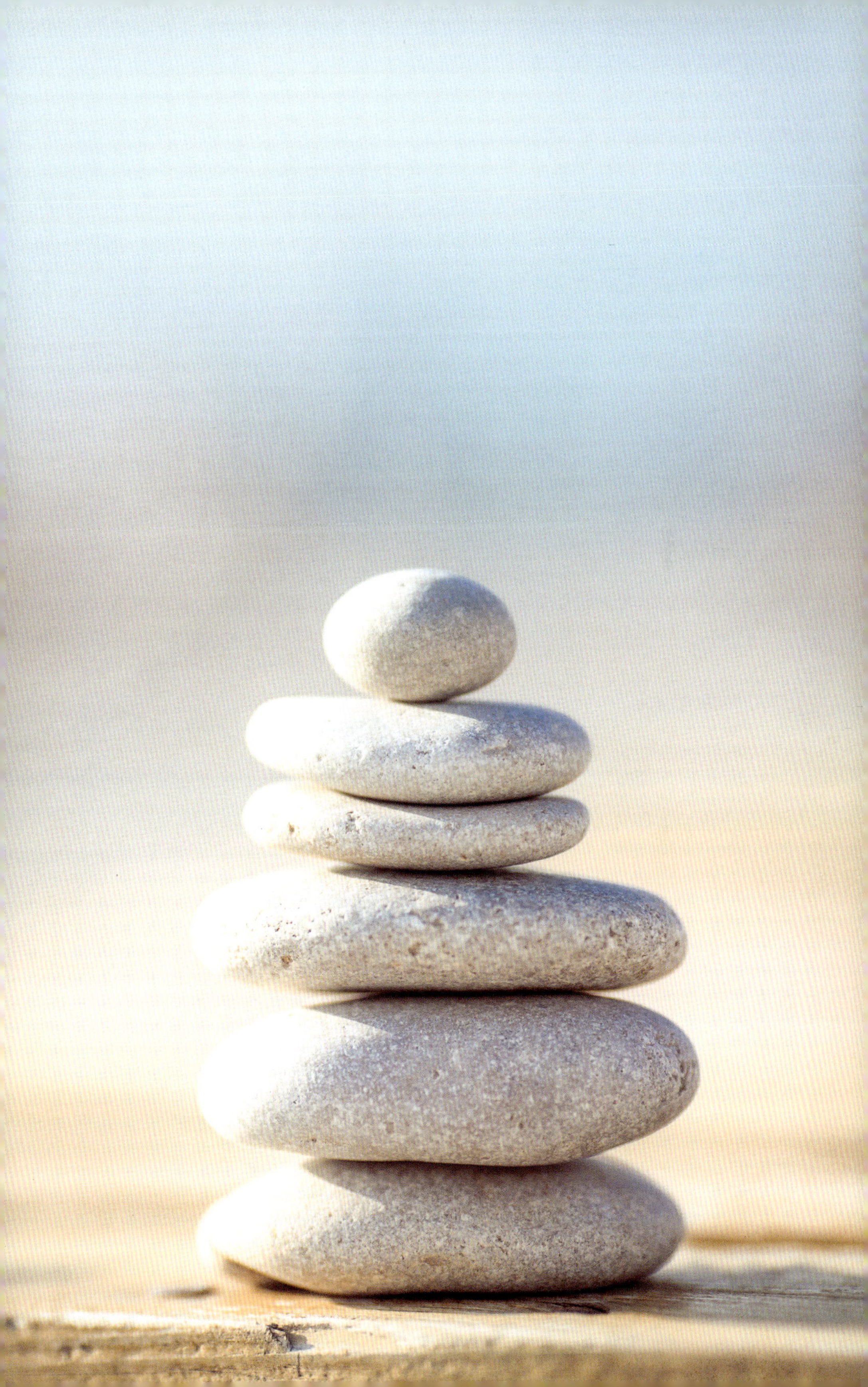

22. How to Balance Your Chakras?

Gerber suggests that if doctors understood that emotional and spiritual blockages are indirectly responsible for organ dysfunction in the body, there would be more attention directed to dealing with the patient's psychotherapeutic needs and not just the pharmaceutical and surgical aspects of a patient's care.[3]

Meditation

Gerber states that all the vibrational therapies such as flower essences, gem elixirs, crystal and colour therapies work at the level of the chakras and subtle bodies in rebalancing energy. He states that one of the simplest and most powerful methods of opening, activating and cleansing blockages in the chakras is through meditation. He explains that meditation opens the mind to the energies of the higher self. It helps to clear the mind of day-to-day concerns of the earthly personality, and allows higher information to be processed through the individual's consciousness.[3]

He describes how meditation can help to balance our chakras:

> *Meditation clears the mind of conscious thought programs to allow higher vibrational sources of information to enter into the biocomputer for processing and analysis. In addition to allowing access to the higher self, the process of meditation causes gradual changes in the subtle energy anatomy of the human being over a long period of time. Specifically, the chakras are slowly activated and cleared, and the kundalini energies within the root chakra eventually make their climb up the subtle pathways within the spinal cord to reach the crown chakra.*[3]

Gerber claims that during the natural course of human development, an individual will gradually open up all the chakras within the body. The degree to which the chakras are opened will depend on the extent to which the person develops his or her abilities to communicate with others, to express ideas creatively and artistically, to love both self and others, and to strive towards the higher meanings of life.[3]

Traumatic emotional events may hold one's growth, resulting in a blockage in one of the chakras. He describes how the release of the blockage to energy flow through a chakra is due to the cleansing and opening effect of the *kundalini* forces, but also related to the gradual realisation of the emotional and spiritual lessons necessary to the proper functioning of that chakra. Gerber states that meditation assists in learning such important life lessons over time as the conscious personality begins to understand the reason for existing energy blockages:

> *Meditation helps to build subtle energy bridges of learning and communication which connect the physical personality to knowledge contained within their own higher vibrational structures of consciousness.*[3]

Rama, Ballentine and Ajana state that one of the most common mistakes made by beginners in meditation is that they try too hard to achieve a goal, when you use your 'ego-will' to force relaxation. This makes calming the mind impossible. They suggest when you use a more passive volitional attitude, by using a relaxed approach, the calming of the mind comes naturally. They explain that when we turn inward to explore the inner space during meditation, we may encounter a stream of thoughts that flow through from the lower mind (*manas*). It is for this reason that in yoga meditation, the student is given a mantra, a special sound, on which you focus your attention. The mantra constantly leads you towards objectivity and non-attachment. As the stream of thoughts fade into the background, the mantra draws you towards a higher state of consciousness.[4]

A chakra meditation

I love this chakra mediation by Dorothea Hover-Kramer and Karilee Halo Shames, authors of *Energetic Approaches to Emotional Healing*.[5]

1. Make sure you are comfortable. Relax and exhale fully, releasing tension from the body and mind.
2. Allow your awareness to rest at the base of your spine. Sense the flow of the colour red moving from the base of the spine to fill your entire body with a sense of aliveness and vitality.
3. Focus your inner awareness with the breath and allow your attention

to move to the lower abdomen. Feel the colour orange filling the area with warmth and let your whole body sense the permission to feel all of the emotions. Note the ones that are comfortable and the ones that are not.

4. Let your attention move to the upper abdomen, feel the colour yellow, and give yourself permission to think clearly. Sense your whole being filled with a sense of power to effectively take charge of your life and relationships.

5. Sense your focus at the heart centre. Imagine the colour green, perhaps a deep forest green, filling your whole being with a feeling of unconditional acceptance. Extend your caring to your loved ones and allow yourself to receive their caring in the heart area.

6. Move awareness to the throat area with the colour of sky blue or turquoise. Feel your creativity expand, notice the things you have made to give you joy and commit to a specific creative activity for the next week.

7. Let your consciousness shift to the brow centre. Connect with your compassion and intuition. Let the colour of indigo blue support your ability to see and hear.

8. Sense the area above your crown and the connection with all that is, the divine plan of your life. The colours purple and lighter shades of lavender, white and silver enhance the expanding consciousness of your being, whole and alive.

9. Gently bring your awareness to your feet and hands, feeling the breath as the connecting link between all the steps. Set your focus and intent for your next task, feeling the support of a friendly universe.

Yoga

Sturgess explains that Hatha yoga is considered foundation to the practice of Kundalini yoga, Kriya yoga and Raja yoga. He explains that Hatha yoga purifies, tunes and stimulates the chakras in preparation for the higher Kriya yoga meditation practices. Hatha yoga balances the sympathetic and parasympathetic nervous systems and tonifies the body organs. Sturgess questions the so-called 'New Age' philosophies that have changed and adapted the meaning and purpose of the chakras to suit their own needs.[6]

He states that the purpose of authentic yoga is:

> ... to awaken kundalini and open the chakras to unfold the powers of the subtle and causal bodies to connect us with our true essential

> *nature and to unite the individual consciousness with Cosmic consciousness.*[6]

He claims that the chakras do not become active and opened during ordinary consciousness. The chakras only become active when the mind and *prana* have entered into *sushumna* through yoga practice which involves meditation.[6]

If you wish to delve into Yogic philosophy and gain a deeper insight into the role of yoga techniques to balance the chakras, I highly recommend Stephen Sturgess's book, *The Book of Chakras & Subtle Bodies*.

It is not in the scope of this book or my level of expertise to delve into the intricate nature of the yoga practices and the influence they have on chakras. There are many books on chakras and yoga that are able to provide detailed explanation of the yoga poses and influences that they have on the chakras. I believe that your yoga journey must begin by finding the right yoga teacher/s for you.

Anodea Judith's Chakra Yoga book provides us with a comprehensive exploration and explanation of each yoga pose and the effects that it has on each chakra. For those beginning their journey into chakras and yoga, you will find the detailed photos of each yoga pose most useful.[7]

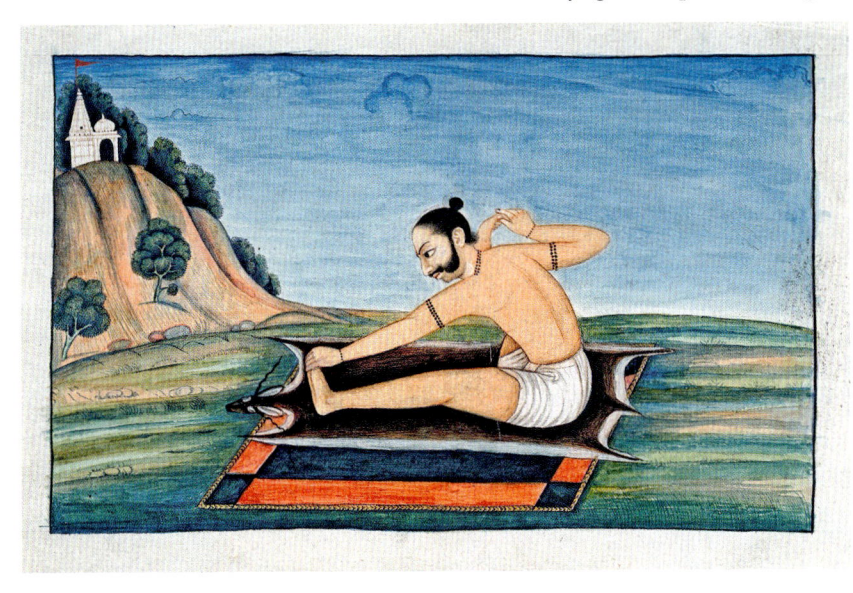

Little states that the greatest danger in yoga is the risk that it becomes mechanical and routine. He asks us to think of yoga as a path leading to mastery, an invitation to evoke mystery and activate a powerful, subtle energy. His book *Yoga of the Subtle Body — A Guide to the Physical and Energetic Anatomy of Yoga* provides us with an insightful understanding of the intricate relation between the physical body, the chakras and the practice of yoga.[8]

Which chakras should I balance?

More than likely several chakras will be out of balance. This leads to the question — which chakra should I balance first?

I like Judith's advice — when in doubt, work from the ground up.[1]

Many consider it best to open the chakras from the lower chakras up. Start with the root chakra and then proceed to the sacral chakra, solar plexus, heart, throat, third eye and finally the crown chakra. The root chakra is the foundation. When the root chakra is open, you're able to feel secure and welcome. Having opened this chakra, you will feel you have territory.

Only when you feel secure and welcome are you able to express feelings and sexuality appropriately, the domain of the sacral chakra. This is generally contact with one person at a time. Feelings get you an idea of what you want and when you are aware of that, you can open the solar plexus chakra to assert your wants, to decide upon them. This assertion is something that's done between people, in groups, in social situations.

Being able to deal with social situations, you can form affectionate relationships, which is the domain of the heart chakra. This tames the aggression of the solar plexus chakra. When relationships are formed, you are able to express yourself by the throat chakra. This is also the basis of thinking, which makes insight possible by opening the third eye chakra. When all these chakras are open, you are ready for the crown chakra, to develop wisdom, self-awareness and awareness of the whole.

What period of time you spend on each chakra is something you will have to find out for yourself. Be aware of how you feel and what you do and don't do. Notice if you really do need to open certain chakras and if you can sustain higher ones.

It is probably a process of years, if not decades, although you will be enjoying benefits immediately. It will not always be necessary to rigidly follow the order of the chakras, as long as you are aware of what is happening with you.

It is mostly a matter of being aware of what your state is. To develop this awareness, it is a good idea to do meditation. That also helps to balance the chakras, and is particularly helpful when you have overactive chakras.

23. How to Use Essential Oils to Balance the Chakras

Making the spiritual connection

Worwood states that when using essential oils for subtle healing or spiritual enhancement, make sure you create a special time to link with the divine energy of the universe. She explains what you do in terms of ceremony or ritual, is not as important as approaching it with the right intention. She says you must empty your mind of negativity, focus on the positive and recognise the divinity in the energy that pervades all living things.[9]

Keim Loughran and Bull also state the importance of intention and visualisation when using essential oils at a subtle level.[10]

Creating a sacred space

Keim Loughran and Bull describe a 'sacred space' referring to a time and/or place that is designated for and devoted to experiencing a connection to the divine. Sacred space is enhanced by the addition of affirmations, candles, colours, crystals, essential oils, flower essences, incense, prayers, chanting, sounds and visualisations. Many spiritual traditions remind us that all space and all time is sacred. Creating a sacred space simply helps us to become aware of the spiritual dimension within and around us.[11]

People need to create their sacred space in order to have a special place to focus on the spiritual. It is a place where you may decide to go back to time and time again. We may go there to seek peace, focus our minds, clear our thoughts or just be. It should be the place where we can open our hearts to the love of the universe that waits to receive us. It is important to create a peaceful, restful place where the mind, body and soul can concentrate on themselves and be whole.

There are several ways to enhance sacred space. The techniques that amplify and focus intention can be incorporated in any of the steps involved in creating sacred space: clearing the area, protecting the area and setting intention.[11]

Clearing the area

Keim Loughran and Bull describe a three-step process when clearing an area to create a sacred space:[11]

1. Initiate a shift in your consciousness, focusing body, mind and spirit on the divine.
2. Release all other thoughts and intentions.
3. Dedicate the area to the divine. This can include specific helpful techniques such as taking a deep breath and releasing it, with the purpose of making a transition into sacred awareness, or using essential oils in a diffuser or mist to cleanse the area and support a sense of spirituality.

Essential oils to clear a space may include Atlas cedarwood, blue mallee eucalyptus, cypress, black spruce, fragonia, frankincense, hinoki wood, juniper berry, lemon, lavender, pine, rosemary, sandalwood or tea tree.

Protecting the area

Protecting the area means creating a safe, comfortable, secure space in which you can give or receive vibrational healing. A contained space has an energetic membrane in which all that supports the sacredness of the space can enter, and all that would interfere is kept out. This is accomplished by physical actions such as turning off the phone, placing a 'do not disturb' sign, or drawing a boundary such as a circle or square, as well as energetically visualising a wall of white light around the area.[11]

Essential oils that are said to protect sacred space include black spruce, frankincense, pine, rosemary and vetiver. They can be diffused or misted in the space.

Intention and purpose

The definitive foundation of subtle energy therapy is the intention to help another person. Thinking about something is the first step in its manifestation, and there is nothing that has ever been accomplished that was not, at first, a thought. For this reason, your intention in giving a subtle energy session needs to reflect the purpose of the session in a positive and restorative way. The most important elements of handling essential oils is encapsulated in three words — thought, intent and purpose. Thought motivates the action of picking up a particular essential oil. Intent is about having positive intentions, and the objective. What you are trying to achieve is the purpose.[11]

Affirmations

Affirmations are positive statements that focus consciousness and intent. They should be said with sincerity, one or several times, silently or out loud. Use affirmations to change old belief systems. Keim Loughran and Bull suggest the following advice when saying affirmations:[11]

- Keep the affirmation brief and clear.
- Work on one thing at a time.
- Avoid the word 'try'.
- Speak in the present tense such as 'I am healing now' or 'Each day …', instead of 'I will be getting healthier' or 'I am going to be healthier'.
- Keep the language positive such as 'I feel strong and confident', instead of 'I don't feel uncomfortable.'
- Make affirmations believable such as 'I am uniquely beautiful', instead of 'I am the most beautiful person in the world'.

Basic techniques for using essential oils

Davis states that you can use essential oils for their subtle effects in any way you like. Well almost! You do not need to be tied to any conventional method of application. What matters is the intent. Each time you use an essential oil for subtle or spiritual purposes, begin with a clear idea of what you aim to achieve and how you want the oil to help you.[12]

In subtle aromatherapy, the therapist may not be required to use massage — in some instances there may not even be a need for a therapist, as in the use of essential oils in diffusers as a meditation aid or in ritual bathing.[12]

Davis provides us with the following guidelines:[12]

- Work safely — observe all the safety rules that apply to the normal uses of essential oils.
- Use very little oil — when using essential oils for their subtle properties, less is better.
- Use very good quality oils.
- Work ethically.

Massage

Massage is fundamental to the practice of aromatherapy. Davis states that if you wish to evoke a subtle response, you should only use 1% or less of essential oil to a carrier oil. This is the equivalent of 2 drops to every 10ml of carrier oil.[12]

Davis recommends that you omit any deep strokes and concentrate on light effleurage and long sweeping strokes. Let your hands come to rest on any area of the body that feels as if it needs special healing. You should also pay particular attention to extremities: hands, feet and head, drawing off any negative energy present. Don't forget to give your hands a brisk shake each time you do so.[12]

At the end of the massage, include some strokes that do not touch the surface of the body — hold your hands just above your client's body and move them slowly, sensing any areas that are cold, hot, blocked or troubled in any way. Always finish with some long, sweeping strokes from below the feet to above the head, just above the body. End by holding your client's feet for a minute or more, to ground his or her energy and allow a gentle return to the everyday reality.[12]

Ritual baths

Davis states that you should create the appropriate ambiance for your bath. Choose a quiet time, light a candle, keep the lights dim and add three to five drops of the appropriate chakra blend to a tablespoon of dispersing bath oil, then add this to the batch, ensuring it is mixed in well.[12]

Enter the bath and lie still for 15 to 20 minutes. The time should not be spent for washing, if you need to clean, do this before you get into your bath. Ritual baths can be used to 'clear' after a bad experience, or to clear the aura after being in a crowded place, where you may be in proximity to energies you would not welcome into your space.[12]

Once again, when it comes to subtle aromatherapy less is best. Davis states that while preparing a bath to help ease muscular aches it would be appropriate to use 6 to 8 drops of essential oil to a bath; however, to prepare a ritual bath you should only use 3 drops or less.[12]

Anointing

This means placing a drop of the essential oil blend you have chosen directly on the body.[11] However, if you are concerned about sensitivity, as I am, please dilute the essential oil blend in a carrier oil such as jojoba (5 drops to 10 ml of carrier oil). Add to a rollerball bottle, as this will make it easy to apply the oil.

Anointing is a very ancient practice, commonly used in many religions and spiritual traditions. Usually the oils are applied to areas of the body that hold some symbolic significance, such as the head, chest, hands or feet and to the areas that correspond to the chakras.[11]

Inhalation

Davis states that inhalation and using essential oils to scent a room or space is the most suitable way to use essential oils in subtle aromatherapy as it only involves the aroma of the plant, which represents its energy.[12]

Aroma mists

An aroma mist can be made by adding essential oils to an essential oil solubiliser in a bottle and then adding water to this mixture before shaking well. This can then be used as a body mist or a room spray. Avoid spraying directly into the face or the eyes. Aroma mists are usually made with an essential oil dilution of between 1 to 2%. Aroma mists can be very effective whenever we do not have access to an essential oil diffuser.

Direct inhalation

Simply inhaling the chakra blend from the bottle is one of the most effective ways of changing our state of awareness. Sniffing the oil direct from the bottle can be overpowering, so you may just add a drop to a tissue or handkerchief. Inhaling is the best way to assist meditation, visualisation and strengthening affirmations. Inhale the blend before the visualisation, meditation or affirmation and inhale deeply again at the end to anchor the experience.

Vapourisation or diffusion

Davis states that diffusing essential oils is similar to the traditional use of incense. Depending on the essential oils diffused, you will create a sacred healing space more conducive to producing feelings of tranquillity and assisting meditation.[12]

Always follow the instructions provided by the manufacturer of the oil burner or the diffuser before using. The ultrasonic diffuser does not involve heat. This does not damage the essential oil molecules.

Crystals and gemstones

Davis states that crystals will enhance the action of the essential oils that you are using. The quartz crystals and gemstones can be used for the purpose of healing, energising and gaining access to higher dimensions of consciousness.[12]

Coloured crystals and gemstones are attuned to a narrower range of vibrations that corresponds to their colour. They can be used to influence chakra energy and are selected according to their colour correspondence with the chakra. Clear quartz crystal can be used with any chakra blend and can resonate with any of the chakras.[8]

You may simply carry the gemstone or crystal with you or the appropriate crystal can be placed around the chakra as a way of balancing the chakra. Davis states that crystals will enhance essential oils by amplifying the aroma. She suggests that just one drop of an essential oil on a crystal will perfume the entire room.[12]

Work safely

Please ensure you observe and know the safety issues associated with the use of the essential oils. While the majority of essential oils can be safe to use, there are a few essential oils which can be hazardous and contraindicated for a range of conditions.

This includes pregnancy, babies and children, people with epilepsy, people with high blood pressure and people with sensitive skin. I agree with Davis who states that it is important to become familiar with the physical properties of essential oils before you use them for subtle purposes. For example, Davis states that while rosemary is a psychic protector, it is a strong stimulant and should not be used in the evening as it may lead to disturbed sleep.[12]

To understand and learn more about the physical properties and safety of essential oils, I refer you to my books, *The Complete Guide to Aromatherapy* and *Aromatree*.

Work ethically

Davis advises us to not attempt subtle aromatherapy techniques just for fun or out of curiosity. You should only embark on this work if you have a genuine desire for healing, insight, personal or spiritual growth.[12]

You should also never make a claim to heal an illness through subtle aromatherapy. As Davis explains, physical healing may indeed take place as a result of subtle therapies, but it should not be the role or principle aim of the subtle treatment.[12]

24. Afterword

As VanSteenhuyse states, fully comprehending the complex philosophy underlying chakras is not something that can be achieved in one book. It requires long-term study, practice and dedication.[13]

Cohen refers to chakras as databases that hold information about our life experiences. He explains that life energy flows up and down the chakras; however, painful life experiences can block the chakras, creating limitations and the development of dysfunctional beliefs and attitudes about oneself and the world. He suggests that the chakra system can provide a valuable map of the human energy system, which can then be used as a catalyst for healing and growth.[14]

Prendergast suggests that the chakras offer an elegant body-based system for understanding a vast array of human experiences. He believes that understanding the significance of the chakras should encourage therapists to more deeply attend to and value their own body sensations, knowing that they may be subtly resonating with their clients' experience. He states that conscious access to these subtle energy centres can help people to foster a trust in their deeper nature as spiritual beings. Chakras can serve as a bridge between ordinary thoughts, feelings and sensations and spiritual intuition and insights.[15]

Judith also describes the chakra system as a map. She explains that she cannot tell us where to go. Using our knowledge of the chakras, she suggests that we should trust the divine intelligence that is embedded within us. The chakra system shows us how we can reconnect ourselves to the world. She suggests that it leads us to divine realisation while reclaiming our rights to pleasure, power, creativity and love.[7]

I hope that this book will take you on a wonderful journey exploring how you can use essential oils with chakras as a powerful catalyst for restoring the long-lost connection between body, mind and spirit, to promote healing and nurturing and support personal growth.

May this book inspire you to use essential oils with love and wisdom.

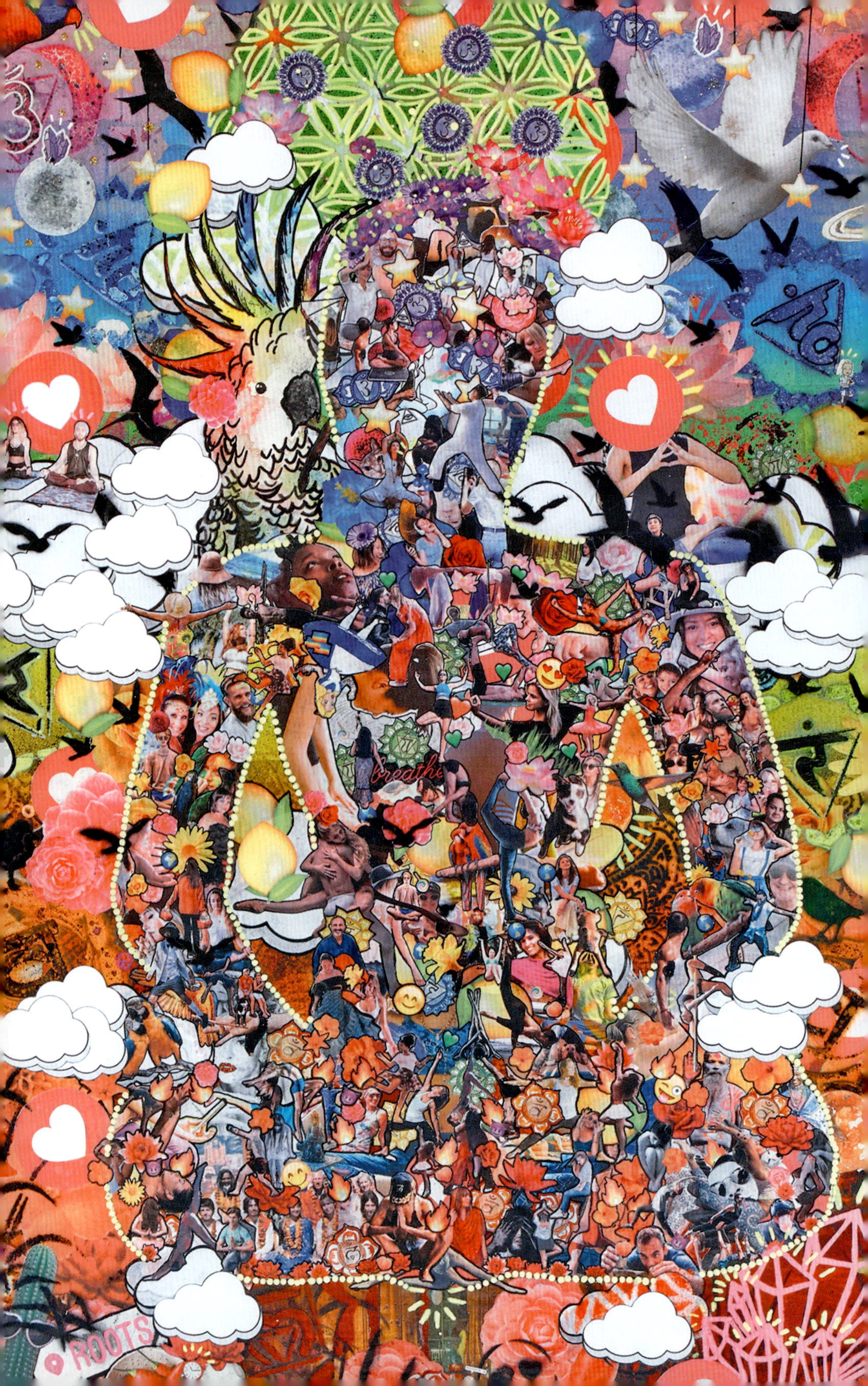
breathe
ROOTS

Part [5]
Resources

Glossary

Potions to keep your chakras balanced

Books by Sal

Stay inspired

Glossary

Ajna
The third eye chakra, located at the eyebrow centre. Also called the sixth chakra.

Akasha
Space, ether element, infinite void.

Anahata
The fourth or heart chakra.

Asana
Seat, posture; pose for meditation.

Astral body
A subtle body, composed of subtle energy. Sometimes referred to as the aura.

Atman
The inner most true self. The spirit or soul.

Bhakti yoga
A spiritual path within Hinduism. Bhakti yoga consists of concentrating one's mind, emotions and senses on the divine.

Bindu
The point at which creation begins; the point around which the mandala is created, representing the universe.

Bija
Seed, source.

Buddhi
Intellect or discernment. Buddhi is one of the four aspects of consciousness.

Chitta
One of the four aspects of consciousness, the mind.

Dhyana
The seventh limb, or requirement, to attain full self-realisation as outlined in the yoga sutras.

Gunas
One of the three qualities of prakriti, or nature, which are rajas, tamas and sattva.

Hatha yoga
A system of purifying techniques and yoga postures to control the body and mind through the control of prana. Sturgess explains that Hatha yoga is a preparation for Raja yoga, the path of meditation.

Ida
One of the three major nadis, which runs on the left side of the spine, from the Muladhara chakra to the Ajna chakra.

Indriyas
Sense organs and work organs.

Jnana yoga
One of the spiritual paths in Hinduism that emphasises the path of knowledge, also referred to as the path of self-realisation.

Kosha
The sheath that encloses pure consciousness of spirit in its material manifestations.

Kriya yoga
An advanced meditation technique that leads to self-actualisation.

Manas
One of the aspects of consciousness. A person's perception of the world is meditated through manas.

Manipura
The third chakra, known as the solar plexus chakra.

Mantra
Sound that enables concentration, free from worldly thoughts.

Mudra
A specific kind of muscular practice to aid meditation.

Muladhara
The first chakra, known as the base chakra. Also called the root chakra.

Nadis
Carriers of prana in the body.

Nirvanic body
One of the subtle bodies, referred to as the bodiless body.

Nosodes
Homoeopathic remedies used as an alternative to vaccines. They are made by taking the bodily matter, such as blood, pus, saliva, tissue or excrement, from a person infected with the illness.

Padma
Sanskrit word for lotus.

Pingala
One of the three major nadis, which runs on the right side of the spine, emerging opposite ida, from the right side of the Muladhara chakra and intersecting each chakra until it reaches the right side of the Ajna chakra.

Prakriti
The ultimate primal matter 'below' human consciousness or the ultimate cosmic energy.

Prana
The cosmic vibratory life force that is omnipresent and sustains the universe.

Pranayama
The practice of breath control, the conscious awareness of breath.

Qi
A term used in traditional Chinese medicine, referring to the life force.

Rajas
One of the three gunas or 'modes of existence', which is associated with the innate tendency or quality that drives motion, energy and activity.

Raja yoga
Commonly known as ashtanga yoga, or the 'eightfold path' that leads to spiritual liberation. The royal path of yoga, that leads to a state of peace and contentment that comes from yoga practice and meditation.

Sahasrara
The seventh chakra, known as the crown chakra.

Samadhi
A state of meditative consciousness.

Samsara
A Sanskrit word that means 'wandering' or 'world' with the connotation of cyclic change. It also refers to the concept of rebirth and the cyclic nature of life.

Sattva
One of the three gunas or 'modes of existence', which is associated with the qualities of balance, harmony, goodness and purity.

Shakti
The vital power and energy of consciousness. The active creative female principle of the universe.

Shiva
One of the main deities of Hinduism. He is one of the supreme beings within Shaivism, one of the major traditions within contemporary Hinduism.

Shoonya
A Sanskrit word that means emptiness or void.

Sushumna
The main subtle channel running through the spine, along which six chakras are located. When the kundalini sakti is awakened, it rises through the sushumna.

Svadhisthana
The second chakra, known as the sacral chakra.

Tamas
One of the three gunas, which is associated with the qualities of inertia, dullness or lethargy.

Tantra
An esoteric tradition of Hinduism and Buddhism, dating from the seventh century or earlier.

Tattvas
An element or aspect of reality.

TCM
Traditional Chinese medicine

Upanisads
From part of the tradition of the Vedic literature. They were composed from around 700 BCE.

Vedanta
One of the most prominent of the six schools in Hindu philosophy.

Vishnu
The all-pervading one, name of one of the gods of the Hindu trinity. He is the preserver and descends to the earth in the form of a divine incarnation when the world especially needs his grace.

Vishuddha
The sixth chakra, known as the throat chakra.

Yantra
Symbol used as a focal point for concentration and meditation.

A note on Sanskrit terminology

As this book is about the Western Chakra System, I have decided to use the simplified anglicised Sanskrit terms. The Sanskrit terms are shown in italics without the appropriate diacritical marks. I do apologise for this omission.

Names assigned to chakras

Chakra number	Sanskrit name	English name
First	*Muladhara*	Base/Root
Second	*Svadhisthana*	Sacral
Third	*Manipura*	Solar plexus
Fourth	*Anahata*	Heart
Fifth	*Vishuddha*	Throat
Sixth	*Ajna*	Third-eye/Brow
Seventh	*Sahasrara*	Crown

Potions to keep your chakras balanced

	Location	Purpose	Aroma	Perfect Potion essential oil blends
Base	base of spine	Survival, courage, vitality, support, stability, good physical health, connection to nature	Earthy, woody and warm	**Balance** — Feel grounded and connected to nature with: black pepper, vetiver, sweet orange, patchouli, lavender, Atlas cedarwood
Sacral	lower abdomen	Confidence, freedom, sensuality, sexuality, passion, pleasure, emotional intelligence, charisma	Rich floral, sweet citrus and warm spicy	**Allure** — Channel your creativity and passion with: jasmine absolute, ylang ylang, cardamom, patchouli, mandarin, sandalwood
Solar plexus	solar plexus	Self-esteem, ego, optimism, self-control, individuality, personal power and responsibility	Fruity and spicy	**Harmony** — Strengthen self-confidence with: aniseed, juniper berry, lemon, Roman chamomile, vetiver, frankincense
Heart	centre of chest	Unconditional love, forgiveness, compassion, harmony, peace, empathy	Delicate floral and light citrus	**Compassion** — Open your heart to unconditional love with: bergamot, rose absolute, ylang ylang, lavender, may chang, neroli
Throat	throat	Self-expression, communication, organisation, creative expression, following one's dreams	Herbaceous and woody	**Expressive** — Speak your truth with: German chamomile, basil, sandalwood, sweet orange
Third eye	forehead	Insight, wisdom, intuition, learning from experiences, mental clarity, memory	Herbaceous	**Insight** — Trust your intuition with: clary sage, fragonia, lavender, rosemary, sage, bergamot
Crown	top of head	Wisdom, spiritual awareness, enlightenment, open-mindedness, consciousness	Woody, resinous and light citrus	**Cosmic** — Make space for wisdom with: frankincense, lavender, cold-pressed lime, sandalwood

Essential oils are available individually or as a pack.

The Chakra Balancing range is ideal to use before meditation, while practising yoga or when you feel the need to rebalance your seven energy centres. Further balance your chakra energies by serving the three pillars of life — rest, nourishment and energy. The Chakra Balancing range contains pure essential oils of:

bergamot, Atlas cedarwood, cypress, everlasting, frankincense, geranium, ginger, jasmine, juniper berry, lavender, lemon, cold-pressed lime, mandarin, may chang, neroli, sweet orange, patchouli, pink lotus absolute, rosemary, rose absolute, rose otto, clary sage, sage, Australian sandalwood, vetiver, ylang ylang

1. **Chakra essential oil kit**
   This beautiful boxed set contains seven pure essential oil blends and a booklet to help guide you to balance your chakras.

2. **Chakra balancing essential oil blend**
   A unique blend of 26 essential oils that will help to rebalance and harmonise your chakra energy centres.

3. **Chakra balancing balm**
   Massage into your temples, pulse points, over your chakras or use as a solid perfume.

4. **Chakra balancing mist**
   Spray your body from head to toe, use as a room spray, or on your yoga mat for a ceremonial yoga session.

5. **Chakra balancing massage oil**
   Pour a small amount into your hand and massage into any areas of tension.

6. **Chakra balancing gift pack**
   Give the gift of balance with our ultimate chakra gift pack including Chakra Balancing Mist, Chakra Balancing Balm and Chakra Massage Oil.

7. **Chakra balancing bath soak**
   Enjoy soaking in this fragrant balancing bath of pure essential oils and rose petals.

8. **Chakra balancing herbal tea**
   Rebalance and harmonise your chakra energy centres with this unique blend of 18 organically grown and wild harvested herbs, seeds, roots and flowers.

available at www.perfectpotion.com.au

Green Goddess Blend

In 2011, to celebrate Perfect Potion's 20th anniversary, we decided to do the impossible — to create the 'perfect' Perfect Potion signature scent. The thought of creating a blend that represents the quintessence of Perfect Potion was so overwhelming that I asked all the Perfect Potion team to help. I ran a competition to see who could come up with the 'perfect' blend. I loved all the blends so much I decided to combine them all together. The result was magic — a unique synergy of 23 essential oils that embodies the passion of the Perfect Potion team and epitomises the spirit of all green goddesses. It is not surprising that this blend is able to harmonise all the chakras.

Atlas cedarwood — base chakra, solar plexus chakra
Australian sandalwood — all chakras
Bergamot — heart chakra
Cinnamon bark — solar pelxus chakra
Clove bud — solar plexus chakra
Fragonia — third eye chakra
Frankincense — all chakras
Geranium — solar plexus chakra, throat chakra
Ginger — solar pelxus chakra
Jasmine absolute — sacral chakra
Lavender — heart chakra
Lemon-scented iron bark — solar plexus chakra
Mandarin — sacral chakra
Melissa — heart chakra
Neroli — heart chakra, crown chakra
Patchouli — base chakra, sacral chakra
Pink lotus absolute — crown chakra
Roman chamomile — throat chakra, third eye chakra
Rose absolute — sacral chakra, heart chakra
Rose otto — heart chakra, crown chakra
Sweet orange — sacral chakra
Vetiver — base chakra
Ylang ylang — sacral chakra

available at www.perfectpotion.com.au

Books by Sal

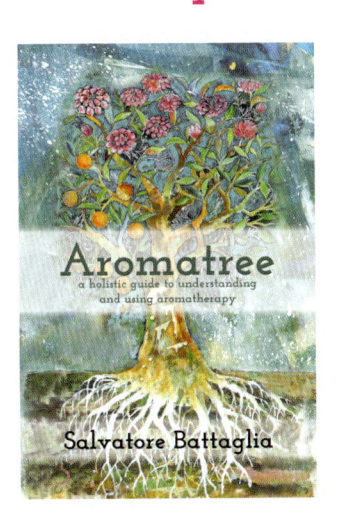

Aromatree
a holistic guide to understanding and using aromatherapy

The *Aromatree* book has been 30 years in the making. It started out as an idea to make learning aromatherapy enjoyable and informative. Over the years it has evolved to reflect the complexity and diversity of aromatherapy. It provides us with a very comprehensive and up-to-date knowledge and understanding of aromatherapy.

As an educator, I would often notice how frustrated people would become when they had to learn the individual properties and actions of essential oils. The Aromatree identifies the relationships that exist between the individual oils and the different parts of the Aromatree — the roots and rhizomes, resins, woods, seeds, fruits, leaves and flowers.

We examine the relationship and pattern between the botany of the plant, traditional folklore, symbolism, mythology of plants, aroma, chemistry, pharmacology, essential oil safety, our psyche, our personality, the chakras, the energetics according to traditional Chinese medicine and Ayurveda, and blending tips.

It embraces all aspects of aromatherapy. Whether you are just starting out or a professional aromatherapist, you will gain an incredible insight into using essential oils.

www.salvatorebattaglia.com.au

The Complete Guide to Aromatherapy
Third Edition

The Complete Guide to Aromatherapy is internationally acclaimed as the most comprehensive textbook on aromatherapy.

VOL I – Foundations & Materia Medica

Volume I includes the most comprehensive and detailed evidence-based monographs on over 110 essential oils. Each essential oil monograph includes a detailed description of the botany and origins, organoleptic profile, chemical composition, history and traditional uses, a comprehensive review of pharmacological clinical studies, actions and indications, blending tips, dosage and administration, safety, precautions and contraindications and more. Other topics covered in Volume I include:
- the role of aromatherapy in promoting health and wellbeing
- detailed history of aromatherapy
- the botanical origins of essential oils
- the methods of essential oil extraction
- quality of essential oils for aromatherapy use
- guidelines for the safe practice of aromatherapy
- how to use essential oils in aromatherapy.

VOL II – Science & Therapeutics

Coming 2021

Volume II will provide you with the knowledge required to understand how aromatherapy works and provide you with the knowledge and skills required for the practice of aromatherapy. This will be achieved by providing you with the:
- latest research into the chemistry, pharmacokinetics and pharmacology of essential oils
- latest research and clinical trials in aromatherapy
- guidelines for establishing an optimal healing environment and encounter
- skills for blending essential oils
- examination of the role of aromatherapy within a professional health care environment
- most up-to-date, clear and detailed guide to the treatment of a wide range of conditions.

VOL III – Psyche & Subtle

Coming October 2020

Volume III will provide you with a comprehensive understanding of the influence that aromatherapy has on our psyche and spiritual wellbeing. This will be achieved by:
- integrating the principles of traditional Chinese medicine (TCM) with your aromatherapy knowledge and skills
- examining the relationship between spirituality and scent
- examining the role of spirituality in promoting health and wellbeing
- examining the subtle effects of essential oils
- examining the relationship between essential oils and personality
- reviewing the mechanisms of olfaction.

Stay inspired

I hope that *Aromatherapy and Chakras — balancing your body's energy centres for optimal health and wellbeing* has inspired you to examine ways in which you can incorporate essential oils into your daily rituals to reconnect you with your chakra energy centres. The following list of books will help you on your journey. Please enjoy.

Bach E. *Heal thyself — An explanation of the real cause and cure of disease.* CW Daniel Company, Saffron Walden, 1931.

Battaglia S. *The complete guide to aromatherapy, Vol I — Foundations & materia medica.* 3rd edn. Black Pepper Creative, Brisbane, 2018.

Battaglia S. *Aromatree — A holistic guide to understanding and using aromatherapy.* Black Pepper Creative, Brisbane, 2019.

Brennan BA. *Hands of light — A guide to healing through the human energy field.* Bantam Books, New York, 1988.

Davis P. *Subtle aromatherapy.* CW Daniel Company, Saffron Walden, 1991.

Fischer-Rizzi S. *Complete aromatherapy handbook.* Sterling Publishing, New York, 1990.

Gerber R. *Vibrational medicine.* 3rd edn. Bear & Company, Rochester, 2001.

Johari H. *Chakras — Energy centers of transformation.* Destiny Books, Rochester, 2000.

Judith A. *Eastern body, Western mind — Psychology and the chakra system as a path to the self.* Celestial Arts, Berkeley, 2004.

Keim Loughran J, Bull R. *Aromatherapy anointing oils.* Frog, Berkeley, 2001.

Keim Loughran J, Bull R. *Aromatherapy and subtle energy techniques.* Frog, Berkeley, 2000.

King D. *Heal yourself — Heal the world.* Atria Paperback, New York, 2017.

Leadbeater CW. *The chakras.* 2nd edn. Quest Books, Wheaton, 2013.

Leland K. *Rainbow body — A history of the Western chakra system from Blavatsky to Brennan.* Ibis Press, Lake Worth, 2016.

Myss C. *Anatomy of the spirit — The seven stages of power and healing.* Bantam Books, Sydney, 1996.

Nardi D. *Jung on yoga — Insights and activities to awaken with the chakras.* Radiance House, Los Angeles, 2017.

Oschman JL. *Energy medicine — The scientific basis.* 2nd edn. Elsevier, Edinburgh, 2016.

Rama S, Ballentine R, Ajaya S. *Yoga & psychotherapy — The evolution of consciousness.* Himalayan Institute, Honesdale, 2014.

Sturgess S. *The book of chakras & subtle bodies.* Watkins Publishing, London, 2014.

Tubali S. *The seven chakra personality types.* Conari Press, Newburyport, 2018.

References

Introduction

1. Leland K. *Rainbow body — A history of the Western chakra system from Blavatsky to Brennan*. Ibis Press, Lake Worth, 2016.
2. Samuel G, Johnson J. eds. *Religion and the subtle body in Asia and the West*. Routledge, Abingdon, 2013.
3. Schnaubelt K. *Medical aromatherapy*. Frog, Berkeley, 1999.
4. Kaptchuk TJ. *The web that has no weaver — Understanding Chinese medicine*. 2nd edn. McGraw-Hill, New York, 2000.
5. Hoffmann D. *Medical herbalism — The science and practice of herbal medicine*. Healing Arts Press, Rochester, 2003.
6. Bach E. *Heal thyself — An explanation of the real cause and cure of disease*. CW Daniel Company, Saffron Walden, 1931.
7. Fischer-Rizzi S. *Complete aromatherapy handbook*. Sterling Publishing, New York, 1990.
8. Burr C. *The emperor of scent*. Random House, New York, 2002.
9. Smith CW. *Energy medicine united.* Complementary Therapies in Nursing & Midwifery, 2003; 9(4): 169-175.
10. Korotkov KG. *Human energy field — Study with GDV bioelectrography*. SPIFMO, St Petersburg, 2000.
11. Wisneski LA, Anderson L. *The scientific basis of integrative medicine*. 2nd edn. CRC Press, Boca Raton, 2009.
12. Bones K, Mills S. *Principles and practice of phytotherapy*. 2nd edn, Elsevier, Edinburgh, 2013.

Part [1] Energy, Subtle Bodies and Subtle Therapies

1. Gerber R. *Vibrational medicine*. 3rd edn. Bear & Company, Rochester, 2001.
2. Kotsirilos V et al. *A guide to evidence-based integrative and complementary medicine*. Churchill Livingstone, Sydney, 2011.
3. Chaoul A. *Opening channels, healing breath — Research on ancient Tibetan yogic practices for people with cancer.* In Samuel G, Johnson J. eds. *Religion and the subtle body in Asia and the West.* Routledge, Abingdon, 2013: 100-114.
4. Binder S. *Energy medicine going mainstream.* Retrieved 26 Sept 2018 from

https://www.faim.org/energy-medicine-going-mainstream.

5   Oschman JL. *Energy medicine — The scientific basis.* 2nd edn. Elsevier, Edinburgh, 2016.

6   Rubik B et al. *Biofield science and healing: History, terminology, and concepts.* Global Advances in Health and Medicine, 2015; 4(suppl): 8-14. doi: 10.7453/gahmj.2015.038.suppl.

7   Kafatos MC et al. *Biofield science: Current physics perspectives.* Global Advances in Health and Medicine, 2015; 4(suppl): 25-34. doi: 10.7453/gahmj.2015.011.suppl.

8   Jain S et al. *Biofield science and healing: An emerging frontier in medicine.* Global Advances in Health and Medicine, 2015; 4(suppl): 5-7. doi: 10.7453/gahmj.2015.106.suppl.

9   Srinivasan TM. *Energy medicine.* International Journal of Yoga, 2010; 3(1): 1. doi: 10.4103/0973-6131.66770

10 Warber SL et al. *A consideration of the perspectives of healing practitioners on research into energy healing.* Global Advances in Health and Medicine, 2015; 4(suppl); 72-78. doi: 10.7453/gahmj.2015.014.suppl

11 Hover-Kramer D, Halo Shames K. *Energetic approaches to emotional healing.* Delmar Publishing, Albany, 1997.

12 Gerber R. *Vibrational medicine for the 21st century.* Piatkus, London, 2000.

13 Wright S, Sayre-Adams J. *Sacred space.* Churchill Livingstone, Edinburgh, 2000.

14 Samuel G, Johnston J. *Religion and the subtle body in Asia and the West.* Routledge, Abingdon, 2013.

15 Samuel G. *The subtle body in India and beyond.* In Samuel G, Johnston J. eds. *Religion and the subtle body in Asia and the West.* Routledge, Abingdon, 2013: 33-47.

16 Woodroffe J. *The serpent power — The secrets of tantric and shaktic yoga.* 4th edn. Ganesh, Madras, 1950.

17 Marques A. *The human aura — A study.* Office of Mercury, San Francisco, 1896.

18 Leland K. *The multidimensional human.* Spiritual Orienteering Press, Boston, 2010.

19 Sturgess S. *The book of chakras & subtle bodies.* Watkins Publishing, London, 2014.

20 Minich D. *The medicine of the future is light: Recent research on what photons can tell us about health and disease.* retrieved 10 Jun 10 2019 from https://www.huffpost.com/entry/the-medicine-of-the-future-is-light-recent-researc h_b_58d93c5ce4b06c3d3d3e701f

21 Van Wijk EP et al. *Anatomic characterization of human ultra-weak photon emission in practitioners of transcendental meditation (TM) and control subjects.* Journal of Alternative and Complementary Medicine, 2006; 12(1): 31-38.

22 Srinivasan TM. *Biophotons as subtle energy carriers.* International Journal of Yoga, 2017; 10(2): 57-58. doi: 10.4103/ijoy.IJOY_18_17.

23   Thaler K et al. *Bach flower remedies for psychological problems and pain: A systematic review*. BMC Complementary and Alternative Medicine, 2009; 9: 16. doi: 10.1186/1472-6882-9-16.
24   Keim Loughran J, Bull R. *Aromatherapy & subtle energy techniques*. Frog, Berkeley, 2000.
25   Cooper AJ. *Colour the cosmic code*. Unicorn 2000/Aura Light, England, 1999.
26   Newton J. *Aromatherapy and colour*. Aromatherapy Today, 2000; 13: 42-45.
27   Leadbeater CW. *Man, visible and invisible*. Quest Books, Wheaton, 2000.
28   Klotsche C. *Color medicine — The secrets of color/vibrational healing*. Light Technology Publishing, Flagstaff, 1992.
29   Carlos KD. *Crystal healing practices in the Western world and beyond*. Honors Undergraduate Thesis. 283, 2018. https://stars.library.ucf.edu/honorstheses/283.
30   Davis P. *Subtle aromatherapy*. CW Daniel Company, Saffron Walden, 1991.
31   Keim Loughran J, Bull R. *Aromatherapy anointing oils*. Frog, Berkeley, 2001.
32   Tisserand R. *The art of aromatherapy*. CW Daniel Company, Saffron Walden, 1977.
33   Price S. *Practical aromatherapy*. Thorsons, London, 1983.
34   Price S, Price L. *Aromatherapy for health professionals*. Churchill Livingstone, Edinburgh, 1995.
35   Rose J. *The aromatherapy book*. Herbal Studies Course, California, 1992.
36   Holmes P. *Energy medicine*. The International Journal of Aromatherapy, 1998/1999; 9(2): 53-56.
37   Worwood VA. *The fragrant heavens*. Transworld Publishers, London, 1999.

Part [2] A Brief Overview of Chakras

1   Leland K. *Rainbow body — A history of the Western chakra system from Blavatsky to Brennan*. Ibis Press, Lake Worth, 2016.
2   Wallis CD. *The real story on the chakras*. Retrieved 6 Jul 2018 from http://hareesh.org/blog/2016/2/5/the-real-story-on-the-chakras.
3   Frawley D. *Opening the chakras: New myths & old truths*. Retrieved 10 Jun 2015 from https://yogainternational.com/article/view/opening-the-chakras-new-myths-old-truths.
4   Wallis CD. *Tantra illuminated — The philosophy, history, and practice of a timeless tradition*. 2nd edn. Mattamayura Press, Petaluma, 2013.
5   Woodroffe J. *The serpent power — The secrets of tantric and shaktic yoga*. 4th edn. Ganesh, Madras, 1950.
6   Satyananda S. *A systematic course in the ancient tantric techniques of yoga and kriya*. Yoga Publications Trust, Munger, 1981.
7   VanSteenhuyse E. *Understanding the subtle body: Examining how chakras are most generally understood, through the lens of tantric/hatha/kundalini yoga, in the modern West*. Retrieved 5 Jun 2019 from https://www.academia.edu/6959581/UNDERSTANDING_THE_SUBTLE_BODY_

Examining_how_Chakras_are_most_generally_understood_through_the_lens_of_Tantric_Hatha_Kundalini_Yoga_in_the_Modern_West.

8. Satyananda S. *Kundalini tantra*. Yoga Publications, Bihar, 1984.
9. Kempton S. *Awakening to Kali — The goddess of radical transformation*. Sounds True, Boulder, 2014.
10. Feuerstein G. *The path of yoga — An essential guide to its principles and practices*. Shambhala, Boston, 2011.
11. Sturgess S. *The book of chakras & subtle bodies*. Watkins Publishing, London, 2014.
12. White DG. *The yoga sutra of Patanjali — A biography*. Princeton University Press, Princeton, 2014.
13. Leadbeater CW. *The chakras*. 2nd edn. Quest Books, Wheaton, 2013.
14. Brennan BA. *Hands of light — A guide to healing through the human energy field*. Bantam Books, New York, 1988.
15. Powell AE. *The etheric double*. The Theosophical Publishing House, London, 1925.
16. Dychtwald K. *Bodymind*. Penguin, New York, 1977.
17. Roney-Dougal SM. *On a possible psychophysiology of the yogic chakra system*. Retrieved 6 Jul 2018 from http://www.psi-researchcentre.co.uk/article_2.html.
18. Wisneski LA, Anderson L. *The scientific basis of integrative health*. 3rd edn. CRC Press, Boca Raton, 2017.
19. Kennedy DO. *Plants and the human brain*. Oxford University Press, New York, 2014.
20. Gerber R. *Vibrational medicine*. 3rd edn. Bear & Company, Rochester, 2001.
21. Maxwell RW. *The physiological foundation of yoga chakra expression*. Zygon, 2009; 44(4): 807-824. doi: 10.1111/j.1467-9744.2009.01035.x.
22. St John G. *The DMT gland: The pineal, the spirit molecule, and popular culture*. International Journal for the Study of New Religions, 2016; 7(2): 153-174. doi: 10.1558/ijsnr.v7i2.31949.
23. Woolfe S. *DMT and the pineal gland: A sceptic's view*. Retrieved 8 Jun 2019 from https://www.samwoolfe.com/2017/09/is-dmt-really-produced-in-pineal-gland.html.
24. Rama S, Ballentine R, Ajaya S. *Yoga & psychotherapy — The evolution of consciousness*. Himalayan Institute, Honesdale, 2014.
25. Drapkin J et al. *Spiritual development through the chakra progression*. Open Theology, 2016; 2(1): 605-620. doi: 10.1515/opth-2016-0048.
26. Myss C. *Anatomy of the spirit — The seven stages of power and healing*. Bantam Books, Sydney, 1996.
27. Judith A. *Eastern body, Western mind — Psychology and the chakra system as a path to the self*. Celestial Arts, Berkeley, 2004.
28. Hover-Kramer D, Halo Shames K. *Energetic approaches to emotional healing*. Delmar Publishers, Albany, 1997.
29. Beshara R. *The chakra system as a bio-socio-psycho-spiritual model of consciousness: Anahata as heart-centered consciousness*. International Journal

of Yoga — Philosophy, Psychology and Parapsychology, 2013; 1(1): 29-33.
30 Best KC. *A chakra system model of lifespan development*. International Journal of Transpersonal Studies 2010; 29(2): 11-27. doi: 10.24972/ijts.2010.29.2.11.
31 Rubik B. *Measurement of the human biofield and other energetic instruments*. Retrieved 9 Aug 2018 from https://www.faim.org/measurement-of-the-human-biofield-and-other-energetic-instruments.
32 Van Wilk R, van Wijk EPA. *An introduction to human biophoton emission*. Research in Complementary and Classical Natural Medicine, 2005; 12: 77-83. doi: 10.1159/000083763.
33 Niggli HJ. *Biophotons: Ultraweak light impulses regulate life processes in aging*. Journal of Gerontology & Geriatric Research, 2014; 3: 143. doi: 10.4172/2167-7182.1000143.
34 Burgos R et al. C*rossing the boundaries of our current healthcare system by integrating ultraweak photon emissions with metabolomics*. Frontiers in Physiology, 2016; 7: 611. doi: 10.3389/fphys.2016.00611.
35 Owens J, van de Castle R. *Gas discharge visualization (GDV) technique*. In Korotkov KG. ed. *Measuring energy fields: Current research*. Backbone Publishing, Fair Lawn, 2004.
36 Kostyuk N et al. *Gas discharge visualisation: An imaging and modeling tool for medical biometrics*. International Journal of Biomedical Imaging, 2011; 196460. doi: 10.1155/2011/196460.

Part [3] The Chakras

1   Brennan BA. *Hands of light — A guide to healing through the human energy field*. Bantam Books, New York, 1988.
2   Judith A. *Eastern body, Western mind — Psychology and the chakra system as a path to the self*. Celestial Arts, Berkeley, 2004.
3   Myss C. *Anatomy of the spirit — The seven stages of power and healing*. Bantam Books, Sydney, 1996.
4   King D. *Heal yourself — Heal the world*. Atria Paperback, New York, 2017.
5   Sturgess S. *The book of chakras & subtle bodies*. Watkins Publishing, London, 2014.
6   Nardi D. *Jung on yoga — Insights and activities to awaken with the chakras*. Radiance House, Los Angeles, 2017.
7   Gerber R. *Vibrational medicine*. 3rd edn. Bear & Company, Rochester, 2001.
8   Satyananda S. *Kundalini tantra*. Yoga Publications, Bihar, 1984.
9   Tubali S. *The seven chakra personality types*. Conari Press, Newburyport, 2018.
10 Johari H. *Chakras — Energy centers of transformation*. Destiny Books, Rochester, 2000.
11 Prendergast J. *The cakras in transpersonal psychotherapy*. International Journal of Yoga Therapy, 2000: 10(1); 45-64.
12 Keim Loughran J, Bull R. *Aromatherapy anointing oils*. Frog, Berkeley, 2001.

13. Keim Loughran J, Bull R. *Aromatherapy and subtle energy techniques*. Frog, Berkeley, 2000.
14. Davis P. *Subtle aromatherapy*. CW Daniel Company, Saffron Walden, 1991.

Part [4] Chakra Healing

1. Judith A. *Eastern body, Western mind — Psychology and the chakra system as a path to the self*. Celestial Arts, Berkeley, 2004.
2. Henderson R. *Emotion and healing in the energy body*. Healing Arts Press, Rochester, 2015.
3. Gerber R. *Vibrational medicine*. 3rd edn. Bear & Company, Rochester, 2001.
4. Rama S, Ballentine R, Ajaya S. *Yoga & psychotherapy — The evolution of consciousness*. Himalayan Institute, Honesdale, 2014.
5. Hover-Kramer D, Halo Shames K. *Energetic approaches to emotional healing*. Delmar Publishers, Albany, 1997.
6. Sturgess S. *The book of chakras & subtle bodies*. Watkins Publishing, London, 2014.
7. Judith A. *Anodea Judith's chakra yoga*. Llewellyn Publications, Woodbury, 2015.
8. Little T. *Yoga of the subtle body — A guide to the physical and energetic anatomy of yoga*. Shambhala, Boulder, 2016.
9. Worwood VA. *The fragrant heavens*. Transworld Publishers, London, 1999.
10. Keim Loughran J, Bull R. *Aromatherapy & subtle energy techniques*. Frog, Berkeley, 2000.
11. Keim Loughran J, Bull R. *Aromatherapy anointing oils*. Frog, Berkeley, 2001.
12. Davis P. *Subtle aromatherapy*. CW Daniel Company, Saffron Walden, 1991.
13. VanSteenhuyse E. *Understanding the subtle body: Examining how chakras are most generally understood, through the lens of tantric/hatha/kundalini yoga, in the modern West*. Downloaded 5 June 2019 from https://www.acedemia.edu/6959581/UNDERSTANDING_THE_SUBTLE_BODY_Examining_how_Chakras_are_most_generally_understood_through_the_lens_of_Tantric_Hatha_Kundalini_Yoga_in_the_Modern_West.
14. Cohen R. *Using the chakras system in psychotherapy*. Portland, 2006.
15. Prendergast J. *The chakras in transpersonal psychotherapy*. International Journal of Yoga Therapy, 2000;10(1):45-64.

Statement to Readers

One of my many references is Satyananda. In 2014–2015, Case Study 21 of the Royal Commission into Institutional Responses to Child Sexual Abuse investigated and reported cases of child sexual abuse by the leaders of Satyananda Yoga that occurred during the 1970s and 1980s at the Satyananda Yoga Ashram, at Mangrove Mountain, New South Wales, Australia.

The Australian Royal Commission into Institutional Responses to Child Sexual Abuse revealed widespread and systemic institutional abuse, not just at the Satyananda Yoga Ashram at Mangrove Mountain, but in many faith-based organisations across the country.

A statement from Yoga Australia [https://www.yogaaustralia.org.au/royal-commission/] strongly condemned the acts of sexual misconduct as presented in testimony in Case Study 21. In a statement, Yoga Australia upholds high teaching standards and requires all registered teachers to abide by the Code of Professional Conduct and clear ethical standards set out in its Statement of Ethics. The cornerstone of these policies is the teacher–student relationship, including the responsibility of teachers to avoid any behaviour that compromises the integrity of the relationship.

Yoga Australia also strongly recommended that all Yoga Australia training providers and registered teachers take the following actions:

1   be transparent about all the abuse that occurred within Satyananda Yoga
2   acknowledge the multiple testimonies, findings and recommendations of the Royal Commission as they relate to Satyananda Yoga.

Yoga Australia recommends that all teachers trained in Satyananda Yoga be mindful of the cultural and systemic issues identified by the Royal Commission as these factors enabled the abuse to occur, and that these issues be addressed in their practice.

Yoga Australia also states that it will continue to support all teachers trained in Satyananda Yoga and will continue to register teachers who meet the registration standards. Yoga Australia will also support their teachings and keep alive the good and sound aspects of Satyananda Yoga within the ethically sound framework of Yoga Australia's Statement of Ethics and Code of Professional Conduct.

A paper by Josna Pankhania, an initiated Satyananda Yoga teacher, examines the question of ethical leadership and questions many of the spiritual traditions associated with Satyananda Yoga. Pankhania states that the ethical way forward for Satyananda Yoga, an international organisation, should involve the current head undertaking the process of reparations in earnest. Pankhania is concerned that gurus are in positions of power and often seen as healers, and states that it is vital that their relationships with disciples encompass ethical boundaries.

Pankhania also quotes a statement issued by the London-based Nidra Network coordinated by Satyananda's most senior swamis, who have made a statement clearly stating their position in relation to the ethical crisis of Satyananda Yoga. They express their unequivocal support for the victims and condemn the perpetrators of the abuses, as well as those who knew that it was occurring and did nothing to protect the victims. They state that for the Indian leaders of the Satyananda Yoga organisation to plead ignorance is disingenuous, and their refusal to accept responsibility is an extended expression of denial and contempt for those concerned and affected, whether as first degree victims or as naive, trusting devotees. Satyananda Yoga Ashram at Mangrove Mountain has dropped the name Satyananda and now calls itself the Academy of Yoga Science. Pankhania states that it is important for institutions with a history of child sexual abuse to now display honesty and transparency.

The Royal Commission clearly stated that the founder and guru of Satyananda Yoga worldwide must accept responsibility as he was the ultimate authority at the Mangrove Mountain Ashram.

Pankhania states that it is difficult to imagine how the sense of mystique and blind worship advocated by Siva Yogasvami, which is prevalent throughout the Satyananda movement from inception, can now be maintained. Pankhania states that it remains to be seen whether Satyananda's successor will demonstrate the vision and courage required to engage in the healing and nurturing process of reparations.

References

Royal Commission into Institutional Responses to Child Sexual Abuse. *Report of Case Study No. 21. — The response of the Satyananda Yoga Ashram at Mangrove Mountain to allegations of child sexual abuse by the ashram's former spiritual leader in the 1970s and 1980s.* Commonwealth of Australia, Sydney, 2015.

Yoga Australia statement. Downloaded on 22 November 2019 from https://www.yogaaustralia.org.au/royal-commission/.

Pankhania J. *The ethical and leadership challenges posed by the Royal Commission's revelations of sexual abuse at a Satyananda Yoga Ashram in Australia.* Research in Ethical Issues in Organisations, 2017;17:105-123.

Image Credits

Front Cover: Chakras. By Paola Milani, © Perfect Potion

Inner jacket: Pink lotus in pond in Xiamen Garden Expo. © Jinhua Xu | Dreamstime.com

Page v: Tantric painting. Credit: Wellcome Collection

Page x: Sending chakra healing energy. © Nikki Zalewski | Dreamstime.com

Page xxii: Chakras — Buddhist painting Thangka from Nepal. Credit Werli Francois | Alamy Stock Photo

Page 7: Electromagnetic spectrum. © Peter Hermes Furlan | Shutterstock

Page 9: Kirlian photograph of a stinging nettle leaf. © Adrian Davies | Alamy Stock Photo

Page 12: Acupuncture chart. Credit: Wellcome Collection

Page 14: The astral body of the developed man or woman. © Charles Walker collection | Alamy Stock Photo

Page 18: Human aura. © Miro Kovacevic | Shutterstock

Page 23: A practitioner of mesmerism. Wood engraving, Mesmer, Franz Anton 1734 — 1815. Credit: Wellcome Collection

Page 28: A light splitting prism. © Magnetix | Shutterstock

Page 36: Quartz crystal. © Sebastian Janicki | Shutterstock

Page 38: Amethyst crystal. © Photofun | Shutterstock

Page 44: Theosophica Practica — Gichtel. © Art collection 2 | Alamy Stock Photo

Page 49: Indic manuscript 347. Credit: Wellcome Collection

Page 53: Two drawings: the easiest method to practice pranayan. Credit: Wellcome Collection

Page 63: Goddess Kali brandishes a sword and a severed head in two of her four arms as she tramples her consort Shiva underfoot in a display of her dominance. Ravi Varma, 1848 — 1906. Credit: Wellcome Collection

Page 65: A simplified view showing the three major nadis, the ida, sushumna and pingala which run vertically in the body. © Alex-Engraver | Wiki commons

Page 68: Beautiful pink lotus flower in pond. © Thananum Leungchayi | Dreamstime.com

Page 70: Helena Blavatsky, founder of the Theosophical Society, 1889. Artist: Anon. © Heritage Image Partnership Ltd | Alamy Stock Photo

Page 72: Charles Leadbeater. © The Historic Collection | Alamy Stock Photo

Page 76: Maslow's pyramids of needs. © Artellia | Shutterstock

Page 80: Chakras and the nervous system. © Chronicles | Alamy Stock Photo

Page 104: Sal's GDV energy field. © Salvatore Battaglia

Page 105: Sal's GDV chakra energy levels. © Salvatore Battaglia

Page 106: My friend's GDV energy field. © Salvatore Battaglia

Page 106: GDV energy centres before smelling essential oil blend. © Salvatore Battaglia

Page 107: Chakra energy centres a few minutes after inhaling Green Goddess blend. © Salvatore Battaglia

Page 108: Sapta Chakra, 1899. © Historic Collection | Alamy Stock Photo

Page 110: Base chakra mandala. By Paola Milani © Perfect Potion

Page 114: MS Sanskrit 391. Authored by Swami Hamsasvarupa 1900s. Credit: Wellcome Collection

Page 122: Sacral chakra mandala. By Paola Milani © Perfect Potion

Page 125: MS Sanskrit 391. Authored by Swami Hamsasvarupa 1900s. Credit: Wellcome Collection

Page 135: Solar plexus chakra mandala. By Paola Milani © Perfect Potion

Page 139: MS Sanskrit 391. Authored by Swami Hamsasvarupa 1900s. Credit: Wellcome Collection

Page 149: Heart chakra mandala. By Paola Milani © Perfect Potion

Page 153: MS Sanskrit 391. Authored by Swami Hamsasvarupa 1900s. Credit: Wellcome Collection

Page 162: Throat chakra mandala. By Paola Milani © Perfect Potion

Page 166: MS Sanskrit 391. Authored by Swami Hamsasvarupa 1900s. Credit: Wellcome Collection

Page 175: Third eye chakra. By Paola Milani © Perfect Potion

Page 178: MS Sanskrit 391. Authored by Swami Hamsasvarupa 1900s. Credit: Wellcome Collection

Page 187: Crown chakra mandala. By Paola Milani © Perfect Potion

Page 190: MS Sanskrit 391. Authored by Swami Hamsasvarupa 1900s. Credit: Wellcome Collection

Page 202: Reiki. © Microgen | Shutterstock

Page 207: Zen stones. © Golyak | Dreamstime.com

Page 211: An Indian person of high rank in a yogic posture. Gouache painting. Credit: Wellcome Collection

Page 222: Chakra collage © Jill Psenitza

Inspiration behind the chakra collage by Jill Psenitza

My inspiration for this piece was Perfect Potion's Chakra Essential Oils kit. When I began working for Perfect Potion, many things started to fall into place. I no longer just understood, but experienced subtle energy and how crucial it is to look after our physical, mental and emotional health. Connecting with our spirituality through the magic of sacred rituals and self-care practices also became important to me.

Coming from struggle and inner conflict, immersing myself in the studies of the chakras through meditation, essential oils and especially through this artwork, was like finding a map. It helped me to facilitate the shift and transformation needed to find more balance, peace and inner harmony. The background in my artwork represents my personal journey, which took nearly two years, revealing all my resistances and imbalances that wanted me to nearly abandon the art piece many times. Only when I began teaching creative meditations and collage art workshops regularly did my ideas begin to flow. I had the idea to use another collage as the top layer of the person meditating, which then turned into a community effort, including many images of family and close friends. Collages are one of the most expressive, fun and easy art forms, simply by assembling various images to create a new picture that tells a story.

Making collages taught me how to work with what I've got, how to stand back and always see the bigger picture, while simultaneously getting involved in all tasks, minute or mundane. This artwork in particular has taught me how to do one thing at a time, mindfully and with persistence, consistency and patience. It taught me to continue to show up for myself, especially when it's hard, when I don't like myself or what I'm creating, and how to let go and let the creative process, and life, unfold as it does. It taught me on a personal level and allowed me to share the insights from my experiences at a community level as well.

Instagram: @embody.yourself.au

About the poems

With scientific mind
Love for numbers
And engineering degree
I never knew writing poems
Would be my thing
But this is what I get
When I connect
To the flow of the Universe
And follow
The whispers of my Soul

Marzena is passionate about yoga, self-compassion, the power of the human mind and conscious living. She loves to learn about ancient practices and natural therapies as well as the scientific discoveries that explain and support them.

Marzena holds a Master of Business Engineering degree and has worked in sourcing in Europe and Australia. She is a yoga teacher and Reiki practitioner. In the process of self enquiry and inner healing, she has found herself tapping into unexpected creative power manifested in intuitive poetry.

Marzena lives in Brisbane with her husband and two children. To connect with Marzena visit her website www.marzenaskowronska.com or Instagram account @myyogarhythm

Index

A
Acupuncture 11-13, 82
Ajna 64, 93, 94, 98, 175-186
Ahankara 86
Anahata 94, 149-161
Angelica root 118, 195
Aniseed 29, 30
Astral body 16-19
Aura 16-19
Ayurveda 3, 22

B
Babbitt, Edwin 22
Bach, Dr Edward 25
Bach flower essences 25-27
Bailey, Alice 71
Base chakra 96, 110-121
    Activities to strengthen 120-121
    Affirmations 121
    Archetypes 114
    Aromatherapy blends 118
    Behavioural characteristics 116-117
    Element 112
    Essential oils 118
    Health issues 117
    Location 111
    Physical association 112
    Psychospiritual 112
    Purpose 111
    Symbology 113-114
Basil 30, 32, 170, 182
Bay laurel 31, 182
Benzoin 29, 118, 157, 195
Bergamot 30, 118, 157
Biofield science 3-5, 101-107
Biophotons 21
Black pepper 29, 144
Blavatasky, Helena 23, 50, 70-71
Buddha wood 118
Buddhi 86
Buddhic body 19
Buddhist Tantric practice 13
Burr, Harold 8-9, 23

C
Cajeput 30, 195
Cardamom 29, 30, 130, 144
Caraway seed 29
Carrot seed 29, 30
Causal body 19
Cedarwood, Atlas 29, 118, 144, 182, 195
Chakras
    Balancing 208-213
    Bio-socio-psycho-spiritual model 92-94
    Blockages 206
    Buddhist tradition 15
    Centres of consciousness 88-90
    Correspondences 52
    Definition 46
    Eastern system xiv, 49, 50, 55-69
    Endocrine system 78-81
    Imbalances 205-206
    Nerve plexus 78-81
    New Age xii, 53
    Origins 46-54
    Psychotherapy 91
    Saiva tradition 15
    Spiritual development 89-91
    Symbology 67-69
    Western system 46-54, 70-77
    Yoga 54
Chamomile, German 31, 170
Chamomile, Roman 31, 144, 170, 196
Chitta 86
Cinnamon 31, 144
Citronella 30
Clary sage 182
Clove bud 31

Colour therapy 27-35
  Blue 31, 34
  Breathing 32
  Chakras 34-35
  Green 30
  Healing 32
  Human aura 33-34
  Indigo 31, 34
  Orange 29, 34
  Red 28, 34
  Violet 31, 34
  Visualisation 28
  Yellow 29, 34
Consciousness 86-91
Coriander seed 118, 130, 144, 182
Crown chakra 97, 187-200
  Activities to strengthen 198-200
  Affirmations 200
  Archetypes 191-192
  Aromatherapy blends 196-197
  Behavioural characteristics 194-195
  Element 189
  Essential oils 195-196
  Health issues 195
  Location 189
  Physical association 189
  Psychospiritual 190-191
  Purpose 188
  Symbology 190-191
Crystals 35-41, 218-219
  Aromatherapy 40
  Chakras 38-39
  Cleansing 38-39
  Colours 38-39
Cypress 29, 144, 182

D
Dill seed 30
DMT 83-85
Dychtwald, Ken 76-77

E
Ego 87-88, 95
Einstein, Albert 7
Electromagnetic spectrum 7
Endocrine system 78-81
Energy healing 91-92
Energy medicine 2-3
  Definition 3
  Mainstream medicine 4
Essential oils
  Anointing 218
  Diffuser 218
  Inhalation 218
  Massage 217
  Ritual bath 217
Etheric body 17-19
Eucalyptus 31, 157, 182
Everlasting 157, 182

F
Fennel, sweet 30, 144, 170
Fir 182
Five Elements 11
Flower remedies 25-27
Fragonia 182
Frankincense 32, 118, 182, 196

G
Gap junctions 81-82
Galbanum 196
GDV 21, 103-107
Geranium 30, 130, 144, 171
Ginger 29, 30, 118, 130, 144

Grapefruit 30, 32, 182

H
Hahnemann, Samuel 24
Heart chakra 93, 96, 149-161
  Activities to strengthen 160-161
  Affirmations 161
  Archetypes 153
  Aromatherapy blends 158-159
  Behavioural characteristics 155-156
  Element 150
  Essential oils 157-158
  Health issues 156-157
  Location 151
  Physical associations 149
  Psychospiritual 151
  Purpose 150
  Symbology 152-153
Homoeopathy 24
Human biofield 101-102
Human subtle bodies 16-19
  Astral body 19
  Atmic body 19
  Buddhic body 19
  Causal body 19
  Etheric body 19
  Nirvanic body 19
Hunt, Valerie 6, 24
Hyssop 31, 32

I
Ida nadi 64-66, 78, 98
Indriyas 86

Index 249

J
James, Williams 95
Jasmine absolute 29, 131
Jung, Carl 95
Juniper berry 32, 144, 183, 196

K
Kali 62-64
Kirlian photography 9, 103
Koshas 19
Kundalini 58-62

L
Lavender 32, 157, 196
Leadbeater, Charles 23, 33, 46
Lemon 30, 144, 183
Lemongrass 30, 183
Lifespan development 95-97
Lime 196
Lotus 67-69

M
Manas 86
Mandarin 29, 31, 131, 171
Manipura 135-148
Mantras 67
Marjoram, sweet 31, 157
Maslow's hierarchy of needs 75-77
Meditation 98-100, 208-210
Melatonin 85
Melissa 30, 158, 196
Mesmer, Franz Anton 22, 23
Muladhara 60-61, 110-121
Myrrh 29, 118, 171, 196
Myrtle 31, 183

N
Nadi 13, 64-67, 78-79
National Center for Complementary and Alternative Medicine 2
Neroli 131, 158, 183, 196
Neurotransmitters 78, 84
Nirvanic body 19

O
Oakmoss absolute 118
Orange, sweet 131, 158, 171

P
Palmarosa 30, 158, 183
Parasympathetic nervous system 78
Patchouli 32, 118, 131
Peppermint 30, 144, 171, 183
Pert, Candice 6, 24
Peru balsam 118, 131
Petitgrain 30, 144, 183
Pine 29, 31, 144
Pineal gland 82-85
Pingala nadi 64, 65, 78, 98
Powell, Arthur 74-75
Prana 4, 5, 8, 13, 16, 59
Pranayama 99
Psychotherapy 91-94

Q
Qi 4, 5, 8, 11
Quartz crystal 35-37

R
Reich, William 6
Rescue remedy 26
Rose 29, 131
Rose otto 131, 158, 196
Rosemary 145, 183, 196

S
Sacral chakra 96, 122-134
   Activities to strengthen 133-134
   Affirmations 134
   Archetypes 126-127
   Aromatherapy blends 131-132
   Behavioural characteristics 128-129
   Element 123
   Essential oils 130-131
   Health issues 130
   Location 123
   Physical association 124
   Psychospiritual 124
   Purpose 123
   Symbology 125-126
Sahasrara 60-61, 93, 187-200
Sage 29, 32, 183
Saiva tradition 15
Samskaras 89
Sandalwood 29, 30, 32, 118, 131, 145, 158, 171, 183, 196
Sat-Chakra-Nirupana 50
Serpent power 50, 70
Shiva 62
Solar plexus chakra 96, 135-148
   Activities to strengthen 147-148
   Affirmations 148
   Archetypes 140-141

Aromatherapy
blends 145-146
Behavioural
characteristics
141-143
Element 137
Essential oils
144-145
Location 137
Health issues 143
Physical association
137-138
Psychospiritual
138-139
Purpose 136-137
Symbology 139-140
Spikenard 158, 196
Spruce, black 145
Subtle aromatherapy
41-43
Subtle energy system 20
Sushumna nadi 64-66,
78
Svadhisthana 122-134
Sympathetic nervous
system 78

T

Tantra 55-57
　Definition 57
　Features 57
TCM 3,10-13
Tea tree 30, 31, 145
Theosophical society
70-73
Theosophy 19
Therapeutic touch 6
Third eye chakra 82, 85,
97, 175-186
　Activities to
strengthen 185-186
　Affirmations 186
　Archetypes 179-180
　Aromatherapy
blends 183-184
　Behavioural
characteristics
180-181
　Element 177
　Essential oils
182-183
　Health issues 181
　Location 177
　Physical association
177
　Psychospiritual
177-178
　Purpose 176
　Symbology 178
Throat chakra 97,
162-174
　Activities to
strengthen 173-174
　Affirmations 174
　Archetypes 167-168
　Aromatherapy
blends 171
　Behavioural
characteristics
169-170
　Element 164
　Essential oils
170-171
　Health issues 170
　Location 164
　Physical associations
164-165
　Psychospiritual 165
　Symbology 166
Thyme 29, 145
Turin, Luca xxi

U

Ultraweak photon
　emission (UPE) 21,
　102-103

V

Valerian 158
Vedic model of
　consciousness 86-87
Vetiver 30, 118
Vishuddha 93, 162-174
Vogel, Marcel 36-37

W

Woodroffe, John 15-16,
　46

Y

Yarrow 31, 158
Ylang ylang 131, 145
Yoga 53, 98-100,
　210-212
　Bhakti yoga 99
　Hatha yoga 58
　Jnana yoga 99
　Kriya yoga 59
　Kundalini yoga 58,
　66
　Psychology of 86-88
　Raja yoga 99
　Tantric yoga 58, 59
Yoga sutras of Patanjali
58
Yoga Upanishads 60

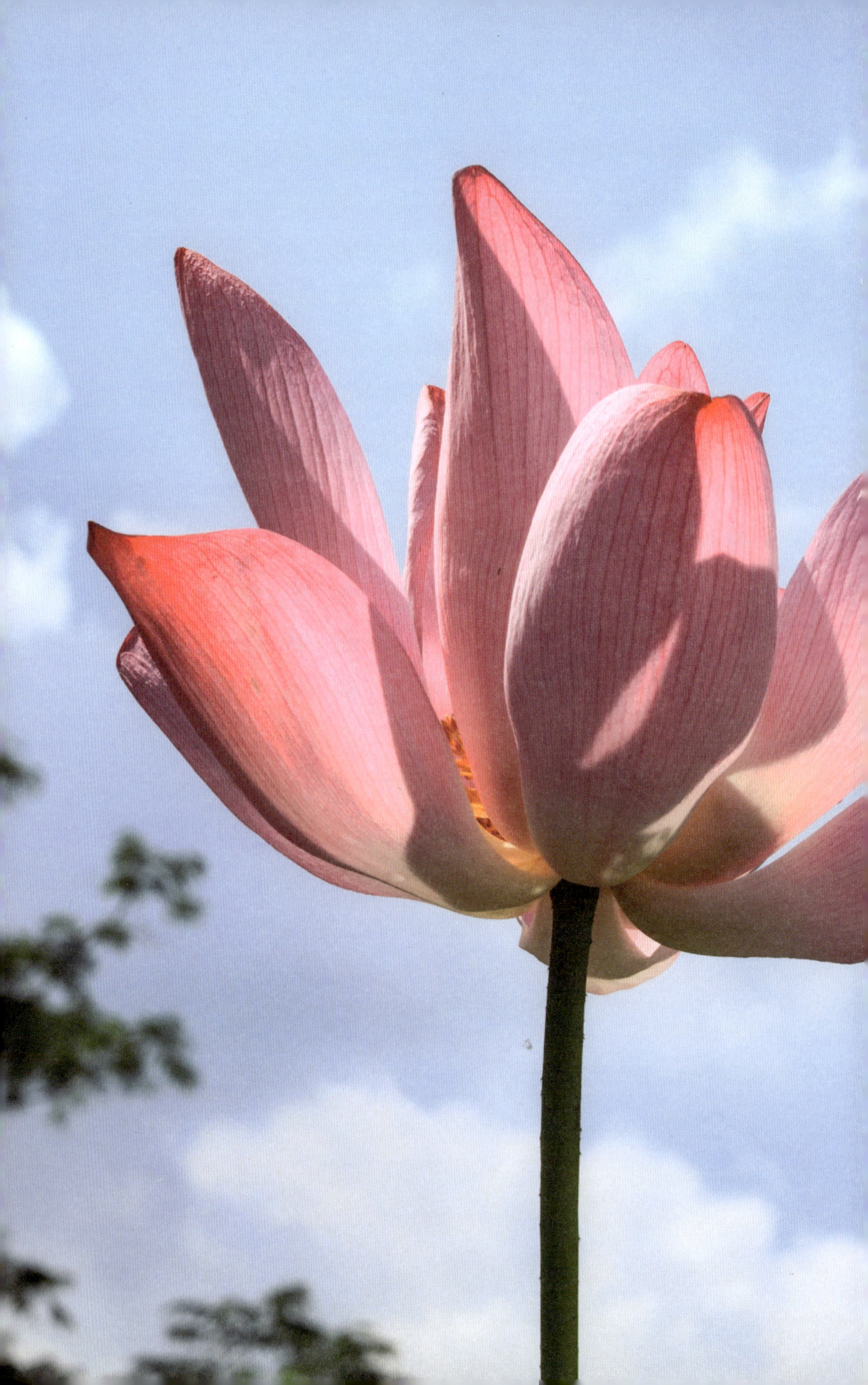